Anchored By This Hope

Our Life With Jesus

Anchored By This Hope

Our Life With Jesus

'We have this HOPE as an anchor for the soul, firm and secure' (Hebrews 6:19a, CSB).

Jennifer Sessums Stockman
Carol Alawine Sessums

Stay Anchored in Jesus!

Jennifer Sessums Stockman

Copyright © 2024 by Jennifer Sessums Stockman and Carol Alawine Sessums

All rights reserved.

ISBN: 9798305802368

No part of this book may be reproduced, stored in a retrieval system, or transmitted by any means without the expressed permission of the author.

Unless otherwise noted, all scriptures are from the HOLMAN CHRISTIAN STANDARD BIBLE, Copyright© 1999, 2000, 2002, 2003 by Holman Bible Publishers, Nashville Tennessee. All rights reserved.

Scripture quotations marked (KJV) are taken from the KING JAMES VERSION, public domain.

Scripture quotations marked (NKJV) are taken from the NEW KING JAMES VERSION®. Copyright© 1982 by Thomas Nelson, Inc. Used by permission. All rights reserved.

Scripture quotations marked (CSB) are taken from the Christian Standard Bible®, Copyright © 2017 by Holman Bible Publishers. Used by permission. Christian Standard Bible, and CSB® are federally registered trademarks of Holman Bible Publishers.

Dedication

We'd like to dedicate *Anchored By This Hope* to

David Sessums
January 18, 1945 - May 20, 2017

Although David is no longer physically with us here on Earth, he was aware of our book being in progress and his steady encouragement still rings in our ears. He had great confidence in our ability to get this book written and finished. As a matter of fact, he always had faith that we could accomplish any project we decided to tackle, and never hesitated to express his confidence in us.

It is with much love, appreciation and gratitude to God for David's life, that we now dedicate this accomplishment to him. We're sure he already knows about it though.

We miss him in our lives every day.

"Father, I desire those You have given Me to be with Me where I am. Then they will see My glory, which You have given Me because You loved Me before the world's foundation." –Jesus
(John 17:24, CSB)

Table of Contents

Stronger Than We Think 1
Fear Not! 3
God Says Stand 5
God's Warrior 7
Victory God's Way 9
Consecrate Yourself...and Go! 11
What Would You Have Me To Do, Lord? 13
It's A Heart Thing 15
Tell What You Saw 17
Our Helper Comes 19
A Discussion With God 21
Sing and Clap 23
I Am and I Will 25
God Fights Our Battles 27
Believe It and Claim It! 29
Descendants 31
Death Is Just A Doorway 33
Queen Esther 35
Praising In Prison 37
Walking With Jesus 39
Plunge In! 41
Just Ask Mary 43
Be Like The Leaves 45
Don't Forget Your Overcoat! 47
Build A Relationship with God 49
Keep Working! 51
Go Your Way Rejoicing! 53
A Godly Step Daddy 54

Joseph's Obedience	56
Make Godly Choices	58
Attitudes Of Defiance?	60
Unending Provision	63
Listen	64
Observe and Obey	66
Dwell In Him	68
A Story of Faithfulness	70
Ordinary To Extraordinary	72
A Humble Servant	74
Prisoner?	76
Standing Together	78
Wait!	79
Here Am I!	81
So Run, With Patience	83
Ants and Giants	86
Jesus In Our Storms	89
Some Thoughts About Life From My Heart	91
Obey, Even If We Don't Understand	94
Go In God's Strength, Not Yours	96
Arguing With A Donkey	98
Needful Things	100
The Lost Necklace	103
Spirit Or Flesh? Our Choice!	105
Praise Him Now!	107
Elijah and The Widow	109
Daniel's Steadfast Faith	111
Grace and Peace To You	113
On Island Time!	115
Just Obey and Let God Lead	117
Descendants and Prayer	119
Encouragement and Hope	121
Miracles and Ordinary People	122
Adopted by God	124
Obey, Even In Fear	126
Walking In The Midst of The Fire	128
Daniel In The Lions Den	131
Seeking God	133
Choose To Trust God	135

Obedience In Change	137
A Burning Bush and Divided Waters	139
God Uses All Things For Our Good	141
Fear	143
Jesus Prayed for Us	145
Perfect Oatmeal	147
Get Out Of That Boat, But Stay Focused	149
Stop Your Fighting and Know That I Am God	151
Roads and Rivers	153
Shipwrecked!	155
Of Chocolates and Sunsets	157
Untrained But Available	159
'Amazing Grace, How Sweet The Sound'	161
God's Line In The Sand	165
Crocheting Socks	168
Wonders Accomplished from Plans Formed Long Ago	170
Do Not Fear	172
Humble Obedience	174
My Story or His Story?	176
New Year, New Me	178
Between The Inhale and The Exhale	180
Job and Peter, Both Sifted by Satan	182
Jacob, A Changed Man	184
Do You See Miracles?	186
When God Questions Job	188
God We Trust You To Fight For Us!	190
Cleaning Out The Fridge!	192
His Will / Our Willpower	194
In The End	195
The Wisdom Of Gratefulness	197
Pain and Pearls	199
Mistakes and Do Overs	201
God Knows Before We Ask	203
Hard Times and Many Blessings	205
A Half Dollar of Comfort	209
Saltiness and Lighthouses	211
So I Asked, 'But God, What If.....?'	213
Instant Peace	215

Broken Shells	217
Disgraced But Forgiven By Grace	219
One In A Long Line	221
His Will Is Best	223
God Uses Willing People	225
Comforting Scattered Minds	227
My Goal; His Will	229
The Importance of Worship	231
Conversations About Jesus!	233
Praying for Others!	235
Trusting God	237
Facing Grief	239
Local Missionaries Needed!	241
Just Call Him	243
God Cares When We Mourn	245
Our Helplessness, God's Provision	247
Star Gazing	249
I Am Not Home	251
Two Sides Of Gossip	253
Just A Lump Of Clay	255
Boundary Limits	257
Just Do What He Says!	259
Be Deliberate About Worship	261
Don't Waste The Wait!	263
The Comfort Of Christ Through Suffering	264
Jesus Makes The Impossible, Possible	266
Trust, Follow, and Obey	268
Blessings, Even In Loss	271
Why Worry?	273
Rejoice, Rejoice!	275
Prayer... Not Worry!	277
God's Not Finished Yet!	279
Humble Sinner or Arrogant Hypocrite?	281
Walking In Faith	283
Get Behind Me Satan!	285
A Heart Of Flesh	287
God Is Faithful To Finish	289
Hope Grows	291
Hope's Fulfillment	293

Are You Shy or Bold?............................. 295
How Do I Respond To Troubles,
    My Own and Others?........................... 298
Encourage One Another In Christ................... 301
Pray For Opportunities............................ 304
When Things Don't Go Your Way, Obey Anyway..... 306
Time 308
The End Result 310
God Cares 313
Enemies 315
Christians Need Each Other 317
God Listens 319
How Should We Respond To Our Fears?.............. 321
Of Pigs and Prodigals!............................ 323
The True Light 325
God's Order....................................... 327
Encourage One Another In Love.................... 329
Dress For Success!................................ 331
It Is Personal 333
Anchored In Hope.................................. 335
Peace With God Produces The Peace Of God......... 337
He Is Seeking. Am I Hiding? 338
Job: Patient Or Faithful?......................... 340
Surrender Of The Will............................. 342
God Is Faithful................................... 345
Sheltered Through The Storms 349
Tell Somebody About It!........................... 351
Building Only With The Spirit's Strength 353
In The Twinkling of An Eye........................ 355
Rest Easy 357
Overcomer!.. 359
I'm Wanting To Go Fishing 361
Waiting For God................................... 363
Ministry Is Personal.............................. 366
God Gave Everybody A Story........................ 369
Safely Anchored In The Living Hope 372
A True Family Legacy.............................. 374
Foggy Night....................................... 378
A Good, Good Father 380

No Equal To God 382
Peace, When We Learn To Trust 384
Completing Our Work 386
Homecoming! 389
About the Authors 392

Preface

We want to thank you for using some of your valuable time to read this book. It is our prayer for each person who reads this book to be encouraged to draw closer to our Lord and Savior, Jesus Christ. May your relationship with Christ grow ever stronger as your faith increases.

Our faith journey is not ended until we see Jesus face to face one day, but rather, it is a continuous growth process. Sometimes, that process takes us through very difficult times and experiences. God always has a reason and a purpose for those trials He allows in our lives. We tend to not want to be uncomfortable but we always learn more when we are pushed out of our comfort zones. God knows this and He is expert at doing that very thing! Hopefully, we can one day realize that even when He allows hard things in our lives, He has our best interests in His heart and we can accept His will for us.

Our goal in life is to have faith like Job who, near the end of all the trials God allowed in his life, was able to firmly declare "Even if He kills me, I will hope in Him. I will still defend my ways before Him" (Job 13:15, KJV)

If you are not saved, please read the following scriptures and accept Jesus as your Lord and Savior without delay. There is nothing more important in this earthly life than your relationship with the One who loves you more than anyone else in the world.

Romans 3:23
Romans 3:10-18
Romans 6:23
John 3:16
Romans 10:9

Acknowledgments

We would like to express our sincerest thank you to the following:

To Jesus Christ, our Lord for salvation and being the reason for our hope.

To our family for your encouragement and belief that we could accomplish this.

To Dr. Ivan Parke for your encouragement and advice, when we came to you and said "We've written a book and now we don't know what to do with it.".

To Melanie Luke, our dear friend who readily took on the task of editing for us. Thank you for using your knowledge (both Biblical and Grammatical) to make sure our work was correct. Your letter to us means more than you know. We trusted you and you did not let us down.

To Kent Mummert, M.F.A., for accepting our project; for your advice and help with design and formatting.

To those who will one day purchase a copy of this book, thank you for your support.

To the reader, thank you for spending your time reading this book. Your time is valuable and we consider it a precious gift.

Stronger Than We Think

Read Judges 6:11-24

Verse 15. "He said to him, 'Please, Lord, how can I deliver Israel? Look, my family is the weakest in Manasseh, and I am the youngest in my father's house.'"

Gideon was afraid. How often in this life are we afraid? I am often fearful. The people in the Bible that we count as heroes were people just like us. They were afraid. They were busy trying to survive in the day-to-day world. Gideon had excuses for why he was not the one to deliver Israel. Hmmm. We would never give God excuses for why we cannot do things HE asks of us.... or would we? More accurately, do we give excuses? How many conversations have we had with the Lord that sounded remarkably like the conversation between Gideon and the Angel of the Lord? God sees what we can do through HIS strength, not just what we can do on our own. Often we fail to see anything beyond what we can do on our own. Gideon's excuses included his family being the weakest in Manasseh and him being the youngest in his family. How many times do we say, "Oh God, I am too small... or too weak, or too timid, or too scared.". The Angel of the Lord answered Gideon's fears with "But I will be with you.". God's presence with us makes the difference between failure or success. God doesn't fail. We can fail, but not God. Gideon was humble. Gideon obeyed God. And with God's help, Gideon succeeded in the mission God assigned him to do! We, too, will succeed in any mission God assigns us to do; not because of our gifts, talents, or abilities, but because when God is with us, we cannot fail. One plus God is always a majority! When God calls me to do something, may I answer with "Yes Lord", not with an excuse. Sometimes we are called to do hard things, but it will always be worth it to obey God.

Notes: _____

_____

_____

_____

_____

_____

Fear Not!

Joshua 1:9. "Haven't I commanded you: be strong and courageous? Do not be afraid or discouraged, for the Lord your God is with you wherever you go."

God is telling Joshua "Be strong and of good courage;" ..."Fear Not", or words to that effect are used in the Bible 365 times... once for each day of the year! God is trying to tell us that it is very important that we TRUST Him and not be afraid...Be strong, stand strong, stay strong, and FEAR NOT! After all, IF we believe that God is indeed in control of all things (physical, political, spiritual) then we must learn to trust Him and when we learn to totally trust, then the Being, Standing, and Staying strong will gradually come easier and easier for us. We must learn that things are not always, and maybe seldom are, the way we would wish or think they should be. But God, who sees the whole picture from beginning to end, always knows what is best, not only for us but for our families, our communities, our state, our nation, and our world. It is very hard to learn to be, stand, and stay strong. The thing that it requires of us the most is not that we are strong in our own strength, but that we learn to completely lean and rely on God and His provision for us in all ways. Then and only then can we truly be, stand and stay strong...not through any strength we may have of ourselves, not through any status we have in this world, not through any reliance on others; but only through our complete reliance and trust in God for our well-being now and the best of all possibilities for our future. Since God put that Fear Not, Be strong, phrase in the Bible 365 times, it is a reminder to us that we are not strong on our own and that it is a daily thing for us to turn everything over to Him and leave it there. It is not something we can attain, but it is something we have to continuously do over and over every day because we are so weak. In so doing, we do become stronger and more reliant on Him and the running to God with all our daily troubles becomes more and more like a little child running to his parents with a hurt finger or a stumped toe. We find comfort and help there and maybe over time, we tend to run to that Comfort and Help sooner and sooner instead of trying to "fix" things on our own.

Notes: _____

_____

_____

_____

_____

_____

_____

God Says Stand

Read Joshua 1:1-18

Verse 5. "No one will be able to stand against you as long as you live. I will be with you, just as I was with Moses. I will not leave you or forsake you."

Key points to remember as you go through each day:
   (1) Verse 1–Listen for God to speak. Always be ready to hear when HE speaks.
   (2) Verse 2–He may say something you don't expect. HE may ask you to do something big for Him.
   (3) Verses 3 - 4–The rewards will also be big. God is big. He can handle big tasks and He can give big rewards.
   (4) Verse 5–God will be with you. He will never leave you. God, plus you, is a majority that can overcome anything you are up against.
   (5) Verse 6–You can accomplish the job God has assigned to you. Be strong and of a good courage.
   (6) Verse 7–Obey God's laws completely. It takes strength and courage to completely obey, but if you obey God, you will be successful.
   (7) Verse 8–Study the Bible morning and evening and do not stray from obeying it so that God will make you prosperous and successful.
   (8) Verse 9–God has commanded us to be strong and courageous, therefore it is possible. Do not allow yourself to be

afraid or feel overwhelmed. God is with you everywhere you go. (See verse 5!)

(9) Verses 10 - 11–Believe that God is able to do what He says He will do. Then live like you believe it. Make the necessary preparations to possess what He has promised to give. If you ask for rain, buy an umbrella and take it with you–opened up!

(10) Verses 12-16–Remember how God has blessed you in the past. Obey what He has told you to do, even after you receive what He has promised.

(11) Verses 17-18–Obey what God has told you to do and encourage others to obey Him as well. Do not condone disobedience to God by anyone.

(12) Verse 18–Be strong and of a good courage!

Notes: _____

_____

_____

_____

_____

_____

_____

God's Warrior

Read Judges 6:11-40

Verses 12. "Then the angel of the Lord appeared to him and said: 'The Lord is with you, mighty warrior.'"

Verse 16. "'But I will be with you,' the Lord said to him. 'You will strike Midian down as if it were one man.'"

God is sending His angel ahead of Gideon and destroying Gideon's enemy! Oh, the Angel of the Lord! We, (in my family), sometimes call Him "the Big Dude with the big sword!" He is there to protect us and fight for us against our enemies.... both the ones we can see and those which are unseen by human eyes. There are many of both! We so desperately need this Angel standing there in front of us and fighting our battles for us on a daily basis. Yet we think we can handle things ourselves! How silly of us and how human! Wonder how many times He has been out there in the trenches of daily warfare fighting our enemies for us and we never even knew? Wonder how many battles He has won against Satan over us and we never even knew? Wonder how many times we were in grave danger in human terms and yet He shielded us from all harm and we never knew? Wonder how many times He has thrown his shield up to send Satan's poison arrows of deception away from us and we never even knew? We should be asking God daily to send His Angel ahead of us in everything we do and everywhere we go. We may not be aware of just how bad we need God's Hedge of Protection every day, but even though we don't understand all the ways we need Him, we surely need to understand that we DO need Him with us all the time. He is there waiting for us to ask Him to be with us, guide our way and protect us. That is the simple part that we should be able to understand....all we have to do is ask.

Notes: _____

_____

_____

_____

_____

_____

Victory God's Way

Read Judges 7:1-15

Verse 15. "When Gideon heard the account of the dream and its interpretation, he bowed in worship. He returned to Israel's camp and said, 'Get up, for the Lord has handed the Midianite camp over to you.'"

Gideon's people had disobeyed God and God had allowed the Midianites to capture them. The enemy destroyed their crops and they were close to starving. They had little hope, but when they finally turned back to God for help, He chose probably the most unlikely man among them to use to save them. Gideon was weak and timid, living in fear of the Midianites when God called him a 'mighty warrior' and gave him a mission to accomplish. Gideon was called to do something for the Lord. He was willing to go do what the Lord told him to do against incredible odds. Gideon was willing to be obedient. God blessed not only Gideon for his obedience but also Gideon's country. One person's willingness to obey God saved a nation. Why are we not willing to make a stand today? Why are we not willing to obey God today? Gideon started by breaking down his father's altars to Baal. Gideon continued in his obedience to the Lord. God reduced the number in Gideon's army, so that Israel would know that it was the Lord who had saved them. By man's logic, this was crazy. But Gideon chose to do things God's way. If you will take the first step of faith in God, HE will provide the comfort and the victory. When we have faith in God and do things God's way, He will provide a much larger victory than we ever dreamed! God's way is always best. We miss so much by not trusting God!

Notes: _____

_____

_____

_____

_____

_____

_____

Consecrate Yourself... and Go!

Read Joshua 3:8 - 4:18

Verses 15-16. "Now the Jordan overflows its banks throughout the harvest season. But as soon as the priests carrying the ark reached the Jordan, their feet touched the water at its edge and the water flowing downstream stood still, rising up in a mass that extended as far as Adam, a city next to Zarethan. The water flowing downstream into the Sea of Arabah (the Dead Sea) was completely cut off, and the people crossed opposite Jericho."

What happens when we obey the Lord? Amazing things, that's what! Just for a minute, close your eyes and try to get a mental picture. We have all seen at least pictures of rivers flooding over the banks. That's what was happening to the Jordan River. The water at flood stage would have been rushing and dangerous. Rivers at flood stage are hard to cross. It's easy to be swept away if you get in the water. The Lord told them exactly what to do. Do you feel like God is asking you to step into dangerous flood waters by doing something? God told the Hebrews if they did it, they would pass over the Jordan River on dry ground. It took a certain amount of faith to step out into that river. But when they did step into the water, they saw an amazing display of God's power. Water rose up in a heap! They had wondered how they would cross the river. They might have had ideas but they probably never dreamed it would be like that. There's no coincidence that the water stayed piled up just long enough for the people to cross and to get the rocks from the middle of the river bed. It was a miracle! When God gives you something to do, HE also provides a way for you to do it! Our job is to be obedient. HE will take care of the rest. Often HE takes care of the rest in a mighty display of power. Not only are we taken care of, but we get to witness something amazing in the process! Step into the water and see what HE does!

Notes: _____

_____

_____

_____

_____

_____

What Would You Have Me To Do, Lord?

Read Acts 9:1-6

Verses 5-6. "'Who are you, Lord?' he said. 'I am Jesus, the One you are persecuting,' He replied. 'But get up and go into the city, and you will be told what you must do.'"

This is the story of Paul's Damascus road experience. "Lord, what would you have me to do?" Not what would you have someone else to do but ME. How would you have ME to use my time? For my time is not mine but yours. For I have been bought with a price and that, dear Lord, includes my time, my money, my possessions and my all. I wonder how much better my life would have been, if I had asked that question early on in my life. "Lord, what would you have me to do?". I was saved at the age of 14. I was a Christian. But I don't really remember ever just saying "Lord, what would you have me to do?". Looking back now, I wonder what I could have been and what I could have done with my life. I think about how much time and energy have been wasted trying to endure this life instead of letting Jesus have total control. I know I surely have made a mess and of this one thing I am convinced: HE would have done a much better job with control. I have asked that question now. It is better to ask now, than never. I am still waiting for an answer that leaves no doubt. I am sure that HE will answer and HE will guide me. As I have learned to recognize miracles, I wonder how many I have missed along the way. I wonder how many miracles Jesus did that I never saw and never said "thank you" for? I don't want to miss anything else! When confronted by Jesus, we should listen and believe. There are numerous accounts of miracles here in this event, as well as Christians exhibiting great faith . When we exercise faith in God, things happen!

Notes: _____

_____

_____

_____

_____

_____

_____

It's A Heart Thing

Read Daniel 1:1-21

Verse 8. "Daniel determined that he would not defile himself with the king's food or with the wine he drank. So he asked permission from the chief eunuch not to defile himself."

Daniel had purposed in his heart to obey God. He was a captive in a foreign country. His captors did not serve God, nor were they interested in Daniel's goal to serve God. They had other plans for Daniel. Does that sound like things that we encounter in life now? We want to serve God, but other people have different goals for us. We have to make a living. We all face trials in life that seem to make it hard to serve God. Daniel certainly was facing a trial. As a matter of fact, this trial ended up lasting 70 years! Serving God starts in the heart though. Purpose in your heart to serve the Lord. You must purpose in your heart first before the trial comes; then during the trial and after the trial. When you purpose in your heart to do the will of God, He will provide a way for you to obey, even during trials. It is not IF we will have trials but WHEN. Daniel faced trials on a daily basis. I would dare to say that we face trials more days than not. Those trials are probably different from the ones that Daniel faced, but trials of many kinds will hinder our service to God if we allow it. That is why it is so important to continue to purpose in your heart to serve HIM over and over.

You must continually recommit. Example: If you are going to read through the Bible, you will continue to be too tired or have some other problem. You must press on through! It is only with the continual commitment, that you over come and receive the blessing. One of the ways to help you stay committed to the Lord is to chose Godly friends. A Godly friend who encourages you in your walk with the Lord is a true treasure. Daniel had three friends who were also committed to walk with the Lord. Together they stood strong in their commitment to honor God.

Notes: _____

_____

_____

_____

_____

_____

Tell What You Saw

Read Luke 2:8-20.

Verse 17. "After seeing them, they reported the message they were told about this child,"

Why would God choose to tell a bunch of stinky shepherds about the birth of His Son? After all, they were out in the field taking care of sheep. They wouldn't have been the important people, at least not by the world's standards. Maybe it was because HE knew that they would be "simple" enough to believe the angels. Maybe HE knew that when they believed the angels, they would just "have" to come to Jesus. And maybe it was because HE knew that after they had been with Jesus, they would tell people about Jesus. I think sometimes we forget about verse 17 in the story. We remember that the shepherds came to see Jesus and that afterwards they went back to their sheep, praising and glorifying God. We remember that Mary kept all these things in her heart, but we forget something very important. The shepherds TOLD people. It doesn't say who. It just says they made it known abroad. Could it be that an excited bunch of shepherds told everybody who would listen? Shouldn't we who have been saved, who have "come to Jesus" be doing the same things? We should indeed be telling everybody who will listen to our story AND praising God!

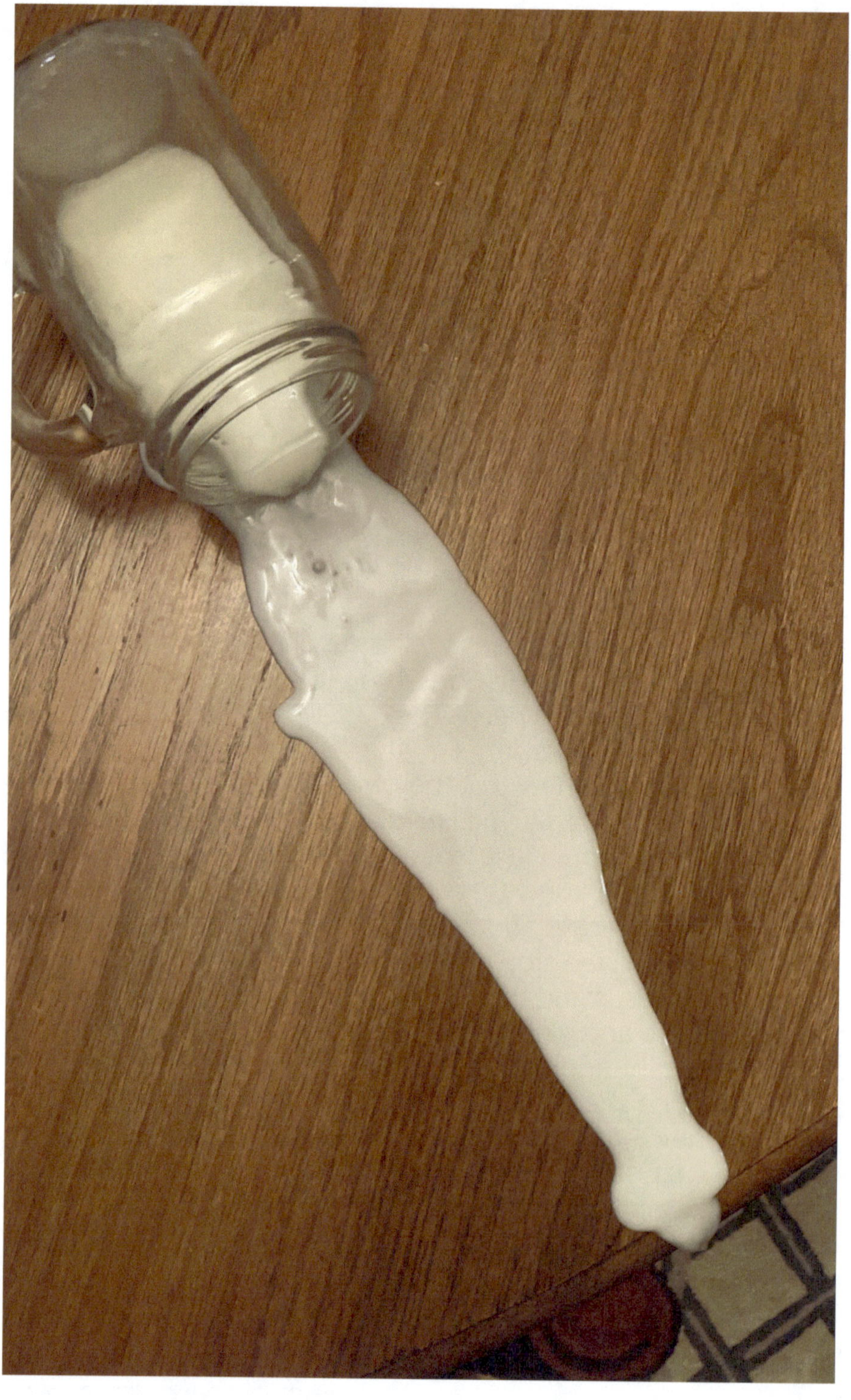

Our Helper Comes

John 16:5-7. (Jesus) "'But now I am going away to Him who sent Me, and not one of you asks Me, 'Where are you going?' Yet, because I have spoken these things to you, sorrow has filled your heart. Nevertheless, I am telling you the truth. It is for your benefit that I go away, because if I don't go away the Counselor will not come to you. If I go, I will send Him to you.'"

Our ability to understand things compared to God's understanding of things is similar to a child's compared to an adult's. I saw a little boy with his family in a restaurant eating supper the other night. He appeared to be very well cared for and loved. His family spoke kindly to him and included him in the conversation, even though he was the only child present. The waitress had brought everyone's drink order and had just finished taking the food order. The little boy accidentally spilled his drink, then immediately started crying. He had made a simple mistake which caused an accident. His mother immediately starting cleaning up the mess and attempting to comfort the little boy who continued to cry, despite the mother's comforting words. The waitress was also there, cleaning up the mess and both were trying to comfort the little boy with kind words. The child did not cease to cry until the mother assured him that the waitress was going to get him another drink. With that reassurance, the little boy immediately stopped crying and was fine. It was only then that the mother realized that the little boy had been crying because he thought he would have to eat his meal with nothing to drink. To the mother, the spilled drink was a simple, very solvable problem that was not cause for tears or sorrow. To the little boy, it was horrible. It was an insurmountable problem that reduced him to tears with no hope. The severity of the problem depended on the knowledge of the person. That is how it is with us and God. We cry and have no hope because we can't see the whole picture. We don't know all that God knows, just as the little boy didn't know that the waitress was already going to bring him another drink but the mother did. She wasn't crying or upset about the drink being spilled because she knew that the little boy would have another drink. She knew that she would never let her little boy go without something that he needed because she loved him. He knows that his mother loves him but for a moment he forgot how much. Really, he doesn't have the ability to understand just how much his mother loves him. But even with his limited understanding, he knows that he always has a drink with his meal and that his mother loves him. He just forgot for a moment. God sympathizes with us the way that mother sympathized with the little boy only on a much larger scale. HE comprehends things that we don't have the ability to understand and therefore we cry. But HE comforts us because HE loves us, not because HE doesn't know what is coming. We need to learn to trust HIM, just as the little boy will learn to trust his mother. It is part of growing up. As the little boy grows up, he will learn to trust his mother more. As we grow up in Christ, we learn to trust HIM more.

A Discussion With God

Read Psalm 63:1-11

Verses 3-4. "My lips will glorify you because Your faithful love is better than life. So I will praise You as long as I live; at Your name, I will lift up my hands."

King David was in the wilderness of Judah when he wrote this Psalm. Maybe he was lonely and fearful for his life as he hid from King Saul and felt the need to call upon God. He knew that praise always lifts us up and puts us in a better place to see that we are actually being well cared for by our Savior even when the human in us is feeling abandoned.

As we obediently begin to praise God, to seek HIM, and to remember HIS many blessings and miracles that HE has bestowed on us, we begin to be comforted. It is not that God has changed, but we have changed. HIS power, HIS help, HIS protection and HIS amazing love for us have been there all along. It is we who must realize that it is there and accept it. We should be comforted and excited by God's power. If we are saved, and thereby HIS children, we know that HE wants the very best for our lives. We can trust God with ALL of our problems, not just our need for salvation. HE can handle our greatest need, and all our other problems after that. Early, we should seek HIM with all that we are, and then we will begin to see HIS power and glory. HE will help us and we can rejoice in HIM, our ultimate rescuer and Savior. We can have joy even in our fearful times if we just learn to voice our praises to Him like King David did!

Notes: _____

_____

_____

_____

_____

_____

_____

Sing and Clap

Isaiah 55:11-12. "'so My word that comes from My mouth will not return to Me empty, but it will accomplish what I please and will prosper in what I send it to do. You will indeed go out with joy and be peacefully guided; the mountains and the hills will break into singing before you, and all the trees of the field will clap their hands.'"

The Mountains burst forth into singing and the trees clap their hands! WOW! These scripture verses are most intriguing and exciting to me. I can hardly imagine what that event will be like to be a part of and witness, but I think it will be an awesome thing to experience. The very elements of nature and the very growing things of the earth will be singing and clapping their hands (Bet you didn't know before now that trees have hands!) and praising the very God of their creation. The people of the ages who have denied God or failed to trust Him, will be mourning and wailing and crying out for mercy, while those who belong to the Lord will be joining with all of nature and all of creation in giving praise to the one and only God of all! What an amazing scene this will be and I can hardly wait to be involved! I KNOW, and have great security in the fact, that I will be one of those singing, clapping and praising! My prayer is that as you read this, you also have the security of knowing that you will be among the happy ones when that day comes, and it definitely WILL come! If you do not have that security, now is the time to ask the Lord, Jesus Christ, for forgiveness and to come into your heart and life. It is a simple thing but so important to know that you are saved and have this security. What a day that will be! Don't take a chance and find yourself in the wrong crowd that day. Make sure you are there clapping your hands with the trees and singing with the mountains!

Notes: _____

_____

_____

_____

_____

_____

_____

I Am and I Will

Isaiah 41:9-10. "I brought you from the ends of the earth and called you from its farthest corners. I said to you: You are my servant; I have chosen you and not rejected you. Do not fear, for I am with you; do not be afraid, for I am your God. I will strengthen you; I will help you; I will hold on to you with My righteous right hand."

This scripture and the old hymn, "How Firm A Foundation", which this scripture inspired John F. Wade (1710-1786) to write, has a lot to say to us even now. It tells us that God has chosen us and wishes to bring us to Him from far and wide and from high and low. Whether we are in distant lands or just down the street; whether we occupy the highest offices of authority or whether we are the poorest of the poor living in the alleyways, He knows who we are and where we are and He is interested in our life. We were created by Him and our purpose in living is to serve Him and bring honor and glory to His name. His desire is that each and every one of us would come to Him and learn to trust Him for our every need. He does not want any one of us to be destroyed by Satan, but rather has made a way of salvation for all of us. But, because He loves us so much, He has given us the choice of whether we want to live eternity with Him or not. He clearly states in these scriptures that IF we choose Him in this life, He will be with us, give us courage and strength, and hold us in His hands. How much more could anyone ask for? To KNOW that you are being held in the very hand of God is such a wonderful and comforting thought to hold on to. "The soul that on Jesus hath leaned for repose, I will not, I will not desert to his foes. That soul, though all hell shall endeavor to shake, I will never, no never, no never forsake!" I have seen it myself....in studying the life of someone who has long ago gone to be with God. He never forsook them and has given them His protection and honor all through the years....and even now still extends His grace to their descendants through generation after generation. This truly is the firm Foundation Christians can stand on!

Notes: _____

_____

_____

_____

_____

_____

God Fights Our Battles

2 Kings 19:34-35. "'I will defend this city and rescue it for My sake and for the sake of My servant David.' That night the angel of the Lord went out and struck down 185,000 in the camp of the Assyrians. When the people got up the next morning–there were all the dead bodies!"

Any of our battles that are real battles are God's battles. David probably had no idea that God would send His angel to fight. He has ways of fighting that we know nothing about. He is bigger, greater, mightier, stronger and wiser than anything we can ever face. And just like that city, if we are saved, we are God's. We belong to HIM. We defend our own families and we never realize that we learned that from God. How often does the "mama bear" come out in us when someone mistreats our child? My son is grown, but the mama bear still comes out in me quickly if someone is mistreating him. And it is the same way for any of my family. I love my own. The instinct to fight for our family is strong. That instinct that we have to defend our own comes from HIM. Once we are saved, we are HIS and HE defends HIS own. Over and over in the Bible, God promises to care for and defend His children. We can read story after story in the Bible of the battles He fought for Israel. Some battles were against enemy nations, and others were against illness. He fought battles alongside His people and provided them with the strength to stand. We still face different types of battles today.

His children are persecuted in many countries around the world and that list is growing. Many dear saints face terrible pain from disease, and the emotional battles of depression and heartache. No matter what type of battle we are facing (and we are all facing one of some kind), God will never leave us to fight the battle alone. He will be there fighting for us every time. Oh, and HE always wins HIS battles!

Notes: _____

_____

_____

_____

_____

_____

Believe It and Claim It!

Isaiah 42:9-10. "'The past events have indeed happened. Now I declare new events; I announce them to you before they occur.' Sing a new song to the Lord; sing His praise from the ends of the earth, you who go down to the sea with all that fills it, you islands with your inhabitants."

When God tells us something, we must believe it and claim it. We must believe it as if we have already seen it come to pass. That is faith. That is really believing God. Believing is a verb. It takes action to be a verb. We cannot simply say we believe something God says, even though that is a start. We must act and live like we believe it. Sometimes we must be obedient to act and live like we believe something God has promised even though our feelings don't match up. It is hard to live as if something has taken place when you are stuck in the before it happens way of life. It is hard to give praise for something you cannot yet see. But we are called to do just that. Abraham believed the promise of God and lived like he could already see it. We read about people in the Bible doing that and forget that years of obedience took place before they saw the promise fulfilled. Why is it so hard for me to walk in faith? Why do I forget to praise God for what I've prayed for before I see it? I have to deliberately choose to put this way of life into practice. If I believe God will do what He says, then I must live like I believe it. Obedience is part of believing. Obeying is also a verb. Our

God is a living God who is active in our lives. HE doesn't just watch and leave us alone to face our trials. He is with us. He is working on our behalf. HE is, HE was and HE always will be... HE is God and that is more than we can even comprehend. HE is the ultimate parent. If you pray for rain, then you need to carry your umbrella with you or get your head wet!

Notes: _____

_____

_____

_____

_____

_____

_____

Descendants

Read Isaiah 44:1-8.

Verse 3. "'For I will pour water on the thirsty land and streams on the dry ground; I will pour out My spirit on your descendants and My blessing on your offspring.'"

A while back, I started praying for my descendants to have faith, serve the Lord and fear not. God made promises to Abraham, David and many others concerning their descendants. Why would He not make promises to our descendants if we asked? How many of us pray for our descendants? Those that we don't know... The ones that haven't been born yet. If we want to leave our children and their children and their children and on, a heritage of faith, now is the time to start. I love my son and I know already that if he ever has children, I will love my grandchildren. It is not something that I have to think about. I just know it. I also know if I were allowed to live to see great-grandchildren and great-great-grandchildren, I would love them too. I know I would love my descendants as long as I lived to know them. So, why do we not pray for them? I believe we will wish one day that we had. I think it is important to start now working on the heritage that we will leave to our descendants. And what better thing can you do for them than to pray for them? Pray that they will be saved and that their faith will be strong. Pray that they will serve the Lord as long as they are on the face of the earth. You do not have to know names. God, who was, who is and who will always be, already knows what their names will be. HE knows what they will look like and what they will face. So pray. Pray everyday. One day in Heaven, they will come to you and thank you. Perhaps your prayer, will be the nudge they need to turn their heart to HIM. After all, Jesus prayed for us before we were born (John 17:20). It is our turn now, to look at that example and pray for our descendants.

Notes: _____

_____

_____

_____

_____

_____

_____

Death Is Just A Doorway

1 Corinthians 15:25-26. "For He must reign until He puts all His enemies under His feet. The last enemy to be abolished is death."

1 Corinthians 15:55. "Death, where is your victory? Death, where is your sting?"

Death. It is something we will all face eventually....death.... unless of course, Jesus returns before we suffer a physical death. It is something none of us understand nor can we comprehend what it will be like. We will all have to "go it alone" so to speak.....but then, not really. If we DO face the death of these physical bodies our souls inhabit, we can be assured that we will not really be alone. Sure, we can't go with our loved ones across the river of death but we can know for sure that Jesus is with us and them. He is standing just inside the doorway waiting with outstretched hands for us. This image is so real to me. After my Dad died, I struggled many nights not being able to find peace and rest. I couldn't sleep well and often would fall asleep for a few minutes only to wake up shortly and remain awake most of the rest of the night. It was beginning to wear me down. I KNEW without a doubt that my Dad was with Jesus in Heaven for he was a strong Christian, but I think because he died in the middle of the night in his hospital room with none of the family in the room with him, somewhere in my mind I felt like he struggled alone before his death. It disturbed me to feel like he died alone. I had prayed for peace and asked God to help me to come to terms with my feelings and doubts...to help me to understand and give me comfort about losing my Dad. One night, after praying, I actually fell asleep very soundly and was resting peacefully. But suddenly, I awoke fully with a strong feeling that someone was there with me...standing alongside my bed and patiently waiting and watching me sleep. I sat up and felt someone's presence and with a completely clear vision, saw my Dad standing near the doorway. He didn't speak out loud so there was no audible sound, but my spirit understood what was being communicated to me. He had so much joy and peace shining on his face and he told me that I should be at peace about the process of death. He told me that it was not hard...that actually it was easy because Jesus was there and it was simply like stepping through a doorway that Jesus had opened and taking His hand to pass through. He said not to worry anymore about him and that all anyone needed to have the assurance that death was not a bad thing, is to KNOW Jesus as our Savior. I don't know how any of this came about. I know my Dad was not really there. I don't understand much about it at all. What I do KNOW is that it happened and I know that since that night, I have had a complete peacefulness about death. I believe God caused it to happen to comfort me and assure me that my Dad was fine. For the Christian, I am convinced that death is simply stepping through the doorway into the arms of Jesus. I hope you have that assurance also.

Notes: _____

_____

_____

_____

Queen Esther

Read Esther 5-8.

Verse 4:14. "If you keep silent at this time, liberation and deliverance will come to the Jewish people from another place, but you and your father's family will be destroyed. Who knows, perhaps you have come to your royal position for such a time as this."

Esther was young and afraid. She was an orphan who was raised by her cousin Mordecai. Due to circumstances she had no control over, Esther was chosen to be Queen to King Xerxes. When the lives of her people were in danger, she had an opportunity to intervene to help them. She loved her people but the king was powerful. She also believed God. Her faith in God overcame her fear of the king. The king could kill her but it was worth the risk to do what she felt was God's will for her. It was her duty. This courageous young woman sets a very good example for us today. We face fears. We all fear something. We fear losing our jobs, sickness, financial issues and the list goes on. But we must remember that God is more powerful than any of these things. HE has control of all things. HE is all powerful. HE sees, HE hears and HE loves us. Esther continued to be Godly and humble also during this time. Even in victory, the Jews continued only to defend themselves. They did not take the spoil. We can be encouraged to obey God as we read about

Esther. God saved Esther and her people. HE used her to do it! We can all be used by God if we will just obey HIM! Even when we are afraid, if we just do our best to obey God's will for us, we will face down our fears and see the results God has planned. Trust God and follow His direction. He's always in control of the outcome.

Notes: _____

_____

_____

_____

_____

_____

Praising In Prison

Read Acts 16:9-31.

Verse 25. "About midnight Paul and Silas were praying and singing hymns to God, and the prisoners were listening to them."

After Paul had a vision of a man in Macedonia begging him to come and help them, he immediately made plans to go there. Luke and Silas were with him. They went to Philippi where he met with Lydia and her prayer group along the riverbank. Word spread of their presence and teaching and a young slave girl who had a demonic spirit started following them, shouting as she followed, calling attention to them everywhere they went. This young girl was able to predict things that would happen because of the spirit which possessed her. Paul healed the girl of the evil spirit and because her owners were no longer able to make money with her predictions, they went to the court and had Paul and Silas cast into jail. Even while in prison, Paul and Silas were praying and singing hymns to God. How many times do I sing praises to God during the thick of my trials? After all, Paul and Silas were in prison for doing God's work. This is an amazing story full of miracles which all happened because Paul listened to the Lord and followed HIS directions. They always do! A young girl was healed; people were saved; an earthquake opened the prison doors; the jailer and his family were saved, and as news spread of the miracles, people were excited by God's power. If we are saved, and thereby are His children, we know that He wants our best. We can trust God with ALL of our problems, not just with our need for salvation. He can handle our greatest need, and all other problems after that. Early we should seek Him with all that we are and then we will begin to see His power and glory. When that happens, often others are impacted also and people are saved. That is our ultimate job and goal, isn't it? He will help us and we can rejoice in Him as we do what he tells us to do and leave the rest to Him!

Notes: _____

_____

_____

_____

_____

_____

Walking With Jesus

Read Luke 24:13-49

Verses 33-34. "That very hour they got up and returned to Jerusalem. They found the Eleven and those with them gathered together, who said, 'The Lord has certainly been raised and has appeared to Simon!'"

Later on the same day after Jesus' tomb had been found empty, Cleopas, who had been following Jesus, together with another believer, was walking along the road to Emmaus, discussing the things that had happened. They were discouraged, thinking Jesus was dead, and trying to understand it all, when Jesus Himself began to walk with them. Because they were so distraught, they didn't recognize Him as He explained the necessity of all that had happened. When it was almost dark, they asked Him to stay with them and eat supper. As He took the bread, blessed it, and gave them a piece, their eyes were opened to recognize Him, but He was immediately gone from them. They realized their hearts had felt His amazing presence while He'd been walking with them and they immediately went back to Jerusalem to tell the others they'd been with the risen Jesus. Their fear of traveling after dark was overcome by their excitement at having been with Jesus. As they were all together talking about these exciting events, Jesus appeared in the room with them, saying, 'Peace to you.' Showing them His pierced hands and feet, He said 'It is I.' Isn't this the way our Savior always works? Just when we are at our most hopeless and lowest point, He comes alongside us speaking peace and assurance to us, giving us the strength and courage to keep going even when our circumstances are still scary! Fear turns to bravery and we have to tell the Good News of salvation!

Notes: _____

_____

_____

_____

_____

_____

_____

Plunge In!

Read John 21:1-25

Verse 7. "The disciple, the one Jesus loved, said to Peter, 'It is the Lord!' When Simon Peter heard that it was the Lord, he tied his outer garment around him (for he was stripped) and plunged into the sea."

Peter, distraught, ashamed and broken because of the death of Jesus and his own denial of Him, went back to the familiar life of fishing he'd known. Six of the other disciples were with Peter in his boat that night. Sometimes when we're broken in deep sorrow and can't think what to do, the best thing is to go back to a comfortable routine. It can be a type of therapy and rest to just function in the familiar rather than keep struggling to understand a traumatic event. That's what these hurting men did that night. They just went back out on the water in the boat and fished, but they caught nothing. At daybreak, they saw a man on the beach but didn't recognize that it was Jesus. He told them to try casting their net on the right side of the boat and when they did, their catch was so big (153 fish!), they couldn't even pull the net into the boat. John said, "It is the Lord!", and when Peter heard that, Scripture says he 'plunged' into the water, abandoning his own boat, and swam to shore. Jesus fed them breakfast and used the time to show Peter He was still loved and valued, and that he still had a place and a purpose in the Kingdom. God will always use us if we abandon ourselves completely to His will and plunge in without holding back, to dedicate our lives to bringing glory to Him, no matter what our past failures have been. He's waiting to give us a huge 'catch' if we just obey where He tells us to 'fish'! Jesus is our Redeemer, our Restorer, our Savior!

Notes: _____

_____

_____

_____

_____

_____

Just Ask Mary

Luke 1:37. "For nothing will be impossible with God."

We forget this sometimes when we pray. We pray and ask God for the impossible but we do not expect it to happen. Why? Why would we ever think ANYTHING was impossible for the ONE who took nothing and made the world? We set our sights too low. We give up on important things of God far too easily. We have a loved one who is not saved, but we think they will never be saved because we can't convince them. If we give up, we are counting God out! Just because something is impossible for us, doesn't mean that God can't do it! We must pray as if we believe ALL things are possible with God. And then we must live like we believe that all things are possible with God. Get up from your knees and go forth expecting your prayers to be answered in God's will! Believe what HE says and then live like you believe it! If we change the way we believe and think, it will change the way we act and live. It will change our attitudes, our lives and the number of people that we reach for Jesus. We will not be able to keep from telling people about all the miracles that Jesus does. Miracles are those "impossible" things that God does and gives us the great privilege of seeing. Once we believe that with God nothing is impossible, then we will start seeing "impossible" things happening!

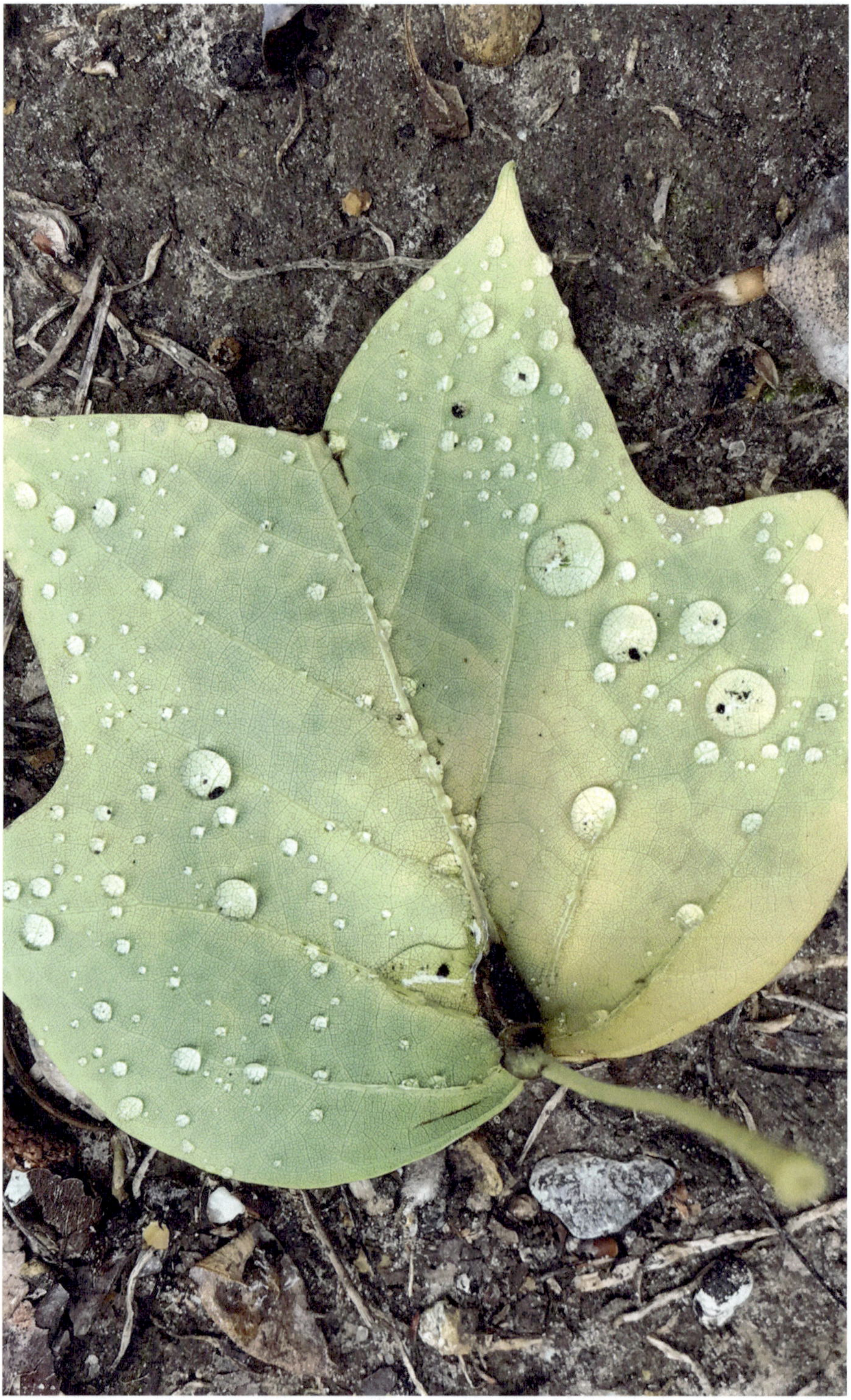

Be Like The Leaves

Ecclesiastes 3:1-2. "There is an occasion for everything, and a time for every activity under heaven: a time to give birth and a time to die; a time to plant and a time to uproot;"

I have been watching as the weather turns from hot to warm and now to cool with cold coming before long. I don't really like the Fall and Winter seasons, but I know that it is God's plan for the renewal of all of nature and so I just try to deal with it. I try to find things to keep my hands and my mind busy in the cold season. But in thinking about Fall, which is the season we are experiencing right now, I have been looking at the trees and all the colors of the leaves as they turn from summer's greens to the varied palette of colors in the earth-tone range. I have to admit, even though I don't really like this season, that God absolutely outdoes Himself with the colors in the dying leaves. There is no way even an expert paint mixer could come up with some of the variations in oranges, browns, golden yellows, and reds. It is an awesome sight to see each year. It seems like to me that God is telling us that even though maybe we are getting older and don't have a lot of time left in our season of life, we can still have a usefulness and be a radiant hue of blessing and joy for Him. We can show our colors and we can make sure they are beautiful and attractive for others to see. It is one way we can radiate our Savior and His great love in our life... by being what He wants us to be and make others think about

Him when they look at us. I have been wondering this Fall what this world we live in would be like if WE, as people created by God in His image, would be as obedient as the leaves are to His commands. After all, He created this world and all of nature along with us human beings, and as we observe His creation, we can see that all of nature obeys His commands for them and their season of life. There is no disobedience. The leaves do as they are supposed to do. What a wonderful place this earth could be if even just those of us who are called by HIS name, would do as the leaves do. They begin their lives and end their lives obeying God. And even in their death and eventual disintegration back into dust of the earth, they are still obeying God and providing nourishment for the next generation of leaves to come. We should take a lesson from the leaves of the trees and do the same. Will our descendants be able to gain nourishment and courage and faith by observing how we have lived our lives?

Notes: _____

_____

_____

_____

_____

_____

Don't Forget Your Overcoat!

Read Ephesians 6:10-18.

Verse 18. "Pray at all times in the Spirit with every prayer and request, and stay alert with all perseverance and intercession for all the saints."

The first thing Paul tells his readers in this message is to Be Strong...not in our own power, but in the Lord and His power. That's first and foremost and the key to be able to stand in this world and what it constantly bombards us with. We have to have God's armor and we must make a conscious decision to 'put it on' each and every day because scripture tells us our enemy, the devil, is going about all the time like a roaring lion seeking prey to devour. Unless we put on God's armor before we encounter the devil, there is no way we can stand against his onslaught. We aren't really standing against flesh and blood people, rather, we are fighting against the evil powers that control those people who are against God and His Kingdom. We have to remember that God loves each person, even those against Him, as much as He loves us. Paul knew these people well, because they constantly followed and harassed him as he traveled in his ministry to the early churches. Some of them were the religious leaders of Paul's day, who were unconvinced that Jesus was the Messiah and felt threatened by the growth of Christianity. Their zeal should have been for God but instead was misdirected against early apostles like Paul and others who were working to help establish churches and see souls being saved. Paul advised his readers two times in these verses to 'put on the armor of God' in order to be able to stand against the evils of the day. Good advice for them, and good advice for us in our lives today. We, too, have many evil forces around us daily which are trying to cause us to stumble and fall. The devil's greatest triumph is to get us Christians to let a little doubt come in or stumble on a temptation which causes us to sin. If you have a job that GOD has given you to do, you WILL face opposition. Our first response should be to pray; second to prepare; third to carry on as if the battle is already won because the battle is God's. If HE wants you to do something, HE will fight the battle for and with you. You need to be available to do the work. God will provide the way. Verse 18 instructs us to pray and bring our needs and requests before God for help. Prayer is the 'overcoat' which finishes up our armor and we should never leave home without it! We would be well advised to take seriously Paul's instructions to the Ephesian church goers, and apply them to our lives daily. We can get advice from many places nowadays, but we'll never find any that's better than what God's Book freely provides for us. God said it, we just need to heed it!

Notes: _____

_____

_____

_____

_____

Build A Relationship with God

James 4:8. "Draw near to God, and He will draw near to you. Cleanse your hands, sinners, and purify your hearts, you double-minded people."

We all know that Jesus comforts us during trying and difficult times, but do we prepare to receive that comfort during the good times? That's right. We have to prepare during the good times to be able to get the most out of the comfort we receive during the hard times. How do we do that? By building a deeper relationship with the Lord during the good times, we feel His comforting presence even stronger during the hard times... the times when we feel like we are just walking in the dark of suffering, barely surviving. We must read and study HIS word everyday. We must spend time in prayer everyday. The more scripture that we have put into our mind and heart, the more the Holy Spirit can call it to our remembrance. If we have read the promises many times, then He can call those promises to memory to comfort us. If prayer is like breathing to us during the good times, it will be natural to pray to Jesus during the hard times. Sure, the Lord sometimes uses hard times to draw us closer to Him, but if we draw closer to Him during the good times, we will find it easier to feel that comfort during the hard times. Relationships must be two-way. We must talk to God but we must also listen. We want Him to know us but we must also want to know Him! We get to know the Lord by spending time in His word, time in prayer and time with others discussing what He has done for us. As we do these things, we begin to see how very much He cares for us. He really meant it when He said He would never leave us, nor forsake us. Others may, but not God. That is a promise you can count on!

Notes: _____

_____

_____

_____

_____

_____

Keep Working!

Read Nehemiah 6:1-15.

Ephesians 6:12. "For our battle is not against flesh and blood, but against the rulers, against the authorities, against the world powers of this darkness, against the spiritual forces of evil in the heavens."

Nehemiah 6:14. "My God, remember Tobiah and Sanballat for what they have done, and also Noadiah the prophetess and the other prophets who wanted to intimidate me."

We see in the scripture from Nehemiah that there were people in high places who were opposed to Nehemiah and his efforts to rebuild the wall. They sent him messages several times and finally accused him of doing wrong and trying to get the people to rebel against their authority. The accusers were some of the people who should have been supportive of Nehemiah as he tried to rebuild the wall and bring the people back to worshiping the true God. Instead they were doing all they could to work against him....basically trying to tear down the confidence of the people and even Nehemiah himself. Nehemiah did not give in to their demands and accusations. He went on with his work and went on with his aim to do the will of God. We see in this story and it is also backed up in the Ephesians scripture, that sometimes the most opposition comes from those who have set themselves up in the "heavenly places"...the religious ones, like the Pharisees who worked so much evil toward Jesus himself. These are the same kinds of people who were called "Generations of vipers" by Jesus. The ones who name the name of Jesus and yet do everything they can against the children of God. Sometimes I think the ones who use their positions of being in the high places of the church to do their evil works, are worse than those who make no claim whatsoever to be a child of God. But if we read verse 14 in Nehemiah chapter 6, we see how he handled their evil deeds. He asked God to remember them and what they had done. And then he went on and finished the wall. That is a wonderful example of how we should handle these kinds of adverse situations. We have to turn them over to God for whatever he has in store for them and then go on with the work He has given us to do. We can be sure that we will all have these kinds of situations come up now and again in our lives... IF we are doing our best to follow God's will. There will always be opposition and it is especially hurtful when it comes from within the church....the one place we should be able to feel love and support. But, when it happens we have to remember, like Nehemiah, to turn them and their deeds over to God, let Him deal with them and then go on with our work.

Notes: _____

_____

_____

_____

_____

Go Your Way Rejoicing!

Read Acts 8:26-39

Verse 39. "When they came up out of the water, the Spirit of the Lord carried Philip away, and the eunuch did not see him any longer. But he went on his way rejoicing."

Can you imagine how excited the eunuch was? God sent someone specifically to explain the scriptures to him. After the scriptures were explained to him, he was saved and wanted to be baptized. Right then, not later. So, Philip baptized him and then Philip was just caught away. The enuch was so excited that he went on his way rejoicing. He had witnessed two miracles. He'd been saved, baptized and witnessed Philip being caught away. We should go our way rejoicing too. We too, have seen many miracles. If we have been saved and baptized, we should go our way rejoicing. That is the greatest thing that could ever happen to us. Do we recognize miracles that we see? Do we publicly acknowledge miracles that we witness or experience? Or do we simply keep those to ourselves for fear that someone will laugh? I wonder how many people would believe that Jesus is the Christ, if we simply talked about the miracles we have witnessed. If we simply went our way rejoicing. Rejoicing to me is exciting! We should be excited! We have a Savior who loves us and if we are saved, we will get to spend eternity with HIM! That is something to be excited about! Rejoice!

A Godly Step Daddy

Read Matthew 1:18-25.

Verse 24. "When Joseph woke up from sleeping, he did as the Lord's angel had commanded him. He married her."

We can learn a lot about the kind of people we should be from these verses. The Bible says that Joseph was a just man. God chose a just person to be the step daddy to His son. Step fathers have a place and a responsibility. We see that Joseph was a kind hearted person, even though he didn't initially understand the situation. Let's think about this from Joseph's viewpoint for a minute. Joseph is engaged to Mary. He loves her and has confidence in her being a virtuous woman, the kind he wants for a wife. He believes she is a virgin. Then he gets the news that she is pregnant. He knows the child is not his. He would have felt hurt and betrayed. He would have been humiliated. All his plans are dashed. He is confused. He has every legal right to have Mary stoned. Some would say he should have gone ahead and "made her a public example." Some would have been telling him that he had to think of his own reputation. But Joseph didn't react immediately. Verse 19 says "Then Joseph her husband, being a just man and not willing to make her a public example, was minded to put her away secretly" (NKJV). He took his time and thought about things. He did not allow his own hurt to cloud his judgment.

He did not choose revenge to hurt Mary. A quiet divorce would have been the least harmful to her. Joseph could have missed the greatest opportunity of his life if he had reacted harshly or hastily. Verse 20 says "but while he thought on these things". While he thought about what to do, the angel of the Lord appeared to him in a dream. Not an angel, but "the" Angel of the Lord! Wow! How awesome would that have been? You are discouraged and hurting, broken hearted and don't know what to do, and you get a personal visit from the Angel of the Lord. The Angel of the Lord says, "Joseph, son of David, do not be afraid to take to you Mary your wife, for that which is conceived in her is of the Holy Spirit. And she will bring forth a Son, and you shall call His name Jesus, for He will save His people from their sins" (NKJV). Joseph now knows that what he believed about Mary was true. The hurt and betrayal are gone. He again believed the best about Mary. Joseph would have known about the promised Messiah. Now Joseph is going to have an active role in this fulfilled prophecy. We also see that Joseph had great faith in God and that he was obedient. Joseph would have faced ridicule himself for marrying Mary. But he chose obedience to God regardless of the hardships. Theirs would have been a strong marriage. Mary's confidence in Joseph would have soared when he told her he was still going to marry her. They would have faced much ridicule together. Joseph was a man who thought through his decisions, who put others ahead of himself and most importantly, who obeyed God, no matter the cost. Step fathers, you are helping to raise a child that is very special to Jesus. Don't take your responsibility to love and protect that child lightly.

Notes: _____

_____

_____

Joseph's Obedience

Read Matthew 2:12-15, 19-23.

Verses 13-14. "After they were gone, an angel of the Lord suddenly appeared to Joseph in a dream, saying 'Get up! Take the child and His mother, flee to Egypt, and stay there until I tell you. For Herod is about to search for the child to destroy him.' So he got up, took the child and His mother during the night, and escaped to Egypt."

Men, if you marry a woman who already has a child, you must commit to love that child as your very own. You must put the needs of that child ahead of your own needs. God chose Joseph to be the earthly father to Jesus. This was not an easy task. The difficulty of the task did not lessen the importance of it though. Joseph would have had to make a living for his family. Moving to Egypt suddenly in the middle of the night would have made that difficult. His faith in what the angel of the Lord had told him about Jesus being the Messiah would have had to be strong to endure all he faced trying to protect Jesus from Herod. But Joseph obeyed God and look at his reward! Women who marry a man with a child, also have to make that same commitment. I believe being a step parent is even harder than being a parent, but can be a precious relationship if handled with love. Many times, the step children need extra grace and help adjusting to new situations.

Obviously, Jesus did not come from a broken home, but many children in the world today do. The children of this world are special to our Lord and they should be to us also. If we fail to be obedient in this job, we will miss so much more than we know. Obedience to the Lord is the only way. It is worth it! He will do amazing things with our lives if we will just surrender our time and energy to HIM.

Notes: _____

_____

_____

_____

_____

_____

Make Godly Choices

Read Genesis 19:4-24.

Verses 12-14. "Then the angels said to Lot, 'Do you have anyone else here: a son-in-law, your sons and daughters, or anyone else in the city who belongs to you? Get them out of this place, for we are about to destroy this place because the outcry against its people is so great before the Lord, that the Lord, that the Lord has sent us to destroy it.' So Lot went out and spoke to his sons-in-law, who were going to marry his daughters. 'Get up,' he said. 'Get out of this place, for the Lord is about to destroy the city!' But his sons-in-law thought he was joking."

Choose carefully where you will raise your children. Choose carefully your surroundings. Lot chose his home based on wealth, not based on a Godly location. Even though Lot was Godly himself, he allowed his family to be surrounded by ungodly people. Therefore, his daughters married ungodly men. These ungodly men would not listen to Lot when it came time to flee because God's wrath was coming. This caused his married daughters to be destroyed. Lot was saved but had children and possibly grandchildren who were destroyed due to unbelief. Be careful of the outside influence on your children. Lot's wealth failed. God saved him but the cost Lot faced for choosing the wealth over the Godly place to live was too great. Choosing to be Godly in all things must be first even above wealth and all other options. Your choices often have eternal consequences for your family. Sometimes our choices mean the difference between life and death or Heaven and Hell. I want my descendants to be in Heaven.

Notes: _____

_____

_____

_____

_____

_____

Attitudes Of Defiance?

First Peter 5:5-8. "In the same way, you younger men, be subject to the elders. And all of you clothe yourselves with humility toward one another, because God resists the proud but gives grace to the humble. Humble yourselves, therefore, under the mighty hand of God, so that He may exalt you at the proper time, casting all your cares on Him, because He cares about you. Be sober-minded! Be alert! Your adversary the Devil is prowling around like a roaring lion, looking for anyone he can devour."

I was thinking about Donald when I was reading over these verses of scripture. Donald was a domesticated mallard duck which my grandson raised from a very young age. First, when they were very small, Donald and his buddy Daffy were kept in a large pasteboard box, and with food and water and an old soft tee shirt in their box, they were pretty content and secure. With time, however, they grew and started getting their "big boy feathers". Then they were kept outside in a cage with a repurposed dog house inside their cage for a secure place. They were still dependent on my grandson for food and fresh water, but you could tell that they were feeling more on their own when moved into the wire cage area. Then before too much longer, he put a big rubber tub inside their cage with water in it and made them a ramp to walk up so that they could get into the tub and swim. At first, they were afraid of this and would not get into the water. Before long they were both swimming in the tub almost all day...only getting out to eat and go inside their "doghouse" at night. They were growing up fast, losing their downy feathers and getting a full grown-up coat. It was decided that they really would be happier free from the cage and so the decision was made to put them in our small fish pond as soon as the time was right. However, they did not know how to fend for themselves or find food on their own. Next on the agenda was to buy minnows and put into their rubber swim tub and then teach them how to dive and catch a meal. This was a funny and interesting process, and it took a little time, but worked! Once they were set free into the big pond at our house, they soon decided they did not need us and did not want a lot of contact with us. We did still put corn out for them just to be sure they had plenty to eat, but they didn't want us to catch them and touch them any more. They were grown....at least in their own minds. Unfortunately, they had never had to worry about predators or danger and Donald, in particular, was so sure of himself that he started venturing out of the pond and into the bushes...even going through the fence and onto a neighbor's property. Daffy was less venturesome, but Donald was strong-willed and he had a lot of influence over Daffy, so he would follow most of the time. A young red fox lived in the woods nearby, and before long, he had discovered the ducks and began keeping a close watch on them. We tried to keep herding them back to the pond, but Donald would not quit his through-the-fence rambling and we knew trouble would come sooner or later. One night the fox managed to get a bite into one of Donald's wings as he stalked and almost caught him. The wing was injured and there was quite a process of healing which ended with the loss of a portion of the wing. This meant that Donald would never fly again. Daffy stayed with Donald, even though he could have flown off at any time. Donald's attitude seemed to get worse and worse, however, after he could not fly and he was dominant and mean to Daffy. One morning, Daffy was simply gone and we never knew if he got tired of Donald's behavior toward him or if the fox had finally managed to have a duck supper. Donald was very defiant and seemed to be just pushing the limits of safety...almost daring the fox to catch him. He seemed to think he was "bullet-proof"....beyond anything bad happening to him. But, with his attitude and defiance of staying in the pond where he would have been more safe, of course, it wasn't long before we found a trail of duck feathers going through the bushes. Donald had not taken the danger or his adversary seriously enough and had paid the ultimate price. I think we are like Donald in a lot of ways sometimes. We think that we don't need to receive instruction; we are filled with pride and arrogance; and we think that we can handle anything that comes our way on our own. But the truth is, like the scripture says, the devil DOES exist and IS out there just lurking and watching and waiting for us to get just a little too far from the safety God provides for us. If we would only learn that we are in grave danger when we rely on ourselves and push God out of our lives and daily routines. We need his protection and help and provision every second of every hour of every day! We cannot survive on our own. But if we keep ourselves in the "shadow of His wings" and trust Him for our safety and well-being, how much easier our lives would be! When our time on earth is up, then we know we will be with Him for eternity. Dear Lord, please help us not to be like Donald and end up devoured by our enemy, the devil.

Notes: _____

Unending Provision

Deuteronomy 8:4. "Your clothing did not wear out and your feet did not swell these forty years."

God put the Israelites through 40 years of wandering in the wilderness, using that journey to test and teach them. He wanted them to learn to obey and depend on Him and keep the commandments He had given them. He fed them with manna, a super food from Heaven, when they were hungry. Manna was something they'd never seen before. He even caused their clothing to last all those years and not wear out! (And I thought my closet has some old clothes!) Even their sandals held up regardless of all that walking and their ankles didn't swell like mine do if I'm standing on my feet too much! This teaches us that God is in control of ALL things! Do we really believe this? We say we do but do we really? God is even in control of when our clothes wear out! That is an amazing thought. God made the Israelites wander in the wilderness for 40 years.

    I hope it doesn't take us 40 years in the wilderness of life to learn to believe, trust, follow, and obey Him! But, when we realize that we are still lost in that wilderness, remember it is not too late to turn to Jesus today and ask for His help in leading us out. He is waiting and He doesn't want us to wander aimlessly through life without His direction and guidance.

Listen

Deuteronomy 9:1-4. "Listen, Israel: Today you are about to cross the Jordan to go and drive out nations greater and stronger than you, with large cities fortified to the heavens. The people are strong and tall, the descendants of Anakim. You know about them and you have heard it said about them, 'Who can stand up to the sons of Anak?' But understand that today the Lord your God will cross over ahead of you as a consuming fire; He will devastate and subdue them before you. You will drive them out and destroy them swiftly, as the Lord has told you. When the Lord your God drives them out before you, do not say to yourself, 'The Lord brought me in to take possession of this land because of my righteousness.' Instead, the Lord will drive out these nations before you because of their wickedness."

"Listen"...the first word of verse one in this Scripture. It's not a suggestion! I'd consider it a command! God's about to tell the Israelites (and us) some very important things to remember and we need to listen and pay attention. They are going across the Jordan River and they'll be facing strong giants ahead. They're probably a little anxious and afraid of being defeated. I've had that feeling when facing my own giants and not knowing how I'll fare against them. He tells them (and us) what to do and what to expect: (1) He always goes ahead of us when He sends us into difficult situations; (2) He fights the battles for us when we allow Him to; (3) He subdues and destroys those wicked hindrances to His will for us; (4) He expects us to obey Him; (5) He alone deserves all the honor and glory for the victory. We are cautioned to always give the recognition and credit to Him. We are never to assume the victory was because we were worthy or because of our righteousness. The defeat of evil in our life is always and only won by His righteousness, not due to anything we've done. We gain the victory only through His grace, mercy, faithfulness and strength. We are not worthy of any praise. Only Jesus deserves that honor.

Notes: _____

_____

_____

_____

_____

_____

_____

Observe and Obey

Deuteronomy 11:22-25. "For if you carefully observe every one of these commands I am giving you to follow—to love the Lord your God, walk in all His ways, and remain faithful to Him—the Lord will drive out all these nations before you, and you will drive out nations greater and stronger than you are. Every place the sole of your foot treads will be yours. Your territory will extend from the wilderness to Lebanon and from the Euphrates River to the Mediterranean Sea. No one will be able to stand against you; the Lord your God will put fear and dread of you in all the land where you set foot, as He has promised you."

All we have to do is obey and serve the Lord. Then HE will bless us and do amazing things with us. Why is it so hard for us to believe that? Why is it so hard for us to just keep HIS commandments? The Israelites struggled to obey and keep His commandments. It's easy for us to read about their struggles and wonder why they couldn't just obey Him, at least until we take a long, hard look in the mirror. Then the question becomes directed at us. Why can't I just obey Him and serve Him? Why did I respond that way to the person in the store or the person who passed me on the highway? We all struggle with obedience. We would receive more blessings than we can imagine if we will just keep HIS commandments. I am not speaking of financial blessings necessarily. There are blessings that are far greater than any financial or physical thing we can own on this earth. There is the blessing of God's presence. There are the repercussions of a life lived in obedience and love to the Lord. Some of the blessings of obedience are received in Heaven and perhaps, even through seeing those we have influenced come to salvation. We have the commandments and we know what we should do. Now let's strive to live for the Lord! HE gave HIS all for us and we should give no less than our very best for HIM!

Notes: _____

_____

_____

_____

_____

_____

_____

Dwell In Him

Exodus 33:14-15. "Then He replied, 'My presence will go with you, and I will give you rest.' 'If Your presence does not go,' Moses responded to Him, 'don't make us go up from here.'"

Think about that for a moment. Think about the danger of going anywhere without God. Anywhere physically OR anywhere mentally. God promised Moses and the Israelites that his presence would go with them. God's presence will go with us also, through the Holy Spirit. To go somewhere without God would be to go without guidance, without protection. We want His protection, or at least I know I need it. I can trip over my own feet and fall down just walking. When you think about how close cars pass each other on the highway running 65 miles per hour, it is amazing that more crashes do not take place. You don't have to be a mountain climber to need God's protection and guidance. Everyday life is full of scary places and events. Don't go anywhere without God, not just physically but mentally also. We, as Christians, often pray for the Lord to go physical places with us but we must also pray about where we go mentally. We tend to overlook the places our thoughts can take us. We must not travel in our thoughts to anywhere that the Lord will not go with us. Thoughts on revenge or covetousness or lust. We must allow the Lord complete control in our lives. Control of our thoughts by the Lord will keep us where we need to be. Allowing the Lord to control our thoughts does not happen overnight or the instant we get saved. It is a learned and deliberate thing. It requires continual prayer and obedience but the reward will be worth it. It becomes personal at that time. And personal is just what a relationship with Jesus is. It is not something from long ago. It is now, every minute of every day. It is about loving Jesus. And if we love HIM, we love HIM every minute of every day and we want to be with HIM constantly.

Notes: _____

_____

_____

_____

_____

_____

A Story of Faithfulness

Read Matthew 1:18-25.

Verse 24. "When Joseph got up from sleeping, he did as the Lord's angel had commanded him. He married her."

What if Mary and Joseph had lived today in our society? Would Mary have been pushed to have an abortion? In the Jewish culture they lived in, Joseph could have had Mary stoned. What did her parents say? What did Joseph's parents say? We all think about the ridicule that Mary faced. What about Joseph? Once he married Mary, he would have faced slander also. The stares. The heads shaking as he walked by. The whispers behind his back. It would have been so easy to have just quietly divorced Mary and gone on with his life. Thankfully, they didn't live during a time where abortion was an option. Thankfully, Joseph was a man who was willing to listen to and obey the Lord. As a result of Joseph's willingness to listen to the Lord, he was able to be part of one of the greatest (if not the greatest) miracles God performed. Now we know that when Jesus comes back, He won't come as a baby. What might we be a part of now if only we would slow down a little and just listen for God's instructions? What could we have a front row seat to and be called from the audience to participate in if only we forgot what the world has to say and go with what Jesus says? Our ticket to a relationship with Jesus and entry into Heaven has already been bought and paid for. We just have to accept Him. But we can have a much deeper relationship if we listen for and obey His instructions. After that, there are no limits to what is possible. Obedience definitely comes with rewards. Joseph, step father of Jesus Christ! And all because he made a choice to listen and go with what the Lord said, which just happened to be against the world's advice.

Notes: _____

_____

_____

_____

_____

_____

Ordinary To Extraordinary

Read I Corinthians 1:24-31.

Verses 24-25. "Yet to those who are called, both Jews and Greeks, Christ is God's power and God's wisdom, because God's foolishness is wiser than human wisdom, and God's weakness is stronger than human strength."

Our pastor made the following statement one Sunday morning from the pulpit: "God takes ordinary people and does extraordinary things." We need to make ourselves available to God for HIS purposes. It is not about us, but about what GOD does through us. If we are only willing to be available and willing to do what HE says, then there is NO LIMIT to what GOD can and will use you to do. The miracle is God's business. Our only business is complete obedience to God. We must remain completely open to what HE might call us to do. It does not matter how impossible or how simple it may seem. We must be willing to do it. Whether it is something that we would do and think the desired result was impossible or whether it is something that HE would want us to do that in our eyes would not generate any result. It could be something huge or something as simple as hitting our knees wherever we happen to be at the moment and praying. Perhaps it would be something that no one would ever see or know about. It doesn't matter. The outcome is God's business. We are not responsible for the outcome or the consequences. It doesn't have to make sense to us prior to or afterwards. We simply must be willing to obey God's call. God is large enough to deal with and handle the results. It is not our responsibility to be great but to be willing to say "Yes Lord", and then to obey. It does not matter how small or how large a task that HE asks of us but only that we are willing. After all, HE was willing to give HIS life on the cross for us. What sweet fellowship we get from simply obeying. I wonder how many blessings I have missed during my life because I didn't simply obey. I know that I don't want to miss any more blessings that HE has for me going forward.

Notes: _____

_____

_____

_____

_____

_____

A Humble Servant

Philippians 2:8. "He humbled Himself by becoming obedient to the point of death—even to death on a cross."

If Jesus humbled himself and became obedient unto death, even the death of the cross, how much more should we be, not just willing, but determined to be obedient to God. How much more should we be humbled by the opportunity to have God even convey HIS will to us that we might obey? If Jesus was willing to humble Himself to the point of going from the God of the universe to dust, to being a man, to living in the body of a man in order to serve man, people who mocked Him, beat Him and NAILED Him to a cross until He died, how willing should we be to serve Him? We should be so humbled that He would even consider sharing what His will is with us and allowing us to be a part of it. We should be so excited about that opportunity that there would be a line of people waiting for a turn to worship Him and to pray. We should be like children scuffling over who gets to go first at doing His will! How wonderful and how amazing it is that each of us can have the opportunity to hear from Almighty God, from Jesus Lord of everything! So, yes, "Hallelujah Praise the Lamb"! Not, tell me what you want me to do first and I will decide then if I am willing to do it BUT "Yes Lord, I will do WHATEVER, you want me to do", so please show me Your will for my life. Not only please show me Your will for my life but thank YOU so much that You are willing to share Your will with me. Thank YOU that YOU would share any shred of anything with me. Hallelujah praise the Lamb! Rejoice my heart, the Lord of all is willing to speak to me!

Notes: _____

_____

_____

_____

_____

_____

_____

Prisoner?

Read Genesis 39:7-21.

Verses 19-20. "When his master heard the story his wife told him—'These are the things your slave did to me'—he was furious and had him thrown into prison, where the king's prisoners were confined. So Joseph was there in prison" (NKJV).

This is the story of Joseph. Joseph was sold into slavery as a teenage boy by his own brothers. Our pastor preached from this passage of scripture this past Sunday. His sermon was from a different angle than I have ever heard. He reminded us that all of us end up in prison sometimes. And sometimes when we end up in prison, it is through no fault of our own. Prison is different for each of us but we all have our prisons. Your prison may be your job, your marriage, your physical health, or your emotional health. Your prison sentence may feel more overwhelming on some days than others. Today is one of the pressing prison days. Prison for me today is torturous. Today's passage shows us Joseph, who went to prison for doing good. Joseph was thrown into prison for resisting the advances of his master's wife. He stood for his Godly beliefs. The scorned woman lied about him, causing his prison sentence. That may be your case today. No matter what your prison is like, you can take comfort in knowing that God is in the prison with you. Verse 21 tells us "But the Lord was with Joseph and showed him mercy" (NKJV). I am so glad that the Lord is with me today in my prison. And HE always shows me mercy. We can learn from Joseph's example. While he was in prison, he still did his best to serve God. Verse 23 tells us that "the Lord was with him, and that which he did, the Lord made it to prosper." May we remember that the Lord is always with us, and that we should do our best to serve Him. What is it to us if it is His will that we should serve Him in the prison? He will still be with us!

Notes: _____

_____

_____

_____

_____

_____

Standing Together

Read Daniel 1:3-8;11-13.

Verses 11-12. "So Daniel said to the guard whom the chief official had assigned to Daniel, Hananiah, Mishael, and Azariah, 'Please test your servants for 10 days. Let us be given vegetables to eat and water to drink.'"

Choose your friends carefully. We see in this scripture that some of the children of Israel have been carried into captivity in Babylon. Out of those children, four chose to stick together and to stand for their belief in the living God. All of the children of Israel should have believed in God, so why did only four stand for their beliefs? That question remains unanswered, however, it is worth noting that those four chose their friends wisely. It is important as Christians that we choose our friends wisely. We should choose other Christians who will encourage us to do God's will and also to stand for God's will. We know that those four went through trials for their stand, as we surely will for any stand that we make for the Lord. But we also see that they received many blessings for that same stand. Would any of the four friends have stood for the Lord alone? Probably so, but we will never know for sure. But it is surely a good thing to have friends encouraging you to stand firm in God's will. You can be sure the stories around their campfire were real and full of excitement! So, too, can be the case in your life, if you choose to completely surrender to God's will for your life.

Wait!

Read I Kings 17:3-6 and Psalm 27:14

Verse 14. "Wait for the Lord; be strong and let your heart be courageous. Wait for the Lord" (NKJV).

Maybe you are going through a time in your life where you feel like you are barely surviving. You might think it doesn't show on the outside, but you feel that way inside. Maybe it is something you are enduring at home. Maybe it is with a relationship, maybe it is financial or a mix of several things. You might feel like it is in every direction in your life. We all have those times in our life. You can't see the way out or even the way for your next step. You have prayed for direction from God, but all you feel like HE responds with is "wait". You want God to ACT on your problem, not tell you to wait. Waiting requires courage like nothing else. It is harder in ways than fighting, working or anything physical. Waiting on someone to come out of surgery or some other illness...or for a loved one to repent and turn to God. Whatever you are waiting on, remember that if you are waiting on God, you must have courage. Psalm 27:14 tells us to "Wait on the Lord" but it also says to be of good courage and HE shall strengthen thine heart. HE will strengthen us to face whatever we are going through but we must do our part. To WAIT and to be of GOOD COURAGE. That requires trust in the One you are waiting on. In I Kings 17:3-6, we see that Elijah was at his wits' end. He was afraid and alone, or so he thought. God commanded the ravens to feed Elijah. That was a miracle. Elijah had a part to do as well. HE had to obey God and go where God said. God can change things in an instant when HE is ready. The key is that HE does things in HIS timing. We cannot see all things or know all things but we can know GOD and HE is worthy of our trust. Waiting is hard but apparently not impossible. Otherwise, God wouldn't tell us to wait on HIM. When it is time though, the waiting will be over. The hard part is not knowing when the waiting will be over or what will change at that time. For now, you must endure and search for the blessings of this time. We must look for the blessings and rest that HE provides during this time of waiting, for those blessings are surely present. Rest is possible while we are waiting on the Lord but it requires courage. This is the time when your faith grows. HE IS working even if YOU can't see it.

Notes: _____

_____

_____

_____

_____

_____

_____

Here Am I!

Read Genesis 37:13-28, 37:36 and 45:28.

Verse 13. "Israel said to Joseph, 'Your brothers, you know, are pasturing the flocks at Shechem. Get ready. I'm sending you to them.' 'I'm ready,' Joseph replied."

"Here am I." (KJV) Would Joseph have said "Here Am I" if he had known he was going to end up in a pit and then sold into slavery? Joseph loved his father. When his father asked him to do something, his answer was "Here am I". When God calls us, our answer should be "Here am I". We need to be willing to say that knowing that God's will for us may be to spend some time in a pit and then in slavery. But Joseph did not stay in the pit. And his slavery was the means God used to save his family from starvation. When we are in the pit, we cannot see the way out. Joseph could not get out of the pit on his own. If God places us in a pit, we cannot get out until HE removes us. That is something we must accept. When Joseph was pulled out of the pit by his brothers, he was probably glad—but only for a moment. He probably was not glad when he found out he had been sold into slavery. In God's time, HE will remove us from the pit but HE may not be finished with us. He may put us into a situation of slavery. But just as God had a purpose for allowing Joseph to spend time in a pit and then be sold into slavery, He has a purpose if He allows us to spend time in the pit and in slavery. Our reaction should be that of Joseph. We should do our best to serve the Lord and do His will no matter what situation He puts us in. Joseph was allowed to be a part of a great thing that God did because he chose to be obedient to God during his time in slavery. Joseph spent his time in slavery trying to do God's will. God was preparing Joseph for the job that God needed him to do. The preparation started when Joseph was 17 even though the job God had for Joseph to do took place when Joseph was 39. The time of preparation was long and hard. It took 20 plus years of long, hard preparation that Joseph couldn't understand. It took faith in God on Joseph's part and obedience on Joseph's part. But when the time came for Joseph to do the job that God had prepared him for, he understood all the suffering. Would Joseph have said "Here am I" if he could have seen the next 20 plus years of his life before he answered? I don't know, but he couldn't see the outcome and neither can we. God is calling—what will your answer be? I pray that my answer is always "Here am I!" when He calls me.

Notes: _____

_____

_____

_____

_____

_____

So Run, With Patience

Read Hebrews 12:1 and Hebrews 5:14

Verse 1. "Therefore, since we also have such a large cloud of witnesses surrounding us, let us lay aside every weight and the sin that so easily ensnares us. Let us run with endurance the race that lies before us."

The King James version uses 'with patience' in place of endurance. Those two words, 'with patience' really jump out at me. I think of people I know who are athletic and who enter races often. Before they can enter the race though, they must get themselves ready for the race. They must exercise and get into shape. They must train their bodies to perform and endure. They must learn what is good to do and what is not. Exercise and training are essential in the getting ready for the race process. The process of exercising and training ourselves for a race is hard, It is not something that can be achieved instantly or easily. It takes a lot of work and effort to get ready. Hebrews 12:1 is a very intriguing verse to me. It brings into my mind a mental image of a huge crowd of onlookers on the sidelines of a great race which is about to begin. These onlookers are rooting the racers on. They are encouraging them and hoping that each one will run the race well and make it to the end successfully. I believe this great race talked about in this verse is the race of life. I believe the great cloud of witnesses are those who have run this race before us, reached the goal line, and received their prize. They are pulling for us; they want us to finish well and join them. Some of them are our fathers and mothers, our grandparents or other ancestors who have gone before us. They are hoping to see us finish our race well, but they can only look on, they cannot run for us. This great race of life is one that we all must enter and run. We will have to have endurance to make it to the finish line in a manner which will be pleasing to God. It is an ongoing, daily race which we have to be ready to get up and run each day. It is not an on and off thing. We can't run this race well if we are not constantly in shape and toned up, having ourselves prepared for it each day. Slackers won't make it. They will get left behind. The very first and most important step in training to win this great race is to accept Jesus as our Savior. That is number one and the only way we even get to hope for the prize at the end of the race. Without Jesus, there is no hope for us. To run our race well, once we have accepted Jesus as our Savior, then we need patience, training, endurance, and discernment. We have to learn how to run and also how to stand. Patience comes with time as we are running this race. It is not something we attain quickly or easily. It takes time. The training comes from learning the rules of the race; reading the handbook, the manual....God's Word, the Bible. Endurance is gained by the daily experience of running the race. As time goes by, we find that we are running, maybe at a slower pace, but with our eyes more and more focused on the goal line and this keeps us on track. Discernment is a key talent. We need to learn how to discern between those who are running with us and those who might be trying to hold us back or cause us to stumble. The ability to discern well, also comes from exercise and training. Hebrews 5:14 says, "But solid food is for the mature - for those whose senses have been trained to distinguish between good and evil." The term 'of full age' really has nothing to do with a number. It has to do with our standing in Christ Jesus; our maturity in our walk with God. It doesn't necessarily speak of an old person in number, but speaks of a mature person in Christ. 'By reason of use, have their senses exercised to discern' (NKJV) tells us that we learn by using the talent God has given us to discern both good and evil. We have to learn to listen to God's voice and instructions. We have to be responsive to the Holy Spirit nudging us toward the right direction. This is how we exercise discernment. We must use the abilities God has given us to run our race well and make it to the finish line to receive our prize which is spending eternity with Jesus.

Notes: _____

_____

_____

_____

_____

_____

_____

Ants and Giants

Read Proverbs 6:6 and First Samuel 17.

Verse 6. "Go to the ant, you slacker! Observe its ways and become wise."

Verses 49-50. "David put his hand in the bag, took out a stone, slung it and hit the Philistine on his forehead. The stone sank into his forehead, and he fell on his face to the ground. David defeated the Philistine with a sling and a stone. Even though David had no sword, he struck down the Philistine and killed him."

Recently I was listening to Charles Stanley preaching early on a Sunday morning. He was talking about the beauty of nature and all of God's great creation and how when he thought about it all, it caused him to worship the God who is creator of all this. He mentioned large animals and small and talked about God's amazing plan which includes all sizes and shapes of these interesting animals, insects and birds and how he loves to photograph them. He made a statement which really intrigued me saying 'imagine how large we must look to an ant.' As I thought about that statement, I could not help but think about the verse in Proverbs which points to the ant as something we should take note of and learn from. Then I thought about how large we are in comparison to them and my mind went to the young David who stood before Goliath and how he must have compared in size something like an ant to us. If we consider the ant, though, we can surely see that they are created by God for a reason and they do not question, they simply go about their daily life fulfilling the mission they were given by God. They work hard, and work together to do what is best for the colony, and they are very ingenious in finding ways to accomplish their goal. Think about how if you see a line of ants heading somewhere, they are mostly in single file and all moving along one after the other at a fast pace heading toward whatever their mission is at that time. If you take a stick and drag it across the ground disrupting their line, they seem to recover very soon and again go on their way. They do not get delayed or distracted for long before they are back on mission, and it does not seem to discourage them that they are so small compared to just about everything else. They are not afraid; they stand their ground. As a young man, probably in his teenage years, David was tending the sheep for his father. He was doing what he was supposed to be doing, but his father changed his mission and sent him to the battlefield area where his oldest three brothers were fighting in Saul's army against the Philistines. He was sent to take food to them from their father and also to check on their well-being. However, when he got there, the giant Goliath came out and showed himself to Saul's army, as he did daily, taunting and challenging them. He boasted that no one could fight him and win and that he and the other Philistines would destroy them. David, God's giant in teenage disguise, was not frightened or disturbed by Goliath's threats. Moreover, he couldn't understand why the soldiers were intimidated and cowering in fear of this man. His feeling was, how could they let this man ridicule their God and get away with it. He set about to gather the weapons he needed to fight the giant. He gathered smooth stones for his sling, simple things, but he actually already had the only Weapon he needed....he had God on his side and that made him a winner before he ever stepped up to face Goliath. God has provided for the 'ants' of this world, both the ones that crawl on the ground, and those of us on two legs who feel overwhelmed by the giants we face every day. All we have to do is stay focused on the mission He has sent us on and call on Him for the help we need. When we do like David and the ants as talked about in Proverbs, and stand up to face our daily giants, with reliance on God, and realizing there are no giants who can defeat our God, we will be victorious no matter how big and scary the giants we face may look to us.

Notes: _____

_____

_____

_____

_____

_____

_____

Jesus In Our Storms

Read Matthew 14:22-33.

Verses 22-23. "Immediately he made the disciples get into the boat and go ahead of Him to the other side, while He dismissed the crowds. After dismissing the crowds, He went up on the mountain by Himself to pray. When evening came, He was there alone."

Jesus sent the disciples on board a ship and then he sent the crowds away and went up into the mountain to pray. As the disciples were out on the water, a storm came up and tossed the boat violently. They were terrified of being swamped by the winds and waves and afraid that they were going to go down along with the boat. It strikes me that Jesus, Himself, sent them out into the water, knowing there would be a great storm for them to face. They didn't know in advance, but He did. When He sends us out into a storm, or allows us to be overtaken by a storm, we can be assured that as in this instance, He will be praying for us just as He was for the disciples. He will be going before the Father for us just as He did for the disciples. Whether the storms we sometimes face are allowed so that our faith will be strengthened, or whether we have stepped into the storms on our own due to disobedience, we can have confidence that He will be there when we call out to Him for help. The same wind-tossed waves that threaten to wash over us are used by Jesus to walk on as a pathway to our aid. Isaiah 26:3 (KJV) says that He will keep us in perfect peace whose hearts are stayed upon Him. Perfect peace means that if we keep our eyes on Him, the storms of life will not be able to cause us to falter, but will be faith-strengtheners for us. We must learn, though, to keep our eyes on Him and not on the circumstances surrounding us in the midst of the storm. Peter had to learn this as he asked Jesus to allow him to walk on the water to Him. Jesus said, 'Come', just as He says to us, and when Peter obeyed, he was able to do so. But when he took his eyes off Jesus and looked at his surrounding circumstances, the waves overwhelmed him. Oh, if we could only realize and remember that what looks over our head, is under His feet! What peace that could give us. The perfect peace Isaiah talked about. Peace in the storms of life by His power and not our own. We have to remember that He is praying for us...at the right hand of God as our intercessor and advocate, waiting for us to cry out, Save Me! When we, like Peter, let our circumstances overwhelm us and cause our faith to become weak, if we will call out, Lord, save us!, Jesus will respond to us immediately, just as he did Peter, and lift us up to a place of safety. Even the raging waters will obey Him if Jesus so choses to calm the storm, but sometimes He wants His child to be calm and peaceful while in the midst of the storm, simply resting and relying on Him for our wellbeing. How much better off we would be if we could just learn this!

Notes: _____

_____

_____

_____

_____

Some Thoughts About Life From My Heart

Psalm 92:12-15. "The righteous thrive like a palm tree, and grow like a cedar in Lebanon. Planted in the house of the Lord, they thrive in the courts of our God. They will still bear fruit in old age, healthy and green, to declare: 'The Lord is just; He is my Rock, and there is no unrighteousness in Him.'"

Psalm 71:17-19. "God, You have taught me from my youth, and I still proclaim Your wondrous works. Even when I am old and gray, God, do not abandon me. Then I will proclaim Your power to another generation, Your strength to all who are to come."

Ruth 4:15. "He will renew your life and sustain you in your old age. Indeed, your daughter-in-law, who loves you, and is better to you than seven sons, has given birth to him."

Since I've gotten older I think of life almost like the seasons of the year. It's somewhat comparable. When you're young, everything is new and exciting like Spring...full of anticipation of things to come; Summer, (or young-mid adult ages) is busy.. mixed with work to do and fun things...seemingly endless times;

Fall comes and you're beginning to be worn and tired, less enthusiastic and somewhat disillusioned since you've learned that life is often filled with hard times and sadness. There are losses and changes in family structures you don't wish for but cannot stop. Then comes Winter, and life gets harsher, cold even. Your body has aches and pains. You're frustrated because you are no longer able to accomplish all the things you've always done; things you want to do, but can't. You realize that time seems to be passing faster and faster and there are not unlimited days left for you but there are still many things you wanted to do. You still feel inside your soul like the young adult of Spring...but you're not.

    My priorities have changed considerably as I've aged. I value each day I'm given more than I did when I was younger. I try to be sure each of my days has time set aside for Bible study, reflection on the blessings I've been given and praise to God for those. I value what time I have with family and treasure it immensely. I think when you're younger, you sort of assume that your time with family is unlimited and will always be available...it will not.

    Being a widow now has changed my life completely. Too many of my plans and dreams are no longer an option to achieve. I guess we all think we have forever to do things. Having never before lived alone, I've had to learn how to manage that aloneness and not become lonely. I've had to learn how to do so many things I had never before had to do by myself. That is hard.

    I've learned that true joy comes from having a deep peace within your soul. Outside influences can give some pleasure and happiness to your life, but only peace within can give a satisfying joy. Outside circumstances no longer affect that joy within. You can actually be sad or in pain but still feel a peace within which gives joy. I find joy now more in the simpler, quiet things. I don't have to be busy or going somewhere...I can be still and be at peace and joyful within.

    It's all about my relationship with God and that is my number one priority. He is first above all else.

    I have finally learned to accept people as they are and love them without judgment. I'm learning that God loves and values every single person just as much as He loves me!

    I look back and see so many blessings God has given me in my lifetime. I was blessed to be born to Christian parents who loved me. I only regret that when I was younger, I may not have realized just how much God has blessed me. I am much more aware now of how much mercy and grace has been extended to me. My goal in life for the past few years has been to remember this and extend as much grace and mercy to others as I possibly can. I'm trying also to have an attitude of more and more gratitude and give God all the glory. I want to stay as focused as I can on God's will for my life and when my days are finished, I want to hear God say 'Well done! You ended your race well.'

Notes: _____

_____

_____

_____

_____

_____

Obey, Even If We Don't Understand

Read Luke 1:26-38.

Verse 28. "And the angel came to her and said, 'Rejoice favored woman! The Lord is with you.'"

Waiting on God brings good results. You are waiting on one who is faithful. We may not understand the results we get at the end of the waiting period and we may not even understand how the results are good, but we will understand one day when we get to Heaven. Mary had a long scary wait on the Lord after the visit from Gabriel. As an unwed teenage Jewish mother-to-be, she faced the very real possibility of stoning under the accusation of being unfaithful to Joseph, even though she had done nothing wrong. When Jesus died on the cross, it would have broken Mary's heart. I doubt she understood. But when she died, she understood. Mary was afraid and she didn't understand it all but she trusted God. She was willing to sacrifice her life for God's plan. She was willing to die but she was also willing to sacrifice her daily life – the day to day doing whatever she wanted life – for God's plan. She didn't fully understand how God's plan would take place, but she verbally accepted God's plan to Gabriel. Gabriel told her "For with God nothing shall be impossible" (Luke 1:37, KJV). We know that Mary gave birth to our Savior. We know that she and Joseph took care of Him and raised Him. That took time. Jesus was 30 years old when He began His ministry and 33 when He died on the cross. In our instant world, that is a lot of time to pass not understanding a plan. Mary and Joseph could not have done what they did if they had not had a strong commitment to and trust in God. We have the Bible to read and see that plan. They had the Old Testament, but they had to trust God for their future. We too must and can trust God with our future. He has a plan and it is a good one. It is up to us to say "Behold the handmaid of the Lord. Be it unto me according to thy word" (Luke 1:38, KJV). And then be obedient to the plan He has for our life. They did not walk alone and neither do we. God provided encouragement and guidance at exactly the times they needed it and He will for us too! He hasn't changed. He is still awesome!

Notes: _____

_____

_____

_____

_____

_____

_____

Go In God's Strength, Not Yours

Read Numbers 13:17–33.

Verse 30. "Then Caleb quieted the people in the presence of Moses and said, 'We must go up and take possession of the land because we can certainly conquer it!'"

Twelve men went secretly into the Land of Canaan to see what kind of land it was and how hard it would be to overcome the inhabitants. Moses chose twelve men, Shammua, Shaphat, Caleb, Igal, Hoseha (Joshua), Palti, Gaddiel, Gaddi, Ammiel, Sethur, Nahbi and Geuel. They were instructed to see what the land was like, if the people were strong or weak, if the land was good, if their cities were like camps or strongholds, if the land was rich or poor, and if there were forests or not. They were told to be of good courage and bring back some of the fruit of the land. They obeyed one of Moses' requests. They cut down a branch with one cluster of grapes. The cluster of grapes was so big that it took two men to carry it between them on a pole. They also brought back pomegranates and figs. That sounds like a tasty lunch after manna. He also told them to be of good courage. When they gave their report to Moses and the people, they showed the fruit of the land. They said the land truly is good. But the people are strong, the cities are fortified and large. We saw giants there, they said. Caleb interjects at this point – Let's go up at once and take possession! We can do it! Caleb was fully obeying Moses and God. He was full of courage. The other 10 men, said "No way, we can't do this.". They said the land devours its inhabitants and the people are huge. I smell a rat in this comment right off the bat. How is it that a land which devours its inhabitants could also grow giants? If the people would only have stopped and thought about that one comment for a minute, I wonder if their response would have been different. It surely might have taken them 40 years less to enter the Promised Land. I see two very big things they could have done differently to have avoided the panic that took place. They could have refused to count God out. God plus anybody is always a majority. Caleb and Joshua were counting on God to fight their battles. After all, they had just crossed the wilderness and witnessed miracle after miracle. Certainly, someone who could single handedly take out the whole Egyptian army, could take a few giants. God would be with them to fight their battles as long as they obeyed him. The second thing they should have done was stop to analyze the comment that was made. A land that devours its inhabitants certainly could never grow very large inhabitants. That just doesn't make sense. If they had spent time in prayer before they responded, they would have seen the truth. But instead, the people rejected God and His ability to take care of them. They didn't trust God nor His promise to give them the land. The consequence of this was 40 years spent wandering in the wilderness. The next time you are facing giants, spend time in prayer before you give up. Count God IN not out. I think if you pray to see the truth of God's will, you will see that you and God are a majority. You might avoid missing out on a huge blessing. And oh, by the way, Caleb and Joshua lived to enjoy this promised land, while the scared doubters all died in the wilderness!

Arguing With A Donkey

Read Numbers 22:22-34.

Verses 28-29. "Then the Lord opened the donkey's mouth, and she asked Balaam, 'What have I done to you that you have beaten me these three times?' Balaam answered the donkey, 'You made me look like a fool. If I had a sword in my hand, I'd kill you now!'"

Have you ever stopped to think about how low disobeying God will get you? I wonder sometimes if we allow ourselves to become so determined to go on a particular path that we lose track of what we are actually doing. We can sometimes be so enticed with getting material things, whether it is money or an actual object, that we fail to notice even the ridiculous things. Sometimes, when that happens, God uses something drastic to get our attention. This was the case with Eve in the garden of Eden. She had a conversation with a snake. Balaam had an argument with a donkey, and the donkey won the argument! The donkey was actually right in this case. But at some point, you would think that each of them would have stopped to wonder about a reptile and an animal speaking in their own language. I mean, really. I love my dog but if he said something in English, I think I would notice. And donkeys certainly can make some noise. We have one that is living proof of that. But if he said something to me in English, I hope that I would do a double take with the first word instead of waiting until the end of the conversation. In Balaam's case, he had quite the conversation with his little donkey. She must have been a good donkey and very loyal. The scripture says that she saw the Angel of the Lord and tried to go a different direction. The scripture says that the donkey actually saved Balaam's life. His response was to beat her. It doesn't even say that the donkey bucked him off. Balaam was so intent on something material from Balak, that he didn't stop to see what was wrong when his donkey acted abnormally. There is a lesson here that we can learn from Balaam and his donkey. When we are trying so hard to make something happen and something seems to be extremely abnormal, stop to see if maybe you are out of God's will. And yes, I would consider a donkey talking in my language extremely abnormal.

Notes: _____

_____

_____

_____

_____

_____

_____

Needful Things

Read Matthew 6:25-34.

Verse 25. "This is why I tell you: Don't worry about your life, what you will eat or what you will drink; or about your body, what you will wear. Isn't life more than food and the body more than clothing?"

Before our first grandson was born, we were trying to help our daughter find and purchase all the 'things' you need to prepare a place for a new baby. A good friend had partial interest in a shop in another town not too far distant from us and the shop sold such items as baby beds, etc. We made plans together with our friend to go to the shop one Saturday and look for a baby bed and some other baby items. The name of the shop was 'Needful Things'. Even though it has been almost 30 years ago, I haven't forgotten that trip nor the name of the shop. It was very intriguing to me. For some reason, it came to mind recently and I was again intrigued with the name. But in the process of my thinking, I began to wonder just what are Needful Things? Do we really need all the things we think we need? Of course we thought we needed that baby bed and at the time maybe we did, but not now, since the grandson is almost 30 years old. Jesus said in the verses listed from Matthew, that we should not be concerned or worried about 'things' we think we need. He said the Father knows what things we need before we are even aware of them ourselves and ask.

As I get older I see how we clutter not only our homes and property with things, but our very lives also. Not many of these things we acquire are really all that needful, are they? Sure, we need clothing, a roof over our head and food to eat. Those are some of the things Jesus talked about that the Father is well aware of and gracious and loving enough to provide for us even before we ask Him, just as he does for the birds of the air and the lilies of the field. But all these other things we surround ourselves with are certainly not needful. What really counts in this life as needful things on our part, are not really things at all. Trust in Jesus as our Savior; a strong relationship with God; faith in His ability to not only save our souls for eternity, but to provide our daily necessities; and love for our families and fellow men, are actually what we really need. These 'Needful Things' are what we should be searching for and building upon. I wonder how much impact we would have on our own little part of the world, if we were so actively seeking the REAL needful things rather than the superficial ones?

Notes: _____

_____

_____

_____

_____

_____

_____

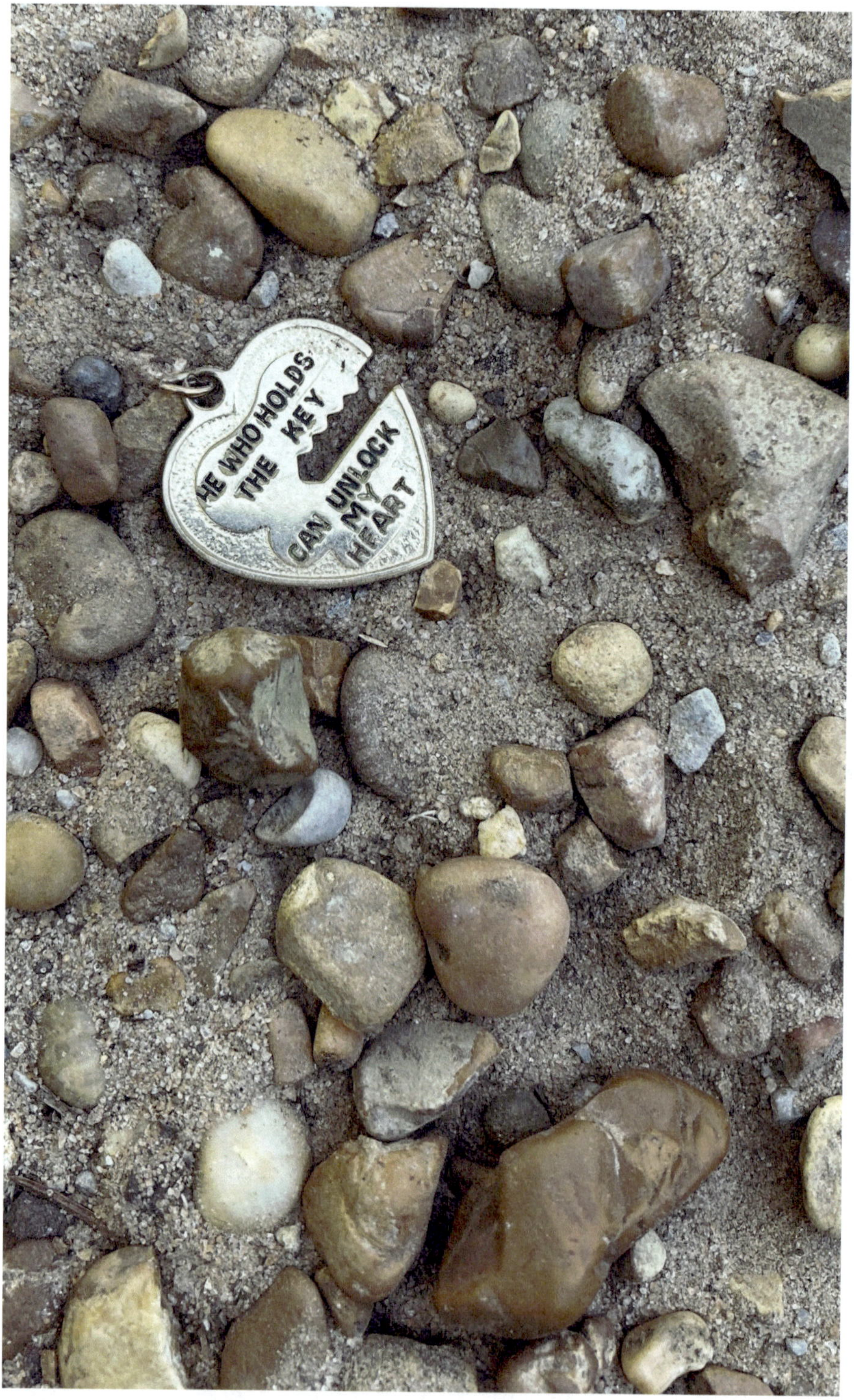
HE WHO HOLDS THE KEY
CAN UNLOCK MY HEART

The Lost Necklace

Psalm 37:4. "Take delight in the Lord, and He will give you your heart's desires."

I have a necklace that my son gave to me when he was a very small boy. It has a heart with a hole cut out for a key. The inscription on it reads, "He who holds the key, can unlock my heart." It is very special to me. I wore it every day for a number of years, and then one day I lost it. To say that I was heartbroken would be a mild statement. I prayed and begged God to give it back to me. I searched for it every day for a week, without success. I searched the house, car, and the yard diligently. I watched for it every step I made. And then, one day, about two weeks after I had lost it, there it was. On top of the ground in the driveway, not far from the front porch, lay the heart charm without the chain. The heart looked perfectly clean as if it had just been dropped a couple of minutes before I saw it. It didn't look like it had been laying in the dirt for two weeks. And I know, without a doubt, that God gave it back to me. He dropped my necklace, unharmed, and clean out of Heaven onto the ground right by my feet. It is not something that would be life or death but it mattered to me. It again shows HIS amazing, tender, compassionate love for me. I know HE smiled this morning when HE did it and then again when HE watched me find it. I know HE also smiled when I told everyone that I did not find it but that HE gave it back to me. I am blessed because of HIS amazing love, over and over and over and over.... again. I think we waste so much of our lives before we really ever think about getting to know God. When we get to know people, we learn their ways of showing love and tenderness, or whether they are tender or not. We should spend that same time and energy getting to know the Lord. It is certainly worth it and look how much additional love we feel that is there. Love can be there and us not feel it if we miss things that show it to us. I have missed so much but I hope not to miss anything in the future. Thank you again, God, for your many blessings on me, and especially for giving my heart charm back!

Notes: _____

_____

_____

_____

_____

_____

_____

Spirit Or Flesh? Our Choice!

Read Matthew 5:5 and Galatians 5:19-26.

Verse 24. "Now those who belong to Christ Jesus have crucified the flesh with its passions and desires."

These verses compare the Spirit and the flesh. Being led by the Holy Spirit produces far different results than being led by the flesh. Everything listed in verses 19, 20 and 21 are results of living a life led by the flesh, bringing pain and sorrow. There are no happy endings listed here as results of being led by the flesh. Those results do not list anything attractive. On the contrary, the results of being led by the Holy Spirit are all happy, positive things. When we are saved, we are called to begin a life led by the Holy Spirit. We are called to lay aside these things in our life listed in verses 19, 20 and 21. These things which all result in unhappiness. This should be easy to do, yet it seems to present quite a challenge for some of us. Could that be the result of not keeping our eyes completely focused on Jesus? Stop and think for a minute. When you are completely focused on Jesus and doing His will, how many of the characteristics listed in verses 19, 20 and 21 do you exhibit? I would dare to say none! And when you exhibit one or more of those characteristics listed in verses 19, 20 and 21, can you honestly say you are completely focused on Jesus and doing His will? Not likely. If you are busy concentrating on Jesus and His will, you will be led by the Holy Spirit. The key here might be to give all that we are to doing the will of Jesus. All the rest will pretty much fall into place.

Notes: _____

_____

_____

_____

_____

_____

_____

Praise Him Now!

Read John 6:66-69.

Verse 68. "Simon Peter answered, 'Lord, who will we go to? You have the words of eternal life.'"

To whom shall we go? We believe and are sure that you are the Christ, the son of God. There is no God like our God. He is the only real God. Who else had the ability to die as payment for our sins? Nobody else qualified to die for my sins, because there was nobody else who was sinless but Jesus. I can never offer repayment. There is no one else who is able to perform the miracle of saving me. There is no one else who could ever deserve my worship. Peter recognized this long ago when Jesus walked the earth and he was never the same. What about you and I? Who else can we turn to but Jesus? There is no one anywhere that is greater. Do we only turn to Jesus during sorrow? Or do we turn back and give Him thanks during and for the blessings? Who else can possibly bless us like He can? There is no one. And who would be willing to bless us like Jesus does? Who could possibly love us anywhere close to as much as Jesus does? Do we stop and thank Him? Do we acknowledge where the good things come from? Or do we just go our way without even saying thank you? I am afraid that I am guilty of not thanking Jesus enough and giving Him enough praise. Who else could we thank for our blessings? There is no one else who deserves our praise more than the One who gave His life for our salvation. If I spend every moment of the rest of my life giving Jesus praise, it would never be enough. That is one thing about being in Heaven that will be so wonderful! I can spend every second praising and worshiping Jesus! Why would I not start now on earth? Gratitude!

Notes: _____

_____

_____

_____

_____

_____

Elijah and The Widow

Read I Kings 17:1-24.

Verse 15. "So she proceeded to do according to the word of Elijah. Then the woman, Elijah, and her household ate for many days."

There had been no rain in the land. At the hand of Elijah, I might add. God sent Elijah to the Brook Cherith where the ravens fed him as he drank from the brook. When the brook dried up, Elijah was sent to Zarephath to a widow who thought that she and her son would die of starvation. The widow was out gathering sticks to make a fire for what she thought would be their last meal due to the lack of flour and oil. But that wasn't God's plan. Elijah told her to make a small cake for him first and then some for herself and her son. That looks a whole lot like tithing to me. God asks that we give Him a small portion of what we have first and then use the rest for ourselves. Elijah told the widow that her flour and oil (food supply) would not run out until it rained (which would provide more). But there was a condition here. She had to trust him. We have to write that tithe check first and trust God that our paycheck will not run out until the next one comes. After all, He provided the first one. The widow decided to trust Elijah and what he told her was true in her life. They all three ate many days from that "one serving" of flour and oil she originally had. But, then her son died. She took him to Elijah asking the question of why?

Basically what have I done? She admits she has past sins but she is still seeking mercy. Aren't we all? Elijah takes the son and asks God to bring the child back to life. God answers and the widow gets her son back. The widow then says "Now I know you are a man of God." Every time I read this passage of scripture, I get to this point and my mind says "Are you just now figuring out that Elijah was sent from God to feed you?" Are you just now figuring out that he was a man of God? God's man? After you ate for days on one meal's worth of flour and oil? And before that thought can become a complete sentence, I think to myself "Are YOU just now figuring out that God is going to take care of you?" After all He has done for me and all the miracles I have witnessed, am I just now figuring it out? And if I have figured it out, why must I be reminded so often?

Notes: _____

_____

_____

_____

_____

_____

_____

Daniel's Steadfast Faith

Daniel 10:12. "'Don't be afraid, Daniel,' he said to me, 'for from the first day that you purposed to understand and to humble yourself before your God, your prayers were heard. I have come because of your prayers.'"

Angels are sometimes sent as answers to our prayers for help. Angels sometimes help strengthen us and other things. Often they help us understand things.. God sends help. Daniel purposed to understand and to humble himself before God. Daniel made a choice. He chose to humble himself before God. He chose obedience. He chose to trust God. He made those choices first. Daniel was a captive in a foreign land. Daniel had been an exiled captive for several years. He had been through a lot. But he still chose to obey God. He purposed in his heart to understand. It took determination to remain obedient to God in a pagan land. I wonder sometimes how well I would do if I was faced with all that Daniel was faced with. He was away from home and family. Daniel was only 15 years old when he was taken captive, far from his home. Daniel could have felt abandoned by God and let go of his faith, but he didn't. Life was hard for him. Life is hard for us too. Daniel had to choose between trying to keep the lifestyle that honored God or pleasing the king. He had an opportunity to serve the king and make life easier for himself. He continued to try to honor God with his life. We have choices to make every day. We can choose to go with the life the world is offering us, or will we choose to honor God? The details may have changed, but the choice still must be made every single day. God still sends help to us, just as He did for Daniel. But we must choose to honor Him. That choice must be made in faith. It takes determination to live for God in this world. It takes determination to stand out in the crowd and be different from the world. You may feel like you're the only one standing sometimes. But God always stands with us. We are never alone. Purpose in your heart today to be humble before God and obey Him even if you're the only one.

Notes: _____

_____

_____

_____

_____

_____

_____

Grace and Peace To You

Read Revelation 1:3-8.

Verse 8. "'I am the Alpha and Omega,' says the Lord God, 'the One who is, who was, and who is coming, the Almighty.'"

We are blessed by reading and hearing scripture, as well as by keeping the words of scripture. It sounds so simple, yet these promises are profound. The Lord Almighty sent Grace and Peace to us through the words of John. The ONE "who is and who was and who is to come" loved me enough to wash away my sins with HIS own blood. That amazes my finite mind to think about the Lord Almighty, who is so powerful, so great that HE created ALL things. To have the privilege of knowing the ALPHA and the OMEGA is more than we could have ever known to request for ourselves, yet GOD planned it that way. The fact that this Lord wants a relationship with us should inspire us to do our very best to live HIS way. We should live for HIM not just each day but each minute of every day. The closer I draw to HIM, the more I realize that I want to be even closer. I want the closest possible relationship. I want to get to know HIM even better. Each step I take towards that closer relationship, I realize a little more of the depth of HIS love for me. I will not know the true depth of HIS love until I get to Heaven but until I go there, it is my wish to make each step pull me closer and closer to HIS will. I want to be In His Service.

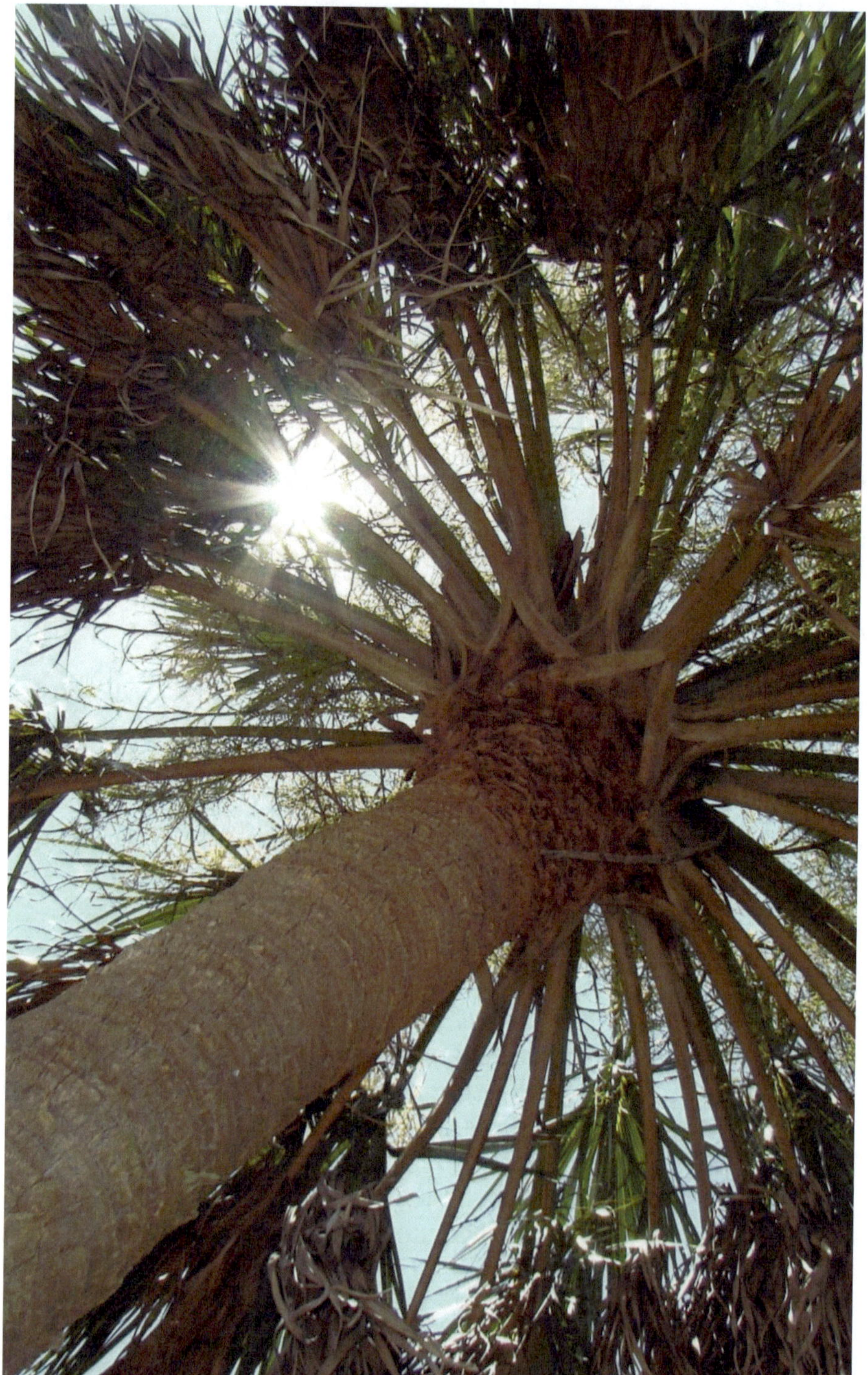

On Island Time!

Read Psalm 46:10, Isaiah 41:1 and Revelation 1:9.

Verse 9. "I, John, your brother and partner in the tribulation, kingdom, and endurance that are in Jesus, was on the island called Patmos because of God's and the testimony about Jesus."

John was alone on an island. I have found that I feel closer to the Lord when I can have some quiet time on my island. John was put on the island of Patmos as punishment for being a Christian. But John received a visit while he was on the island. A very special visit. Jesus did not abandon John nor did He leave John comfortless. Instead, during his time alone on the island, John was in the spirit on the Lord's day. John didn't abandon worship of Jesus because he was alone. Actually, the opposite is true. And Jesus honored that devotion. John received a vision. He was given understanding of things that we still study and try to figure out. So, don't worry if you feel like you are alone on an island. Jesus can still come to you. Also, don't ever think that you can't worship Jesus on an island. John choose to worship no matter his circumstances. For me personally, I love islands. Maybe it is why we subconsciously love islands and celebrate beach trips. Maybe if we tried just a little, we could spend some quiet time alone with Jesus on our island. Maybe, we would see that the blessing we would receive wouldn't be the sun tan we expected but conversation with God. After all, God must like islands. He created islands. Consider taking some of your time on an island, to spend it with Jesus and receive a blessing from HIM!!

Notes: _____

_____

_____

_____

_____

_____

_____

Just Obey and Let God Lead

Read Daniel 1:1-17.

Verse 8. "Daniel determined that he would not defile himself with the king's food or with the wine he drank. So he asked permission from the chief eunuch not to defile himself."

Daniel was determined to obey God no matter where he was or what the consequences were. He asked the prince of the enuchs about not eating the food appointed for him by the king. Although he had found favor with the prince of the enuchs, the prince still told Daniel no because the prince feared for his own life. Daniel asked the next one down in charge. He was determined to obey God. God gave Daniel understanding in all things. God rewards obedience. HE also gave Daniel and his friends favor with the ones over them. But the issue of who they would obey - God or man - came up more than once during their lifetimes. Each time we see it, they were still determined to obey God. We must be just as determined to obey God as they were. It takes courage and sometimes it may be a challenge, however, it is important. God will reward and bless us for obedience. Obedience is the first step in the right direction. When we make that first step toward obedience to God, He will always reach out to us and take our hand to go with us through our trials just like He did for Daniel and his friends all those years ago. Trust Him!

Notes: _____

_____

_____

_____

_____

_____

Descendants and Prayer

Exodus 3:6. "Then he continued, 'I am the God of your father, the God of Abraham, the God of Isaac, and the God of Jacob.' Moses hid his face because he was afraid to look at God."

All through the Old Testament and even in the New Testament, people's genealogies are listed. If it's in the Bible, it must be important. Family is important. We love our children. Do we love them enough to saturate them with the Word of God? How many people do you know with grandchildren? Everyone I know is just crazy about them. Most of them buy presents for their grandchildren, offer to baby sit anytime, and various other things. How much time do you spend teaching your children and grandchildren about Jesus? Why don't we pray for our grandchildren before we know they are going to be born? It is important to pray for our descendants. We provide food, clothes, and anything else they need, plus a whole lot of things they just want. But the greatest thing we can do for them is pray for them. Have we taught our children to love Jesus enough to withstand the fires of life and not be led astray? Have we taught them the importance of loving and worshiping Jesus deeply enough for them to teach their children? Have we instilled the love for Jesus in our children deep enough for them to see the importance of passing that love for Christ to the next generation? How many generations in my family will be Christian after I am gone? My children and grandchildren can't be saved simply because I am. I must teach them about Jesus so they will have such a strong relationship with Him that it will influence the next generation to want the same relationship. I don't want to be the one that fails to teach my children about Jesus. I might not be on this earth to teach grandchildren or great grandchildren. Pray that they will be saved and pray that their faith will be strong. Then, hopefully, we will get to meet them one day in Heaven!

Notes: _____

_____

_____

_____

_____

_____

_____

Encouragement and Hope

Read Psalm 37.

Jeremiah 29:11. "'For I know the plans I have for you'–this is the Lord's declaration– 'plans for your welfare, not for disaster, to give you a future and a hope.'"

We can have hope because God has promised to give us a hope and a future. When God makes a promise, we can count on it. The Psalmist tells us what to expect as Christians. God knows there are evil people on earth and He knows we will encounter some of them. We will face trials at work, trials with our children in school, trials in the neighborhood, the grocery store, difficulties paying bills, health issues, sometimes the loss of friends and even hurts within our immediate family. He knows that things are hard for us but take hope—He has overcome the world. We must trust Him. We must dwell on His faithfulness. That means we must remember back on the blessings He has provided for us and the miracles He has already performed. When we concentrate on what He has done for us and when we concentrate on Him, we take hope. Don't fret over your enemies or people who plot against you—concentrate on God. He is our hope and He is enough. We should encourage each other. We should remind each other of God's miracles and by that we will both be encouraged.

Miracles and Ordinary People

Read Luke 2:1-20.

Verse 11. "Today a Savior, who is Messiah the Lord, was born for you in the city of David."

Jesus always has been and always will be. He always has been God and He always will be God. His birth on earth was full of miracles that occurred to ordinary people. We should expect no less than miracles in our life if we are saved. The Bible is full of miracles that ordinary people witnessed and were a part of. If you believe that miracles only took place during Bible times, you have missed out! Miracles still happen everyday. Each and every day. Just because we do not recognize or acknowledge the miracle, does not mean that the miracle did not happen. We miss so much that God wants to show us. He wants to encourage us and He wants to be close to us. Why else would He bother to leave the splendor of Heaven to come to an earth full of sinners? He loves you that much. Yes, you! He loves me that much too. He loves us enough to keep showing us things to draw us closer and closer to Him. But we must open our eyes and our heart to see Him; to see the things He wants to show us. He also wants us to share Him with others. So, what are we doing while we are here on this earth? What else could possibly be better for us than His perfect will? How my heart craves the miracles! How my heart craves to draw closer and to see those things which nobody can ever take away. Because when you recognize a miracle from God, nobody can ever take that from you. When you have experienced a miracle from God, nobody can convince you otherwise. If you know, you know! You know that nobody ever convinced Mary that Jesus wasn't born of a virgin. And you can be sure that nobody ever convinced Joseph that he had not been visited by an angel. They had to run to Egypt fearing for their life, but you can know they still knew an amazing miracle had taken place. Nobody could take that from them. When we get saved, a miracle takes place and nobody can take that from us! Don't let the excitement die down. Keep remembering it and keep sharing it. You are now part of HIS story! And its a story worth sharing. The shepherds shared it. Mary pondered it in her heart. That means she thought about it a lot! And nobody ever took it from her. Mary's life was not easy and probably neither is yours. But she was not alone and neither are we. Joseph, Mary, the shepherds and many other ordinary people were obedient. Because of their obedience, they witnessed a miracle and shared it with the world around them. Why would we be anything less than obedient to do the same?

Notes: _____

_____

_____

_____

_____

_____

Adopted by God

Read Galatians 4:6.

Romans 8:15. "For you did not receive a spirit of slavery to fall back into fear, but you received the Spirit of adoption, by whom we cry out, 'Abba, Father!'"

When we are saved, we are adopted by God as His child. That gives us the right to cry "Abba, Father". That is "Daddy". We can cry out to our Heavenly Daddy just as we cried out for help from our earthly daddy when we were a small child. What a wonderful privilege that we have to be able to call the God of the whole universe "Daddy!" "Daddy help me!" And you can count on Him to help you not just once, but every time! That is a most amazing privilege! God is awesome and amazing. He created everything! He created the universe and the tiniest insect. He set the earth in motion and hung the stars by just speaking a word. He also created each one of us. We are all incredibly unique, even down to our DNA. Yet, if we accept Jesus as Savior, we get to call the God who created everything, Father. He will take the time to hear and listen to our prayers. He doesn't just create us and abandon us. He loves us with an amazing love. Jesus loved us enough to give up Heaven and come live among us on the earth. Living on this earth came with a lot of suffering for Jesus. He knew this in advance and yet He still came here for us. He came for us!! And because He did that, if we accept His sacrifice for our sins, we have God for our Father and Jesus for our brother. We have the Father who is always with us. And because we can call God "Father", we never face anything alone, not even death!

Notes: _____

_____

_____

_____

_____

_____

_____

Obey, Even In Fear

Read Acts 9:8-18.

Verses 13-17. "'Lord,' Ananias answered, 'I have heard from many people about this man, how much harm he has done to Your saints in Jerusalem. And he has authority here from the chief priests to arrest all who call on Your name.' But the Lord said to him, 'Go! For this man is My chosen instrument to take My name to Gentiles, kings, and Israelites. I will show him how much he must suffer for My name.' So Ananias left and entered the house. Then he placed his hands on him and said, 'Brother Saul, the Lord Jesus, who appeared to you on the road you were traveling, has sent me so that you may regain your sight and be filled with the Holy Spirit.'"

Sometimes when God asks us to do something, we are afraid. It's okay to admit that you are afraid, as long as you don't let that fear keep you from obeying whatever God has told you to do. Ananias was afraid to go to Saul of Tarsus. He had good reason to be afraid. Saul had been persecuting Christians and had papers with him to do even more harm. Saul was on a mission: a Christian killing mission! But then something happened to him on the road…. on the very road to Damascus as he went his way to persecute even more Christians. But could Ananias know what would happen to him if he obeyed God and went to see Saul? That's just it. He didn't. He had to trust God with the consequences of obeying God. Have you ever wondered what would have happened to Saul if Ananias hadn't gone to him and put his hands on him? Could he have possibly even guessed at the number of people that would come to believe on Jesus Christ as their Saviour because he touched Saul's eyes? He couldn't have known because that number hasn't been totaled yet. People are still reading Paul's writing and seeing the truth of our Lord. It seems like such a simple command... yet one that struck fear in Ananias' heart. I can just hear him... "God, now you know that this Saul is out to kill all of us Christians! You haven't mixed him up with someone else, have you God?", And we do read in Verses 13 and 14, the conversation between Ananias and God. It doesn't say that God was angry with Ananias for being afraid. He just answered Ananias and again, told him to go. Ananias obeyed. The rest is history... or some of it. Some of the ones who will read Paul's words and believe may be yet to come. One act of obedience by Ananias and now he has a part in an uncountable number of souls saved. Never discount what God can do with one simple act of obedience. We are not responsible for the outcome... only to obey. I believe we will be in Heaven before we have a clue how many people we have influenced. I pray that mine will be actions of obedience so the influence will be for Christ and not against. Be encouraged. Know that God may be using you in ways that you can't begin to see. HE sees the whole picture, while we only see a small portion. Ananias' obedience was about so much more that day than touching one man's eyes because the results touched more hearts than he could have possibly imagined! You never know the magnitude of your actions, so make those actions obedient to Jesus and leave the results to HIM!

Walking In The Midst of The Fire

Read Daniel 3:1-27.

Verse 25. "He exclaimed, 'Look! I see four men, not tied, walking around in the fire unharmed; and the fourth looks like a son of the gods.'"

Verse 27. "When the satraps, prefects, governors, and the king's advisors gathered around ,they saw that the fire had no effect on the bodies of these men: not a hair of their heads was singed, their robes were unaffected, and there was no smell of fire on them."

Have you ever felt like you were walking on hot coals or in the midst of a fire? Felt overcome by heat and smoke and confused about which direction was the right way to get out of it? Have you ever felt like your life was so confined in the heat of a bad situation that you couldn't move or even breathe? Well, I would say that we should consider God's servant, Daniel and his three young friends. These guys were taken captive, taken from their homeland and put into slavery, far away from home in a foreign land. Their situation seemed hopeless and permanent and they could see no way out. But they didn't let their situation cause them to lose faith in their God. They knew that He was with them even through their bad times and would be with them no matter what the situations of life brought their way. Their faith was indestructible even when their entire way of life had been completely changed. The foreigners who held them captive did not worship the God of Daniel and his friends. They even had a golden image made and convinced the king to make a decree that required every person in the land to bow down and worship that statue made of gold. Daniel and his friends refused to do that, even though they knew the king might have them killed. They had so much faith in the God of all creation, that they told the king, whether we live or whether we die, that is up to our God, but even though it may cost us our life, we will not bow down and worship your golden idol. Daniel's three young friends were thrown into the furnace and extra fuel was loaded into that furnace to increase the heat to the hottest degree. Those boys were in dire circumstances for sure and they had no hope of being able to withstand the fire and live. But, as we see in verses 25 and 27, when the king had someone look into that furnace to see if they had died and burned, the report was not only did they see the three boys walking around in the fire, but there was a fourth figure walking about with them! It was God himself who was in the midst of the intense heat and flames with them and because they were His children and because they had remained faithful to God, He was faithful to His promise to be with them and protect them, and honored their commitment and faithfulness. They not only were kept safe and secure, they were able to be walking about and talking with God even in the very midst of this terrible ordeal. This is so amazing and a very important truth for us to learn from this scripture. We worship and serve the same God as Daniel and his three young friends! When we feel like we are being tried by the fires of adversity and dejection; when we feel like we are being held captive by a horrible and hopeless situation, we still need to keep in mind that the same God who 'walked in the midst of the fire', with Daniel's three friends, is still God! He is our God and we can count on Him just like Daniel and his friends proved all those years ago. He is still the One on the throne and He is still the God of all creation and universe. He still wants to walk and talk with us in the good times and in the trials of life. He still wants to walk through the fires of life with us as we face them. But He won't push His way into our life; He waits until we open the door and invite Him in, but He immediately will come to us and help us when we allow Him to. He is waiting and hoping we will ask Him to join us in the furnaces of our life so that He can walk and talk with us and see us through them. It is up to us whether we try to make it alone and are consumed by the fires of life or whether we call on Daniel's God - indeed Our God - to come and walk through life with us. If we want to come out of the furnace of life as Daniel's three friends did in verse 27, with no burns to our body, no burns to our clothing or the very hair on our heads, and not even smelling like the smoke of the fire, we must have God with us. He is the Master of the fires of life and the only hope we have to come through unscathed.

Notes: _____

_____

_____

_____

_____

_____

_____

Daniel In The Lions Den

Read Daniel 6.

Verse 5. "Then these men said, 'We will never find any charge against this Daniel unless we find something against him concerning the law of his God.'"

We hear about the story of Daniel in the lion's den and we cheer good old Daniel on. We almost look at him as some super hero who felt no fear or pain. That is simply not true. Daniel was a teenager when he was taken away from his home and all he knew. He did have three friends that were also taken at the same time but he was taken from his family. Daniel was royalty. Can you imagine the fear of being taken to a foreign country? He did not speak the language. He did not have the same customs. They did not worship the same God that Daniel worshiped. Yet Daniel chose to remain true to the God he believed in. He took each challenge that he faced and prayed for a way to remain true to the one true God. He probably did not feel like the super hero we think of him as. He was probably afraid. He was probably nervous. From his point of view, this was a great trial. Maybe it was like some of the trials we can face today. Do you feel like a super hero when you are faced with a difficult situation and don't know how it will turn out? We need to realize that Daniel was just like us. He was a human. He was a teenager as a matter of fact. He lived more of his life in captivity than in freedom. He lived 70 years in captivity. Yet through all of it, he remained faithful to God. He faced every situation with prayer. God was with him and answered every one of his prayers. God will answer our prayers too. We need to remember that even though we see Daniel as a super hero that would not have been how he felt going through all that he faced. Daniel was an old man when he spent the night in the lion's den. Go back and re-read the book of Daniel. Read it from the perspective of a scared person in a foreign land who never saw his family again. We see that Daniel's faith grew every time he was obedient. Our faith too will grow every time we are obedient in life's difficult times. Yes, we are afraid but there might be someone watching us who sees a superhero and is encouraged to stand firm in their faith. Will we feel like a superhero? Probably not, but I doubt Daniel did either.

Notes: _____

_____

_____

_____

_____

_____

Seeking God

Read Matthew 6:33, and Philippians 4:1-23;

Verse 6. "Don't worry about anything, but in everything, through prayer and petition with thanksgiving, let your requests be made known to God."

The Bible tells us to do it. But how do we do it? Face it. Life is hard. Jesus knew life was hard when he instructed us to seek His kingdom first. What does that mean anyway? To concentrate and put our efforts toward finding His will for our lives and doing it would be a really good start toward seeking His kingdom. There are some really good instructions for us in Philippians chapter four that help us accomplish seeking His kingdom first. Stand fast in the Lord. Don't give up your faith. Help each other to spread the gospel. Rejoice in the Lord. Life is hard and we don't often have very many positive things to be happy about, but we can always be thankful for our salvation. Jesus didn't have to die for us. He chose to because He loved us that much. But He didn't leave us on our own after that. Not sure about that? Try praying. I mean really praying about everything, like verse six instructs us to do. If we follow verse six, we see that verse seven promises we will have the peace of God in our hearts. Verse eight reminds us of what we are to do with our minds. We are to make an effort to control our thoughts. Yes, that is possible! Verse thirteen reminds us that we are not alone. I can do all things through Christ who strengtheneth me. We cant do all things through our own strength but only with the endless supply of Christ's strength. Our strength runs out but not the strength of Christ. Verse nineteen reminds us that God knows and will take care of our needs...not just some of our needs but ALL of our needs. We should read this chapter often. There are many things here that I need reminding of quite often! It's there for us. We need to rely on His Word. It's our life manual.

Notes: _____

_____

_____

_____

_____

_____

Choose To Trust God

Read Daniel 9:3-23;

Verse 3. "So I turned my attention to the Lord God to seek Him by prayer and petitions, with fasting, sackcloth, and ashes."

Daniel set his face toward God to pray. Now we know that Daniel had chosen to serve God from his youth, but we see that he specifically made a choice again to turn his face toward God to pray. We need to make a heart choice to pray to God. That involves choosing to humble ourselves and get our attitude right before God. It involves repenting of our sins. We have to humble ourselves, admit our sin and repent of it. We also must set our hearts to praise Him in our prayer. We must have faith that He will answer us. Now we see in verse 23, that God began to answer Daniel's prayer while he was still speaking that prayer. How awesome is it that the God of the whole universe would hear us and begin to answer while we are still speaking a prayer. The Lord dispatched the angel Gabriel while Daniel was still speaking. Daniel was just a person, just like we are. But he chose to trust God and serve Him. We can make that choice too. Have you made a deliberate choice to trust God. Trusting God does not come naturally. Honestly, trusting anybody doesn't come naturally for me. I doubt trust comes easily for anyone that has lived past the age of 5 because this world is full of hurt. Trust is something that I must deliberately choose to do. Start praying to God expecting that He will answer. Live like you believe it! If you are praying for rain, then carry an umbrella with you! We must live as if we truly believe God will answer our prayers, because He will! Then watch for His answers and you will see Him answer your prayers.

Notes: _____

_____

_____

_____

_____

_____

Obedience In Change

Read Numbers 13:26-14:25, Deuteronomy 34; and Joshua 1.

Verse 2. "Moses My servant is dead. Now you and all the people prepare to cross over the Jordan to the land I am giving the Israelites."

I personally don't usually like change. I guess I prefer for things to just rock along as it has been, over the unknown of how things will be. I don't think I am the only person who is like that. Most of us fear change. We may know what change will take place, but we don't know the consequences that change will bring. It's in the unknown consequences, that fear grows. I must remember that change is sometimes necessary to do God's will. Joshua must have faced and endured much change through forty years of wandering the wilderness. Sometimes I feel like I am wandering in the wilderness of life. I imagine most of us feel that way. Life is hard, as was wandering in the desert. Joshua was not at fault for the desert wandering. He obeyed and stood for God when all but he and Caleb disobeyed. Sometimes we must continue to walk through the desert of hard times in life. Sometimes those hard times are through no fault of our own. Of course, sometimes we do cause our own troubles. Either way, we must continue to obey God without sight of the reward. But never doubt that the reward is there. God is faithful to keep His promises always. Not sometimes or most of the time but ALWAYS! We do not grow in the valleys of good times but growth comes in the hard times. I must remember that life is not about me being comfortable but about me living to obey Jesus. His will is what my goal should be, not my will. By the way, Joshua did get his reward. He received his inheritance in the Promised Land. And so did Caleb. They were 80 years old when they received it, but they did receive it. And all those who are faithful and obedient will too!

Notes: _____

_____

_____

_____

_____

_____

_____

A Burning Bush and Divided Waters

Read Exodus 3:1-3, and Exodus 14:13-26.

Verses 21-22. "Then Moses stretched out his hand over the sea. The Lord drove the sea back with a powerful east wind all that night and turned the sea into dry land. So the waters were divided, and the Israelites went through the sea on dry ground, with the waters like a wall to them on their right and their left."

I imagine Moses was pretty amazed and awestruck when he saw the bush on fire but not being burned up. That was a miracle of God and no doubt got his attention. What if Moses had stopped there? The Israelites might not have been led out of Egypt. Because Moses chose to obey God, albeit hesitantly, and fearfully, he saw greater miracles than the burning bush. The burning bush was pretty amazing, but he would have missed so much more of God. Too often we receive the gift of a miracle from God and we stop there. We don't take the next step of faith and obedience, thinking that is all He has for us, when actually, that was just the beginning. The burning bush was just the beginning of miracles that Moses witnessed and was a part of, but he would have missed out on the rest if he had not obeyed God. He would have missed the larger miracles.

I do not want to miss anything that God has for me. I don't want to live the rest of my life on one experienced miracle from my past. I want to take the next leap of obedience and watch my awesome God! Moses continued to obey God and witness miracles throughout his life all the way through his death. What an awesome way to live and die, being close to God. God hasn't changed. We can live that way too.

Notes: _____

_____

_____

_____

_____

_____

God Uses All Things For Our Good

Read Genesis 37-47.

Romans 8:28. "We know that all things work together for the good of those who love God: those who are called according to His purpose."

Last Spring, I used the story of Joseph in Genesis to teach the children the meaning of Romans 8:28. I had no idea at the time, how much I would come to cling to that verse and remember those lessons myself. I am glad now that I obeyed God. I studied those lessons that God gave me intensely and did the best that I could to teach the children how God uses things that we don't understand to take care of us. At the time it happened, I am sure that Joseph didn't understand why he was sold into slavery and taken to Egypt away from his family. But Joseph stayed true to God during his time in Egypt. I am sure he missed his family, especially his father and brother, Benjamin. When he was thrown in prison under false charges of attacking Potipher's wife, I am sure he didn't understand. But he continued to serve God, even in prison. We don't always understand God's instructions to us or rather the reasons why. Joseph probably didn't see going to prison as success. The results or consequences of obeying God are not our business. Obedience is our business. Success is God's business. The consequences of God's instructions are God's business. We need to learn to simply obey God. Our simple obedience and trust in HIM is our success. I often forget that obedience to God does not necessarily mean a cushy, easy life. Actually, it often means just the opposite. God measures success differently than we do. If we have obeyed God, then we are successful. Loving and obeying God is the greatest success we can possibly have. Joseph was successful in carrying out God's plan, even though I am sure he couldn't see the plan while he was an imprisoned slave in Egypt. Yet, God used Joseph to feed, not only all of Egypt, but his own family as well. Joseph did come to understand the plan in the end. We may not see the plan until we get to Heaven, but we just need to continue to trust God and obey Him! God's plans are always the best.

Notes: _____

_____

_____

_____

_____

_____

Fear

Read Exodus 14.

Verse 16. "As for you, lift up your staff, stretch out your hand over the sea, an divide it so that the Israelites can go through the sea on dry ground."

It's ok to be afraid when God tells you to do something as long as you don't let your fear cripple your actions. Moses was afraid. That's probably the understatement of the year. Moses was terrified. I mean, what would he have looked like holding a stick out over the Red Sea? And what would that have done with the Egyptians bearing down on them? They could not see them but they knew they were coming. Moses might have expected to use the stick as a sword instead of holding it out over the Red Sea. Yea, right man! What would you look like holding a stick out over Mobile Bay or a lake? What about a pond or a mud puddle for that matter? But God told him to do it and Moses obeyed. Moses held out his stick over the Red Sea. The results were incredibly different than you would expect. Why? Because God had a plan. Because God was involved. When God tells you to do something impossible, HE is not asking you to do it alone. HE is only asking you to do your part of it and have faith that HE will do HIS part. And HE always takes the hardest part. Moses' job in parting the Red Sea was to hold the stick out over it. Yes, it was a particular stick but the power was not in the stick. The power was in God! HE is the same God now that He was then. He has not changed nor has HE lost any strength. Trust HIM enough to obey HIM. HE will not let you fall! And if He tells you to do something that doesn't seem logical to you, do it anyway. Even if you shake with fear while you are doing it! Obey and watch for incredible results!

Notes: _____

_____

_____

_____

_____

_____

_____

Jesus Prayed for Us

Read John 17:20-21.

Verse 20. "I pray not only for these but also for those who believe in Me through their message."

Jesus prayed for the ones who would come to believe through the words of his disciples. That's us! If you are a Christian, you believe, because of the words the Disciples were courageous enough to share and because of the prayer of Jesus. That's pretty awesome. Jesus thought of us before we were ever thought of or born! HE wanted Christians to have unity. Why did He want us to be united? So others would believe! So that more people would come to know HIM and HIS love. Jesus did many miracles and signs. Why? So that people would believe. HIS goal was for people to be saved. That's why HE came to earth and to a horrible death on the cross. HE wanted a relationship with us, but not just with us. He wants a relationship with every person. If it was important enough to Jesus for HIM to leave HIS father and the glories of Heaven, then it should be important enough to us for telling people to be our top priority. It should be our main purpose in life. That purpose is not just for those called to preach. It should be the goal of each and every Christian. It should be constantly on our mind. It should be the reason we live and breathe. It should be our first and last thought every day. We owe a debt that we can never repay. But HE loved us enough to send somebody to show us the way to salvation. How many people can we show? Saved souls is the only thing you can take to Heaven with you.

Notes: _____

_____

_____

_____

_____

_____

_____

Perfect Oatmeal

Micah 7:7. "But I will look to the Lord; I will wait for the God of my salvation. My God will hear me."

I was having one of those mornings, or actually times in my life, that things didn't seem to be going the way I planned. We all have those times. At least, I do. I am organized. I keep things organized in my mind, at least, about how I think things are going to work out. I have plans and if everything clicks along just so, then all should be fine. Right. Not! Not now. Not even normally. Rarely ever does life just cruise along smoothly with all working out like you plan. My life is certainly no exception to that. On this particular morning, I hadn't slept well the night before from all my worries and I just wasn't feeling very spry. I decided to make some instant oatmeal. I was working from home, so I put some water to boil on the stove. Then I went back to my computer. When I heard the kettle whistling, I got up and poured some water into my bowl on top of the packet of oatmeal that I had already emptied. In my haste to get back to my long list of emails, I poured what I thought was too much water. My thoughts immediately were "Well, this is just like my life right now." I have so much uncertainty going on and I can't seem to fix anything in my life right now. Nothing seems to be going the way I planned or would plan. I looked at the water and the oatmeal, and just stirred it, thinking I would just add some more oatmeal to it in a few minutes. But emails were dinging, so I went back to view the latest emergency coming through cyberspace. In a minute, I went back to pour some more oatmeal into my bowl, only to find the perfect bowl of oatmeal ready for me to eat. There was nothing that needed my fixing. Could it be that if I will calmly wait for the Lord, things in my life will work out the same way? Could it be that God's plans will be okay and my life won't require any of my own fixing? God made the prettiest bowl of oatmeal I have ever eaten that day from what I thought was a mess that needed fixing. HE didn't need my help with the oatmeal and HE doesn't need my help to fix my life. His plan is best. His plan is always best. My plan might be good but why trade God's best for my good? God uses all kind of things to teach us if we will just listen to that still small voice. That day, HE gave me peace through a bowl of instant oatmeal.

Notes: _____

_____

_____

_____

_____

_____

Get Out Of That Boat, But Stay Focused

Matthew 14:26-33. "When the disciples saw Him walking on the sea, they were terrified. 'It's a ghost!' they said, and they cried out in fear. Immediately Jesus spoke to them. 'Have courage! It is I. Don't be afraid.' 'Lord if it's You,' Peter answered Him, 'command me to come to You on the water.' 'Come!' He said. And climbing out of the boat, Peter started walking on the water and came toward Jesus. But when he saw the strength of the wind, he was afraid. And beginning to sink he cried out, 'Lord, save me!' Immediately Jesus reached out His hand, caught hold of him and said to him, 'You of little faith, why did you doubt?' When they got into the boat, the wind ceased. Then those in the boat worshiped Him and said, 'Truly You are the Son of God.'"

How many of us make a commitment to do God's will (or get out of the boat, so to speak) and then face boisterous waves? We all face boisterous waves in this life at some point. And sometimes, those waves can be really huge. Our faith remains strong as long as we keep our eyes on Jesus. We read the Bible and try to keep a smile on our face. But what about when the waves threaten to over run us? What about when our problems are large? We all have times when our faith is weaker than others. None of us are immune to feeling overwhelmed when troubles come one on top of another on top of another on top of another. Peter got out of the boat. Was the wind already boisterous when Peter got out of the boat? Possibly. Peter's eyes were focused on Jesus. Peter walked on the water, on top of the boisterous waves... as long as his eyes were focused on Jesus. It was only when his focus changed from Jesus to the wind and waves did he begin to sink. When Peter looked at his problems instead of looking across the problems to Jesus, he begin to sink. When he begin to sink, panic set in and he cried out to Jesus. Peter has been criticized for his momentary panic attack, but he is the only disciple who even dared to get out of the boat and cross the boisterous waves to get to Jesus. Before we are so hard on Peter for crying out in panic, maybe we should consider how well we do. Do we even get out of the boat when the waves are boisterous? Or do we stay safe in the boat? Are we willing to cross the boisterous waves to get to Jesus? Will I trade the safety of the boat for doing the will of my Lord? What should we do when our focus on Jesus is momentarily messed up and the waves are boisterous? Dear frightened one, cry out to Jesus with everything in you! HE sees where we are. HE knows the waves are huge. HE is waiting to stretch out HIS hand to us and save us. HE is master of the boisterous waves in our life. And when it's all safely past, HE will say, "O ye of little faith, why did you doubt?".

Notes: _____

_____

_____

_____

Stop Your Fighting and Know That I Am God

Read Psalm 46.

Verse 7. "The Lord of Hosts is with us; the God of Jacob is our stronghold. Selah."

We often quote the first portion of the King James version of Psalm 46:10, "Be still, and know that I am God". We quote this when we need a reminder to take some quiet time alone, or when we need some rest. We tend to want to take this time when we are on vacation at the beach or by the mountain stream. That verse comes to my mind when things are peaceful and quiet. That is our excuse to sit and talk with God. But I wonder if we miss much of what this verse is telling us by not reading the rest of this chapter. Verse one says "God is our refuge and strength, a helper who is always found in times of trouble." Often when things in my life are not going the way I planned, the last thing I tend to do is be still and know anything. I run around at a mad pace trying to fix whatever the problem is. I have recently lost my job. It was a good job, or so it seemed to me. It was also a high stress job. I worked a lot of long, hectic hours. But, alas, the pay was good and helped provide for my family, along with the benefits the job provided. So, ever since the announcement was made that I would be losing my job, I have frantically started searching for another job. A job that would pay as much and have similar benefits. I was determined to find a new job before this one ended. But that was not God's plan. Now that my job has ended, I find myself frantically searching online, asking people if they know of any open jobs, and going on job interviews. But, if we look at Psalm 46, maybe I am taking the wrong approach. Verse one speaks of God being our refuge and strength, not only in good times, but help in trouble. Verse two and three speak of many very serious things that could happen that would definitely qualify as trouble. The whole Psalm is eleven verses long, but it is not until verse ten that we get to the part about being still. It seems as if the whole Psalm is listing things that could or have happened. Calamity at its finest. But every few verses in this Psalm, we are reminded that God is with us and what HE can do. But then, in verse ten, we are given our instructions. This is what we are to do during troubling times.... "Be still, and know that I am God.". Verse eleven closes by reminding us one last time, that the Lord is with us and that God is our refuge. Maybe, just maybe, I would feel a whole lot less stress, if I committed to spending more time in prayer, not talking, but listening. During this time of trouble, I need to take more time, just knowing that God is God. And that HE is my refuge and my strength. If HE can make wars cease, (verse eight), then HE can surely handle my crisis. Much is definitely going on in the lives of my family right now. We have faced and continue to face much worse than just the loss of my job, but this one thing I know: "The Lord of hosts is with us; the God of Jacob is our refuge" (Psalm 46:12, KJV). HE has it all under control. Even the heathen are under His control. I can certainly take time to worship God and know, beyond any doubt, that HE is God. And HE is worthy of my praise. And HE is a very present help in trouble!

Roads and Rivers

Read Isaiah 43.

Verse 19. "Look, I am about to do something new; even now it is coming. Do you not see it? Indeed, I will make a way in the wilderness, rivers in the desert."

This morning when I read the 43rd chapter of Isaiah, I was in need of encouragement. It seems that I have many problems. This chapter reminds me that God is in control. First of all, HE created me. And then HE sent his Son, Jesus, to pay for my sins, so that I can be saved. Verse one says HE called Israel by name. HE knows my name too, and I am HIS. The Hebrew children knew what it was like to pass through the waters, with the Egyptian army hot on their trail. They were faced with the Red Sea on one side and the Egyptian army behind them. That was a hard place to be. Sometimes, I feel that way too. We all do. Maybe we had a hard job but now, we have lost it. Or maybe, someone in our family was very sick, and now they have gone on to be with the Lord. Maybe, we have bills to pay and now we worry that there will be enough money for them. Maybe you are trying to get through college and you have a difficult class. Maybe your family is scattered all over the country and you miss them. We all seem to have things in our life that just feel overwhelming. Life on this earth is hard sometimes... most of the time. It seems to us that others have their act together. But the truth of it is, that we just can't always see what they are facing. But we all have something. We all have something that feels like being between the Egyptian army and the Red Sea. Verses 16 and 17 says "the Lord, who makes a way in the sea and a path through mighty waters". HE knows exactly where we are in this life. Verse 18 and 19 reminds us not to look back. The Lord doesn't want us to remember the former things. The hard things that overwhelmed us. HE will make a road in the wilderness and rivers in the desert. The Israelites knew what this was referring to. They had passed through the wilderness on the way to the Promised Land. They knew the value of a river in the desert and that only God could provide one. The Israelites needed the reminders in this chapter that God had delivered them from so much and we do, too. We also need the reminders that there is no other god, but our God, the Lord. He is our Redeemer. He is The Holy One. There has never been any other God and there never will be any other God. And HE loves us! You and me! God promises in verses 18-19 that HE will do something new. He will make a way for us to endure. A road in the wilderness and a river in the desert. Water is necessary for life. Be encouraged on this hard road you are walking. God is there with you and HE will make a way. Even when we can't see it, HE can see it.

Notes: _____

_____

_____

_____

_____

Shipwrecked!

Read Acts 27.

Verses 41-44. "But they struck a sandbar and ran the ship aground. The bow jammed fast and remained immovable, while the stern began to break up by the pounding of the waves. The soldiers' plan was to kill the prisoners so that no one could swim away and escape. But the centurion kept them from carrying out their plan because he wanted to save Paul, and so he ordered those who could swim to jump overboard first and get to land. The rest were to follow, some on planks and some on debris from the ship. In this way, everyone safely reached the shore."

Land. Solid ground. Safety from the storm. And so much more in this Chapter of scriptures. Paul had been questioned by Agrippa. Agrippa had found Paul believable and was tempted to trust Paul's God, but not quite. In rejecting Jesus, he uttered some of the saddest words ever spoken...'you almost persuade me to become a Christian'. And so, it was decided that Paul would be taken by ship to Rome to appear before Caesar. A centurion, named Julius, was put in charge of seeing that Paul was delivered to Rome and so they began the long voyage. The early days at sea were somewhat uneventful although the winds began to increase, and it soon became a slow and difficult voyage with the contrary winds. They arrived in port at a place called Fair Havens and stayed there many days. When Paul knew their lives would be in danger at sea, he tried to convince them not to go back out. The centurion was determined to carry out his duty and he listened to the owner of the ship and made the decision to continue the voyage. The storms came and the seas were treacherous. They all feared for their lives. Some devised a plan to escape on the skiff, but Paul told them they had to stay or all would be lost. After fourteen days of severe storms, and fasting and praying, God gave Paul the words they needed to hear. They had done every thing they possibly could, even throwing the cargo and tackle overboard in attempts to lighten the load. Now they were about to see God's deliverance of them! Two hundred and seventy six men on board that ship were about to be saved by God's hands, and so they were. There's a wonderful lesson in this story for us. We, too, sometimes disregard God's warnings and sail our ships out into the stormy seas thinking we can make it on our own. Only after we are in trouble and have exhausted all our abilities, do we cry out for help from the Lord. Too often we listen to the wrong people, putting ourselves and others in danger, or we think we are capable without God. Too often we rely on our own selves or others and what we think are our own 'strong ships'. We will get into treacherous seas and perilous storms every time we do this. We should surely learn that we MUST listen and rely on God for our daily deliverance and safety. When we do, He will do as He promised the two hundred and seventy six souls on the ship that day so long ago. Life is a continuous stream of violent storms and rough seas. It may be that we have to struggle to swim, barely staying afloat, or we may be one of the weaker ones who have to just cling until we get to safety, but HE will deliver us to our safe haven if we obey His word and trust in His deliverance.

Of Chocolates and Sunsets

Read Romans 1:18-21 and Genesis 1:3.

Verse 3. "Then God said, 'Let there be light,' and there was light."

To say that I love chocolate might be an understatement. I often keep small chocolates for times when I need a treat for whatever reason. That being said, the other day I bought a small package of a certain brand of chocolates. I like the chocolates, number one because they just plain taste delicious, but I also like to open the wrapper and read the one line message inside. The first one I opened out of the package said "Never go too long without a sunset." That started me to thinking. I kept the wrapper where I would see it often. The more I thought about it, the more I realized that is very good advice. When I sit and watch the sunset, it reminds me that God is in control of everything and that HE created everything we see. Watching the sunset takes a few minutes and has a calming effect on me. It causes me to just be still and relax for a few minutes. As I watch a sunset, I am reminded of just how awesome God really is. I mean, who else could think through something like that and create such a thing? Romans chapter one verse 20 reminds us that everything that exists is cause for the argument that God exists. It is good for us to sit and just listen to and/or watch nature. Even if you are an unbeliever, God is the only possible explanation for the things we see in nature. Sunsets, birds, ocean breezes, wave after wave rolling onto the shore - each one different from the last.... It is a good thing for me to sit on the beach and watch the sun set over the water. I just relax and praise God as I watch HIS wondrous creation. I think the advice I got in my chocolate–Never go too long without a sunset– is great advice for all of us. It says to me, never go too long without sitting still and praising God in an unhurried way. I'm not saying this worship takes the place of gathering with other believers to praise Jesus. But I am saying that we should be sure to make time for BOTH types of praise to Jesus. The time to gather with other believers AND the time to sit quietly alone or with one or two others, and worship Jesus in a way that words can't describe. I am looking forward to going back outside and just sit for a few minutes. I know that God will show me something that causes me to praise HIM. That will be pleasing to HIM and it will do my heart a world of good also.

Notes: _____

_____

_____

_____

_____

_____

Untrained But Available

Acts 4:13. "When they observed the boldness of Peter and John and realized that they were uneducated and untrained men, they were amazed and recognized that they had been with Jesus."

God uses real people. People who are not trying to fit the mold but people who are willing to be themselves for God. God doesn't call you to fit a mold. He calls you to be yourself for Him, and doing those things you naturally enjoy. That's part of the personality that He gave you. It's ok to enjoy things because along the way, you are going to reach people by connecting with them through some of those things. It's always tempting to think you have to fit a certain mold but you become fake over time trying to do that. It's not that you are not a Christian. It's just that who you are gets lost and you are not as effective. You are always most effective at reaching people for God by being yourself for God. God does not call perfect people. There are none. He works through you. He made you like you are. And He uses you that way too. Our job is to be dedicated to Him and to make ourself available to do what He asks us to do. He will handle the results if we trust Him and just obey His call on us!

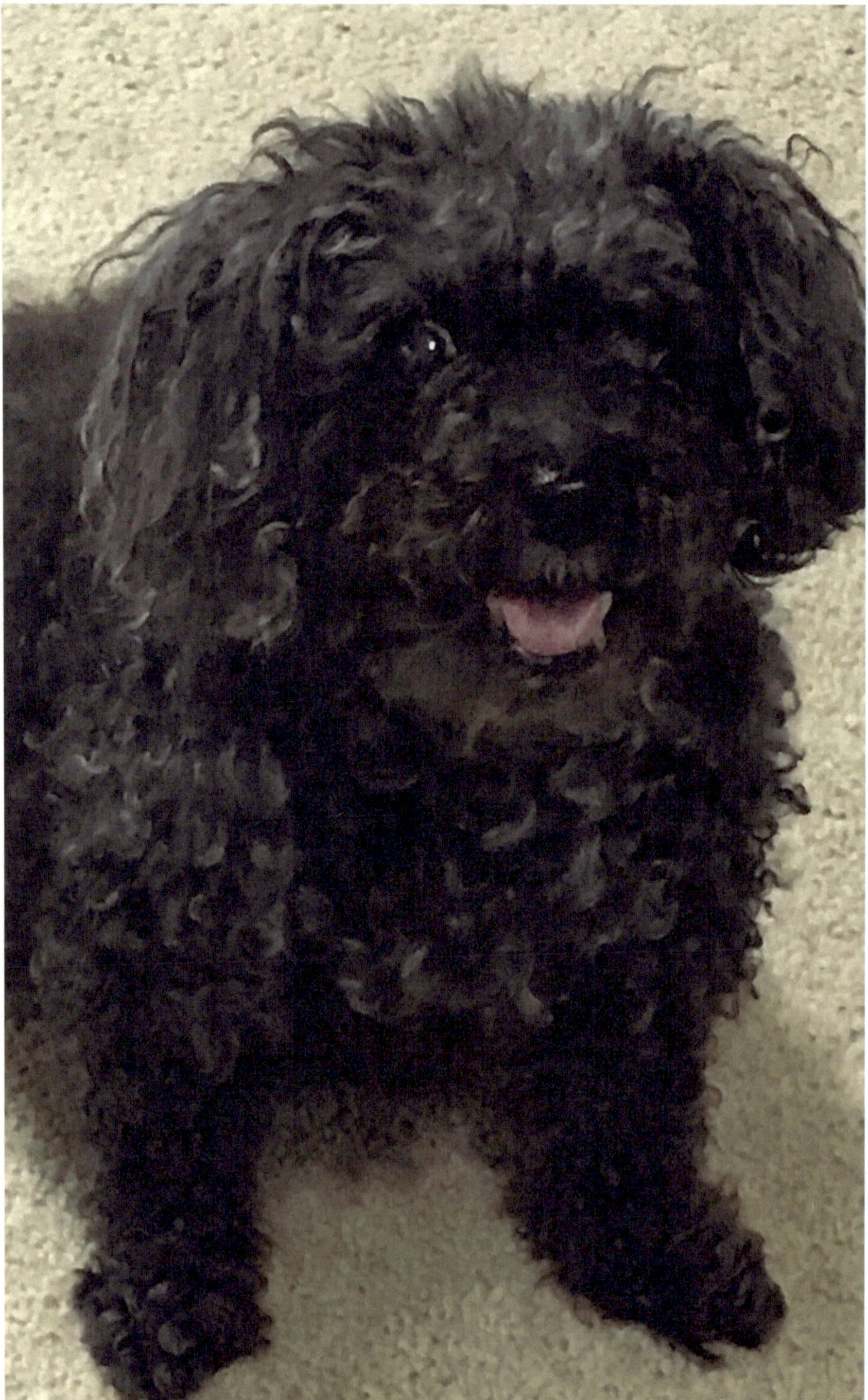

'Amazing Grace, How Sweet The Sound'

Ephesians 2:8. "For you are saved by grace through faith, and this is not from yourselves; it is God's gift."

Beautiful and comforting words from the old hymn that is so familiar to almost everyone I'm sure. It is a complete praise song which puts me in awe of our wonderful Savior. We ALL were lost once and now we are found IF we've trusted Jesus for our salvation. We ALL were blind once, but now we see IF we are keeping our eyes focused on Him. If my little toy poodle, Josey, could give his testimony, I am pretty sure he'd use the words of this great hymn to express how he feels. I wasn't looking for a pet when Josey came to me. I was struggling with the loss of my husband of 52 years to cancer. I was having to learn how to live alone for the first time ever in my life. Also, I had recently fallen and hurt BOTH of my ankles and my doctor had put me in 'walking boots' for three weeks. So, needless to say, I was in a low period of my life......then Josey came. He also was in a very low period in his life. My CPA had found him in a cemetery......a few days after Labor Day in very hot and dry weather. He had been thrown away by the people who once had loved him and he was lost and alone in a cemetery with no water or food and he was BLIND! He had advanced cataracts; probably the cause for him being thrown away. People want the perfect; not the flawed. On her way home that Thursday after Labor Day, my CPA spotted a 9 pound, black ball of fur among the headstones of that cemetery. Nobody was around. It was a strange thing to see so she stopped to investigate. He was hot and thirsty and alone, dehydrated, and needing help for sure. Being a devout dog lover, of course she picked him up and took him home with her. She tried to find the owner but could not. She fed him and sat with him in her lap and comforted him. The next morning she took him to her vet so that they could check for an ID chip. They bathed him and checked him. There wasn't a chip nor a collar with an ID tag. Meanwhile, my daughter had seen her notice about the lost dog she had found and sent her a message telling her that IF she didn't find the owner, she thought that her Mother might need him. So Josey came into my life on Friday, September 8th, 2017. From the very first time we met, we bonded. I think he knew I needed him and I knew he needed me. We became best buds right away. He was almost perfect as dogs go......except that he could not see. His eyesight was so bad, he would bump into door facings and posts especially at night and until he learned his way around the house. He didn't ever run and play because he couldn't see well enough to be sure of where he was. My goal became to get him settled in with me and confident that he wasn't going to be thrown away again......and after a time, to see what could be done for his eyesight. And so, we travelled quite a bit and got comfortable with each other and I made an appointment for evaluation of his eyes with a wonderful veterinary ophthalmologist in Bessemer, AL, in August, 2018. The Tuesday after Labor Day, 2018, one year after he came to me, he had cataract removal surgery and lens implant on the one eye that could still be saved, and when the surgery was over, he could see! It has been amazing to watch him discover things he couldn't see before. On the trip home after the surgery, even though he was still groggy from the anesthesia, he would just look and gaze at me. It was almost like he was thinking, 'So, that is what my rescuer looks like!' He is doing great and now runs and plays and pounces on his toys and can actually be free to be a dog again. Josey's life as it is now has reminded me of the song 'Amazing Grace'. He was definitely once Lost - but

God knew where he was and had his redemption planned....
just as He does with us. He definitely was once Blind - but God
had a plan to restore his sight and let him see ....just as He does
with us. I do wish Josey could speak and tell his testimony. I
remember that Scripture tells us that all creation declares the
glory of God and even the very rocks cry out in testimony.
I'm pretty sure Josey would love to be able to do that, so I am
sharing his story for him. I think we will gaze into the face of our
Redeemer one day with the same look of awe and appreciation
for saving us from a desolate place of blindness and sure death,
that Josey had for me that day. Amazing Grace, indeed! Thank
you Jesus for your indescribable sacrifice and grace!

Notes: _____

_____

_____

_____

_____

_____

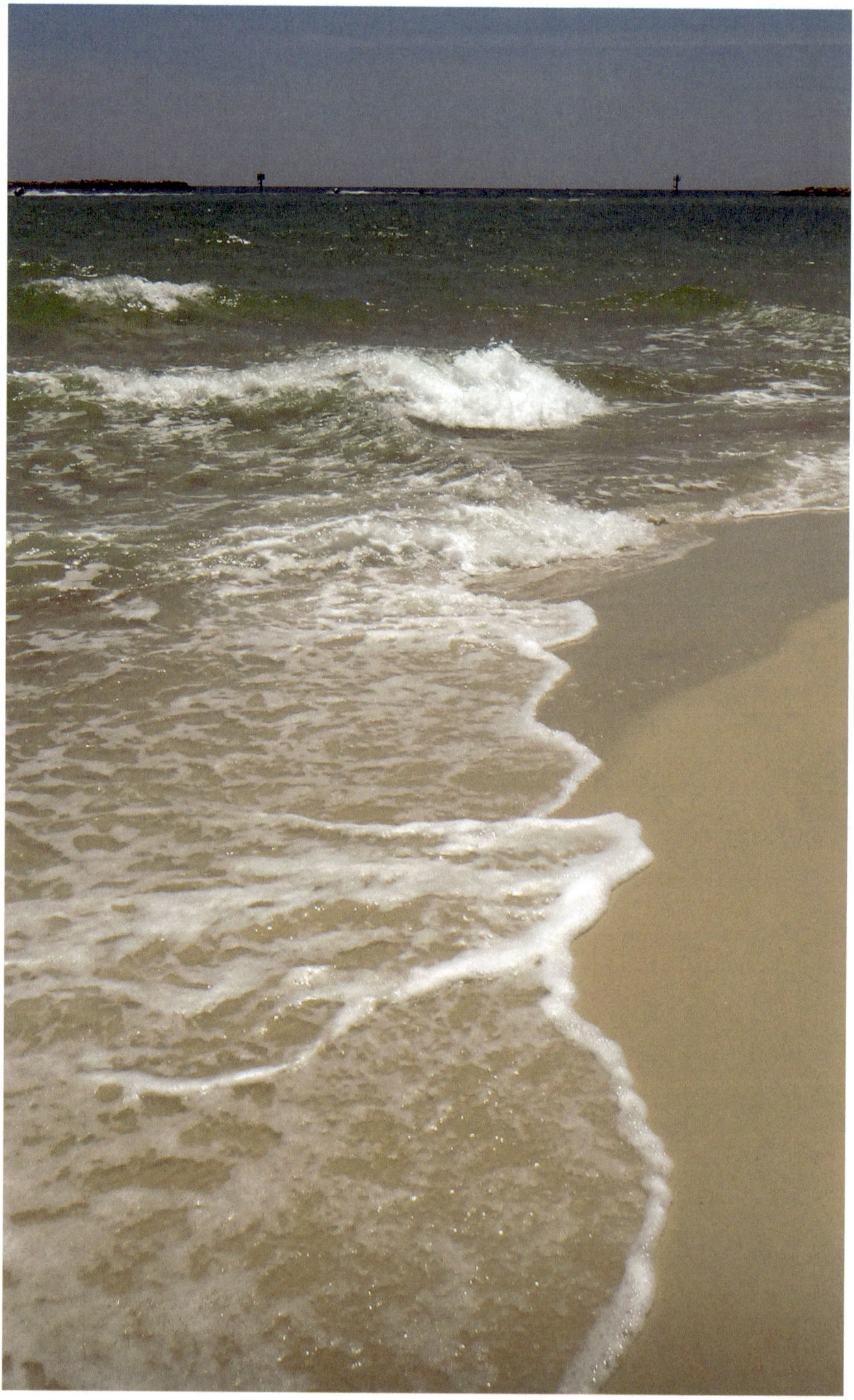

God's Line In The Sand

Read Job 38 and 39.

Job 38:8-11. "Who enclosed the sea behind doors when it burst from the womb, when I made the clouds its garment and thick darkness its blanket, when I determined its boundaries and put it bars and doors in place, when I declared: 'You may come this far, but no farther; your proud waves stop here'?"

Have you ever hurt? Really hurt? Not physically, although often that also causes mental anguish, but I am talking about emotionally. Has life ever just not gone your way? I think the answer to all of these questions for every one of us is a resounding YES! We have all hurt. We have all had major trials during life, honestly probably multiple times during our life. I don't know about you, but when I hurt, I tend to feel sorry for myself. When I face a serious trial, at some point or multiple points during the trial, my bottom lip becomes long enough to drag behind me and clear out my foot prints. I am just plain not good at long term trials. Before you judge me, look at yourself. Who amongst us on Earth is good at handling long term trials. Often, well meaning friends, say things that make us feel worse. This was the case with a man named Job. With friends like Job had, who needs enemies? And before we judge his friends too harshly, haven't we all been guilty of being just like those friends? I can't say the book of Job has ever been my favorite. I mean, who wants to read about a man that was righteous before God suffering greatly. I have read Job more than once but it is not usually where I turn for comfort during trials. I just plain don't want to hear that things in life can go that wrong and we might never know the reason why. I just don't want to read about bad, horrible things happening to "good" people. I like the stories of reward much better. I think we all kind of expect that we deserve something good, I mean, after all, we do the best that we can most days, right? I know that I slip into this mindset way too often.... The mindset of deciding that I am good enough to deserve all happiness and no trials in life. But this is just not Biblical nor realistic. (Romans 3:23).

    I just so happen to be in one of these difficult times of life right now. As a matter of fact, it appears to me that all of my family is in a difficult time. I can't understand why, and I can't see what God is trying to accomplish. I haven't faced all that Job did, not by a long shot, but I catch myself wanting to ask some of the same questions he did. And then, I am reminded of God's answer to Job. First, we need to look at the fact that God answered Job from the whirlwind. I personally am not capable of answering anyone or anything from a whirlwind. So, here is one example out of many of God's greatness. HE alone is great. I have no greatness in me on my own. Secondly, one portion of God's response to Job that always stands out to me is Verses 8-11 of Chapter 38. "Who enclosed the sea behind doors when it burst from the womb, when I made the clouds its garment and thick darkness its blanket, when I determined its boundaries and put its bars and doors in place, when I declared: "You may come this far, but not farther; your proud waves stop here?" The beach has always been my happy place. I can sit on the beach from morning until evening, just watching every wave roll in, one after another, after another, each one different from the last. Each wave seems to reach and stretch to cover all the sand it possibly can, only to roll back out with much dry sand still left. Yet, wave after wave rolls in, each one trying for the same goal. I have no control over how far any wave, not even one, comes ashore. There is nothing I can do to have a wave stop short or come further in. I would not even know where to begin to try such a feat. Yet, God has control of every one. At HIS command, each wave stops at a different place.

I don't know why I must be reminded over and over during every trial of God's greatness, but I do. It seems so illogical that the story of Job would bring me comfort, but God's answer to Job always does. I think it is a comfort to me because it reminds me that I am not in charge. I don't have to be in charge. I don't have to bear that burden, a burden which would, by far, be too great for my weary shoulders. I am reminded of just how awesome God is in chapters 38 and 39 of the book of Job. God's greatness is very comforting. HE alone is God and HE alone is great! When you read those chapters of Job, we see that HE is, indeed, mighty, great, wonderful, powerful and beyond our understanding. After that, it becomes okay that I don't have all or any of the answers. My God has all the answers and that is enough for me.

Notes: _____

_____

_____

_____

_____

_____

_____

Crocheting Socks

Read Second Corinthians 5:17-21.

Revelation 21:5. "Then the one seated on the throne said, 'Look! I am making everything new.' He also said, 'Write, because these words are faithful and true.'"

I don't know if you crochet but I enjoy it. I would not say that it is a great talent for me but it is something that I enjoy. My mother, on the other hand, is an expert at it. She makes beautiful things. Complicated things like sweaters, hats, gloves, and among many other things, socks. Now I have reaped the benefit of many of her crochet endeavors. During my unemployment time, I decided it was time that I learned to make socks. So, with Mother's guidance, I picked out some crochet thread and got started. The colors in the thread are beautiful and seeing the skien of thread made me happy as I envisioned wearing my socks. I got started with her help. I tried hard on the sock and tried the sock on my foot several times during the making of same. I listened closely to her instructions and thought I was following correctly but something just wasn't turning out right. The sock was too big. It was too long and too big around. Still, I continued. I finished that sock and although it looked good, it still didn't fit. I made the second sock to match the first one. Nice pair of socks but they didn't fit right. Well, I thought to myself, I'll just wear the socks anyway. So, I put them

168 | ANCHORED BY THIS HOPE

on and wore them one day. But the socks weren't comfortable. I thought maybe the socks would shrink if I washed them and put them in the clothes dryer. Nope, that didn't work either. So, I laid the socks aside and started a second pair from a different color. This time, I chose the correct sized crochet hook. What a difference that one detail made. The second pair went more smoothly. But even with the correct size crochet hook, there were times that I messed up and had to ravel the stitches out, so that I could try again. Eventually, the second pair, which I made for a dear friend, turned out pretty well. I wore the first pair I had made again but I just didn't enjoy it. So, I raveled out one sock and crocheted it again, this time using the correct sized crochet hook. I worked hard, raveled out stitches when necessary and eventually came out with a sock that I am proud of. So, I raveled out the stitches of the second sock and remade it also. Now, I have a pair of socks that I am both proud of and enjoy wearing. The thread is the same thread that was used the first time. But, the socks have been made new again. This time, they are comfortable, a joy to wear, and fit correctly. Revelation 21:5 quotes Christ as saying "Behold, I make all things new" (NKJV). My heart was made new by Christ when I accepted HIM as my Savior. I believe that verse might be referring to a new heaven and a new earth, but Christ also makes every one new who accepts HIM as their Savior. My body may be the same but my heart is new. Just like the socks, the remade version of my heart is much better. Christ made a vast improvement in my heart. I'm so thankful you can ravel out crochet stitches and make socks new but I'm even more thankful that Christ makes hearts new!

Wonders Accomplished from Plans Formed Long Ago

Read Isaiah 25:1-10.

Verse 1. "Yahweh, You are my God; I will exalt You. I will praise Your name, for You have accomplished wonders, plans formed long ago, with perfect faithfulness."

As I read Isaiah chapter 25 verse 1, I began to think about what all God planned long ago and how HE has accomplished it. Do I know all of HIS plans? Of course not, but I can think about some things I have seen that I know HE planned and accomplished. Some of it is just too amazing for it not to have been HIS doing. God knows what HE is doing in our lives and the lives of others. I have seen some things be accomplished that I know HE planned many generations ago. Things planned long before I was born, yet HE used me to help accomplish the plan. I was involved in a search for a lost grave several years ago. It was something that God laid on our hearts and we just could not let it go. It was one of those things that burned in our hearts, day and night. We did research on the family and where others were buried. We visited many graves of these family members to see if by chance, she was buried in the plot also. We ordered many obituaries, contacted some churches and cemeteries, all without success. But the need to find her grave just continued to burn within us and we knew it was a mission from God. God did eventually show us where the grave was and there is now a marker placed on the grave by the Great Granddaughter of the lady. In the process of the search, we learned much about the dear lady buried there. She was a very strong Christian lady, who witnessed to her husband and children as she lay dying. God knew as she lay dying that the location of her grave would one day be lost to her descendants but it was never lost to God. HE knew where it was the entire time. Many years went by, almost 100, before her grave was again marked. I don't know all the reasons that this was important to accomplish, but it was. Maybe her mother prayed asking God for the grave not to be lost permanently. I don't know. Perhaps, the search was to teach us about God's miracles. HE certainly performed a number of miracles during the search as HE showed us many things. I don't know all the reasons why HE chose us to do the search but it certainly taught me something about HIS faithfulness. God is faithful. HE never forgets HIS children. HE didn't forget this dear Christian lady and HE won't forget us either. The search also taught me to watch for HIS miracles and HIS blessings. Now, I look back on the past few years and I can see many instances of HIS guidance, and how HE has blessed us, even years later, for obeying HIM. After losing my sweet Daddy to Heaven, I am understanding more and more that God has destroyed the burial shroud as discussed in verses 7-9. I look forward to seeing Jesus, face to face, one day and quoting verse 9; "Look, this is our God; we have waited for Him, and He has saved us. This is the Lord; we have waited for Him. Let us rejoice and be glad in His salvation.". I can rejoice now in HIS salvation but I know I will understand much more when I see HIM face to face! As for now, I see HIS plans and how HE has accomplished HIS plans in many things. Not only has HE accomplished HIS plans, but those plans were formed long ago and accomplished with perfect faithfulness. How amazing and awesome to be a part of accomplishing HIS plans!

Do Not Fear

Isaiah 41:9-10. "I brought you from the ends of the earth and called you from its farthest corners. I said to you: You are my servant; I have chosen you and not rejected you. Do not fear, for I am with you; do not be afraid, for I am your God. I will strengthen you; I will help you; I will hold on to you with My righteous right hand."

I think "Do Not Fear" is in the Bible 365 times. That's once a day. So, I believe the Bible. I say I do anyway. That being said, why do I still fear? More accurately, why do I spend much of my life worrying about what might happen and how I will cope with it?

We have a dog named Gilligan that is a boxer-mix. We found him eight years ago on the side of the road, starved nearly to death. He was lost and without hope. He was in a pitiful state and could do nothing for himself. He could only stare up at our car with big eyes. My husband stopped the car and my son jumped out, scooped the then nameless puppy up, and got back into the car. We turned around immediately and brought him into our home. He could never repay us. We fed him some left over chicken and dumplings, which was probably the best food he had ever had. We let him rest while we resumed our journey to a restaurant for supper. Then, when we got back home, Jonathan bathed him. We gave him some attention and tried to comfort him. Then we fixed him a bed in a crate near Jonathan's bed. He was full, clean, and safe. His needs were all met.

Flash forward eight years. Why does my dog, Gilligan, fear being left somewhere and me not coming back for him? He's eight years old. We have never left him and not come back for him, yet his fear is still there. It's real. Verse 9 says "I chose you". God chose us. He chose to come to earth, die an agonizing death on the cross to save us. We chose to pick our dog, Gilligan, up from the side of the road that night when he was just a young pup. We chose to give him a home, feed him, bathe him, get his shots, flea medication, heart worm medication and all around care for him. He has too many toys to count. He has a soft bed both at home at the foot of our bed and at the foot of our bed in the camper. As far as dogs go, his life is pretty near the top. We have blessed him with many things and continue to do so. We have no plans of not taking excellent care of him. Yet, he still fears us not coming back to the camper for him. Why? Are you starting to see a parallel here? Could it be that God looks at us, just as I look at Gilligan, and wonders why we fear?

Verse 10 (and many others in the Bible) says "Fear not". Yet, we still do. The Bible is very plain when it states that God will take care of us. We have many blessings. Too many to count, as a matter of fact. God continues to bless us. When I would worry and get discouraged, my Daddy used to ask me if I had received a letter from God saying He wasn't going to take care of me anymore. The Bible says just the opposite actually. The Bible very plainly states that God will take care of us. God continues to bless me. And yet, I still fear. The picture between myself and Gilligan is amazingly similar. I need to learn to live more in faith than in fear. It's a matter of choice. Do I choose to believe God or not?

Humble Obedience

Luke 1:38. "'I am the Lord's slave,' said Mary. 'May it be done to me according to your word.' Then the angel left her."

Mary was willing to obey. We see her as a super hero in the Bible, but in reality, she was just a normal young girl with hopes and dreams. She had marriage plans. Yet, she willingly said yes to the Lord, when advised of His plan for her life. His plan could have cost Mary all of her plans, dreams and very easily her life. Joseph also had dreams and plans for his life. Yet he too, willingly agreed to the Lord's plans over his own. They were both just normal people but because of their obedience, they experienced God in a unique and wonderful way. God still uses normal people who are willing to obey Him. We have plans, dreams and goals for our life. But God also has a plan for our life. We can't see the results of His plans before we obey. If we could, we would always choose His plans over our own. Just like Mary and Joseph, we should choose to obey God's plan in faith. What would have happened if Mary had said "No" to the angel? What would the difference have been if Joseph had not trusted what the angel said? God could have used different people to carry out His plan, but look what Mary and Joseph would have missed. The same is true of us. If we say "No" to God, what will we miss? There is no way to know what all we miss by disobeying God. When the Holy Spirit leads us to do something, if we will just obey, we will experience amazing things. Obedience is the best worship. I don't want to miss out on anything God has for me!

Notes: _____

_____

_____

_____

_____

_____

My Story or His Story?

Proverbs 20:7. "The one who lives with integrity is righteous; his children who come after him will be happy."

A certain brand of chocolates have different one-line pieces of advice inside the wrappers, so you get double the benefit. The one I ate the other day said, "We're all stories in the end, just make it a good one.". I've thought about that a lot since enjoying the candy. I think I've actually enjoyed the advice more than the candy and that is saying a lot, given my love of chocolate.

What's your story going to be in the end? Your story actually could be the best or worst thing you leave your descendants. Your children usually pay more attention to what you do and how you live your life, than what you say. Aren't we all that way? Don't we all pay more attention to what someone does, than what they say? History is really HIS Story. I want my story to reflect a life lived to honor HIS Story. That's what I want to leave my children, grandchildren and friends. When you come to the end of your life, that's what really matters. Are you preparing your children for the future without you, by living a Godly example before them that they can draw from to walk with the Lord? Or will they be clueless about what really matters, when they face hard times? It's not a matter of when we will face hard times during our life, it's when. That is true for all of us and there is no preventing it. We teach so much more to our children, grandchildren and even those to come we do not live to meet, by how we face difficulties, trials, and even prosperous times than by what we say.

"We're all stories in the end, just make it a good one.". I want to make my story about HIS Story because I want my story to be worth looking back on for advice. Why? Because I want to see my descendants one day in Heaven. Yes, even the ones that haven't been born yet. I know I will love those too!

Notes: _____

_____

_____

_____

_____

_____

_____

New Year, New Me

First Thessalonians 5:14-22. "And we exhort you, brothers: warn those who are irresponsible, comfort the discouraged, help the weak, be patient with everyone. See to it that no one repays evil for evil to anyone, but always pursue what is good for one another and for all. Rejoice always! Pray constantly. Give thanks in everything, for this is God's will for you in Christ Jesus. Don't stifle the Spirit. Don't despise prophecies, but test all things. Hold on to what is good. Stay away from every kind of evil."

January First is the beginning of a new year. As January 1 approaches, many begin to think about making resolutions for the coming year. It is a time to start over on many things. A chance to do better at life. It is just generally a good time to make changes, form new habits and improve on life. I am not immune to considering all of those things. I don't typically just "make resolutions" for the new year but I have considered making some changes in my life. Things in my life are kind of upside down right now anyway. At least, it feels that way from the side of life that I can see. Last year was a hard year. My husband and I both ended up with job changes, which have left us working in different towns. Being apart during the week has not been easy for either of us. A recent doctor's visit involving a cholesterol check, resulted in news that my cholesterol is not where it needs to be, so I decided that January 1 would be the start of a new diet and exercise plan for me. I decided this might be a good year to make some serious attempts to take better care of myself physically. That's very important but even more important is how you take care of your spiritual walk. A few friends and myself took a challenge to read through the Book of Luke, beginning December First. The Book of Luke has 24 chapters in it, so we finished up Christmas Eve night. We posted things that jumped out at us or that we learned new on Facebook every day, after we read. That was a great experience for me, as often, other's comments made me take a second look at something I had missed. We enjoyed our study of the Book of Luke together, enough that we have decided we are going to read through the Bible in this new year. So, today begins a journey through the Bible together, with daily comments from the reading. We did form a group through an app, so that we do not end up with a yearlong Facebook feed. I didn't really make resolutions this year but choices. I am choosing to take better care of myself physically, but more importantly, I am making a choice to do things to grow closer to the Lord. The Bible study will help but as I read my devotion this morning, I read the scripture First Thessalonians 5:14-22. Now, within that scripture, I found the perfect New Year's resolutions! If I follow the instructions within this scripture, I think my choices will make for a better year ahead! I can't control all circumstances, but it's my choice how I respond!

Notes: _____

_____

_____

_____

Between The Inhale and The Exhale

James 4:14. "You don't even know what tomorrow will bring—what your life will be! For you are like vapor that appears for a little while, then vanishes."

I opened a piece of chocolate candy yesterday and printed inside the wrapper, I found this: 'Life happens between an inhale and an exhale.' Certain chocolates are kind of similar to fortune cookies in that inside each one is a statement of some kind. Sometimes encouraging; sometimes inspirational; sometimes funny and sometimes profound, like this simple statement. This one really made me think. At birth, as we come into this world, usually kicking and trying to scream, we inhale our first breath of air. From that moment on, we are beginning our journey toward the last breath we will exhale, and that moment will come very quickly. James says it is like a vapor - a mist that is quickly gone. Having lived 78 years and counting now, I can attest to the fact that life passes quickly. It seems only yesterday that I was a teenager not concerned with the cares of the world and not even thinking about the last exhale. But as time goes by, you begin to realize just how fast it is speeding. I am more conscious with each passing day as to how important it is to live every breath with a passion for the Lord. I need to be aware every moment as I breathe in and out, that any one inhale or exhale could be my last. I need to live the life God gives me in between those, in doing all I can to point others to Him, who through His grace, gives us each breath. It's not the first inhale nor is it the last exhale that matters most; but the life I live in between (Ephesians 5:15-17, NKJV). 'See then that ye walk circumspectly, not as fools, but as wise, redeeming the time, because the days are evil. Wherefore be ye not unwise, but understanding what the will of the Lord is.' I need to be sure I'm redeeming my alloted time wisely!

Notes: _____

_____

_____

_____

_____

_____

Job and Peter, Both Sifted by Satan

Read Job 1:6-12, Job 2:1-7 and for deeper understanding, read the entire book of Job.

Luke 22:31-32. "Simon, Simon, look out! Satan has asked to sift you like wheat. But I have prayed for you that your faith may not fail. And you, when you have turned back, strengthen your brothers."

This may seem like a strange combination of scripture references, but we can learn much from these three passages when considered at the same time. Based on the knowledge that the Book of Job is one of the oldest books in the Bible, we believe that many years passed between the Book of Job and the Book of Luke. This being accepted, we see that Satan diligently tried to turn the hearts of God's people away from Him for a very long period of time by using various trials. Have we any reason to assume Satan has stopped causing trouble for the people of God? Of course not! Poor Job had no clue as to why such awful, horrid trials came about in his life. The trials came one after another, after another, after another. We read the Book of Job and see the whole picture but Job could only see from this side of Heaven. Isn't that true in our lives also? We can only see from this side of Heaven and therefore, cannot even begin to understand the why of things, especially difficult things, that happen in our lives. Jesus warned Peter that Satan had asked to sift him like wheat, and yet Peter still failed. Peter just couldn't understand what was coming, and therefore, didn't recognize it when it happened. Yet, Jesus gave Peter encouragement by telling him that He had prayed for him. Jesus prayed for Peter BEFORE his trial. Peter still failed but he did repent. He did go back and strengthen his brothers after his repentance. Peter came back strong for Jesus. Peter never stopped preaching the gospel and telling others about Jesus as long as he lived. Friend, Jesus has prayed for us also, and continues to intercede on our behalf! We probably won't understand why trials come into our lives, nor what is going on when it happens, but we can rest assured that Jesus loves us. Jesus will never leave us to face the trials alone. Just as he allowed Peter to go through the trial, instead of removing it from his path, we too, will face trials in this life. We may fail during some of those trials, but we can also come back to strengthen our brothers and sisters in Christ, just as Peter did. We can take courage from the Bible. We must read it and study it, as well as spend time in prayer to survive this life. And, we must never forget to strengthen our brothers (and sisters, too)!

Notes: _____

_____

_____

_____

_____

_____

Jacob, A Changed Man

Read Genesis 32:24-33:3.

Verse 24. "Jacob was left alone, and a man wrestled with him until daybreak."

Jacob had normally put his own needs ahead of the needs of others. Jacob had left his father-in-law, Laban, and was preparing to meet Esau. Jacob sent messengers to his brother, Esau, and they returned to tell Jacob that Esau was coming to meet him with 400 men. Jacob was really afraid. Then, we see that he had an encounter with God during the night. Jacob wrestled with Him until daybreak. His name was changed from Jacob to Israel during the encounter. After this encounter, we see that Jacob is different. Jacob was changed for the better. We see that even in his fear, he goes ahead of the women and children to face Esau. If Esau attacks, then the women and children would have a chance to flee. This is the first time we see Jacob put others ahead of himself. He is willing to face the danger himself and take care of his family. When we have an encounter with God, we are also changed. God shows us what He wants from us. We see our sin, and where we need to repent. The encounter between Jacob and Esau goes very well. There is a great reconciliation between them. When we encounter God, we are always better afterwards. Sometimes the change is greater than others, but there is always change. If you want to encounter God, a good way to do that is to spend time studying His word. Some other good ways are to spend time in prayer, or listening to praise and worship music. If we want to spend time with God, He is always willing to meet us where we are. I'm so thankful that He is willing to spend time with me, and that He always leaves me a better person than I was before!

Notes: _____

_____

_____

_____

_____

_____

_____

Do You See Miracles?

Read Mark 9:17-27 and Second Kings 6:4-7.

Verse 6. "Then the man of God asked, 'Where did it fall?' When he showed him the place, the man of God cut a stick, threw it there, and made the iron float."

In the above reference scriptures, we see two very different events. In Second Kings 6: 4-7, we see trees are being cut down with a borrowed ax and the ax head flies off into the Jordan river. Panic sets in on the one who is using the borrowed ax. Elisha asks where the ax head fell. When shown where it fell into the water, Elisha cuts a stick and throws it into the water. The ax head floats. So, the person who was using the ax, has to be told to pick it up. The ax head floating where he can reach is what he needed. But he is probably just too stunned to be able to move, until Elisha's command to pick up the ax head is heard. A miracle has taken place. Ax heads don't normally float.

In Mark 9 verses 17-27, we see a son with a demon that causes him to be mute, to be thrown to the ground, to grind his teeth and to foam at the mouth. The man has brought the son to the disciples but they are unable to drive the demon out of the boy. Now, he asks Jesus if there is anything that He can do to help. The man is asking for help from the One who created the son in the first place. Jesus replies "Everything is possible to the one who believes.". The father cries out "I do believe! Help my unbelief.". Here is a father that desperately wants help for his son. He wants to believe Jesus can heal the boy, but he is afraid. Jesus commands the demon to come out of the boy and never enter him again. The demon comes out of the boy, but it appears the boy is dead. Jesus takes the boy by the hand and raises him up. The boy stands up. A miracle has taken place. Demons don't willingly give up their victims.

In the Bible, the waves are calmed, 5,000 are fed with a small lad's lunch, Lazarus is raised from the dead, an ax head swims, demons are removed from people, and the list goes on. Miracles. All miracles.

You can add to the list of miracles, we are saved, right in there beside the ax head swims. One is just as easy as another for God. Everything named above is on the "impossible" list. Ax heads don't float. Demons don't willingly give up their victims. We can't forgive our own sins. I am sure if you think about it, you can name many things God has done for you during your lifetime. It's actually a very good exercise to make a list of things that God took care of for us. Miracles. Things not possible. But we serve a "possible" God. He's just that awesome! He's just that powerful! And, we should forever be on fire to serve and praise Him and tell others about His great miracles in our own lives!

Notes: _____

_____

_____

_____

_____

_____

When God Questions Job

Read Job 38 and 39.

Job 40:4. "I am so insignificant. How can I answer You? I place my hand over my mouth."

Job has gone through a lot of terrible things. As a matter of fact, I would say Job suffered just about the worst of everything you can imagine. Certainly more than I want to imagine. He doesn't curse God, but he does begin to whine and question God. I am sure nobody reading this has ever done that before. Ha! I know I have questioned God for a lot less suffering than poor Job faced. I have certainly done my share of whining and complaining.... and questioning. My finite mind just cannot comprehend all the ways of infinite God. I tend to forget that sometimes, just like Job did. Well, when God gets around to answering Job (in His own time, I might add), He starts off with "Who is this who obscures My counsel with ignorant words?" That is a good description of my normal whining and complaining. God goes on to ask Job a number of questions, one of which is found in verses 6-11 of chapter 38. "Who enclosed the sea behind doors when it burst from the womb, when I made the clouds its garment and thick darkness its blanket, when I determined its boundaries and put it bars and doors in place, when I declared: "You may come this far, but no farther; your proud waves stop here"? Have you ever sat on the beach and just watched the waves roll in? Each wave is different. Each wave stops at a different spot. There is no predicating where each one will stop, as many sitting in a chair found out when they got wet. God created that and put the stops in place for each wave that has ever and will ever roll onto the shore! That is enough right there to put me in my place. It is one of the reasons that I love to sit on the beach and watch the waves roll in. There is a peace in knowing that God handles all of that and He can handle my life too. Other verses right after those that cause me to pause and think, are verses 12 and 13; "Have you ever in your life commanded the morning or assigned the dawn its place, so it may seize the edges of the earth and shake the wicked out of it?" I very seldom watch the sunrise, although most days I am up in time to do it. I really should take the time to watch it more often. We all should. I could watch it every day but I could never do anything to make it rise or not rise. Not one thing! I cannot alter the time at all. But God handles that every morning. It is beautiful. And then it sets every day. God can handle anything in our life that we face. We may not understand our circumstances or the deep hurts we face, but we can rest assured that God can. He has a plan and a purpose for our life. His part is to work it all out for our good. Our part is to obey Him with complete trust. Think about this the next time you watch the waves roll in or the sun rise or set. Let the peace of God roll into your heart, just as the waves roll onto the beach. Let calm saturate your being, just as the sunlight saturates the day. Trust Him and obey Him. He's has a plan. And you are a wonderful part of it!

Notes: _____

_____

_____

_____

God We Trust You To Fight For Us!

Read Second Chronicles 20: 1-25.

Verse 12. "Our God, will You not judge them? For we are powerless before this vast number that comes to fight against us. We do not know what to do, but we look to You."

Jehoshaphat and God's people were facing a huge army that was coming to attack them. They had no way to defeat that army on their own. They were scared. Actually, they were terrified.

Jehoshaphat stood at the temple and prayed to God for help. His prayer started off with praise to God and then, humbly asked for help. God answered him through a person there. He was told to go out against the vast army but not to be afraid or discouraged. He was told "You do not have to fight this battle".

Jehoshaphat's response was to fall down and worship God. That should always be our response when we hear from God. The very thought that He will answer us is amazing and should provoke our worship of Him.

Then he and the Israelites got up the next morning and went out. Jehoshaphat told them to believe God. He also arranged a group to go before the army singing praises to God. The moment they begin to sing praises of thanks to God, the Lord set an ambush on the vast armies. They completely destroyed each other. Not one man was left standing.

When Judah got to a point they could see, they found only dead bodies. Jehoshaphat told his army to collect the plunder from the bodies. It took them three days to gather the plunder!!!

What originally looked like certain destruction for them became a time of blessing even with lots of plunder. This happened when they prayed, believed, obeyed and then gave thanks to God on faith!

If God can orchestrate that victory for Jehoshaphat, can HE not also give us victory over all battles if we follow what Jehoshaphat did as our example? The victory may not be what we are expecting, but we know that God works all things for our best. HE knows better than we do what is best for us. We must learn to trust HIM in all things, just as Jehoshaphat did.

Notes: _____

_____

_____

_____

_____

_____

Cleaning Out The Fridge!

Psalm 51:10. "God, create a clean heart for me and renew a steadfast spirit within me."

Proverbs 14:30. "A tranquil heart is life to the body, but jealousy is rottenness to the bones."

In the routine of my household chores today, I had to tend to a job I always hate to do. I always dread it, so I wait until there is no choice but to do it. Of course, that makes it worse than it would be if I didn't put it off. It is cleaning out the fridge!

I'm so bad about storing leftover amounts of food in the refrigerator, with the intention that I will probably eat it tomorrow. But, too often that tomorrow doesn't come and I forget that it's in there as it gets pushed back behind the milk jug and other things. As time passes, I begin to notice that my fridge is full and there's no more room for even the good food. That's when I know I have to do what should have already been done. It's always amazing what I find in there and sometimes it is disgusting also! What looked so good and tasty before has turned into a moldy, greenish, stinky, unrecognizable mess that I would never be tempted to eat!

I'm trying to learn that God can speak to me through anything, and so today as I cleaned out the fridge, I asked Him, 'God, what do you want to tell me about this mess'? He answered me by showing me that I need to look at my life and into my own heart like I do that cluttered fridge, and clean out the old, nasty, moldy, ugly, stinky, stale and unlovable things I have stored there. There are plenty of them, too, I hate to admit! But just thinking about all of them as I dumped the bad food items into the garbage bag, made me realize that I need to examine myself every day before God's word and discard every single thing that will cause decay and rottenness in my heart. I don't need to store them inside and allow them to rot there. I need to learn not to hang onto the things in my heart that will not bring a sweet smell to God's nostrils or glory to Him, just like I need to quit sticking back leftover foods until they ruin and are wasted. This needs to be a daily thing for me. With God's help I want to keep my heart fresh and clean and uncluttered so that I can spend my time focusing on Him. Oh, and I'm going to try to do better on the fridge thing too!

Notes: _____

_____

_____

_____

_____

_____

His Will / Our Willpower

First Thessalonians 5:18. "Give thanks in everything, for this is God's will for you in Christ Jesus."

Often when I am studying my Bible I write down my thoughts about what I've studied. It helps me to write it out and be reminded of what God wants me to see in the particular scripture I've read. Here's what I wrote this morning: 'Doing a lot of study today. Need to be doing housework but not wanting to. I feel a strong need to be deep in the Word today and to be talking with and listening to the Author of the Word, the Lord of all creation and circumstances.' 'In everything give thanks; for this is the will of God in Christ Jesus for you.' (First Thessalonians 5:18, NKJV). It's God's will that we give thanks in everything. Sometimes it takes us making it a matter of WILLPOWER to be able to be thankful in ALL things. But He wants us to do this and if we are His, He doesn't allow anything into our lives that is not ultimately for our good. THAT'S what we must keep in mind and THAT'S what we are to be thankful for....that He loves us, is in control of all things, and has a plan for only GOOD for us. So, when we think things are bad for us (and maybe they are), we need to keep in mind that IF we are His child, then whatever is happening, ultimately has a good purpose in our lives. Someday, He will show us the reasons and consequences in His own timing and we will understand more about why things happened the way they did, but meanwhile we need to just grab onto Him and hang tightly!

In The End

Revelation 21:4. "He will wipe away every tear from their eyes. Death will no longer exist; grief, crying, and pain will exist no longer, because the previous things have passed away."

I ate another chocolate the other day. Inside the wrapper was this verse "Everything will be okay in the end. If it's not okay, it's not the end." I thought to myself "There is a devotion in that saying.", but I put the wrapper down in my purse, meaning to write the devotion later. Several days have now gone by, and I had forgotten about the wrapper as well as the devotion. But, when I opened my chocolate today, guess what the wrapper had inside? The same verse. I said, "Okay, Lord, you are right.". And, this time, I carried it home in my hand and followed through on what I should have done days ago. Many people try to comfort others by saying "It's okay" or "It will be okay". Well, sometimes, things are just not okay! My Daddy had pancreatic cancer. He suffered terribly and had much pain. He did not complain very much, and did all he could do to fight to stay with us. He refused pain medication when I am sure he needed it because he chose to be conscious in order to visit with us, instead of taking the much needed pain medication that would have caused him to sleep. There is nothing about what he went through and how bad I miss him that is okay. There is nothing about that dreadful disease that is okay. I know my Daddy is in Heaven with Jesus. I also know that he is no longer in pain or any other kind of suffering. He was a strong Christian and loved Jesus dearly until the end. What he went through was not okay! I don't even like to hear people say "It is okay or It's going to be okay.". But, what Daddy suffered was also not the end. The end for Daddy was to be in Heaven with Jesus, around God's throne with many other saints that have already gone. The end for all Christians will be in Heaven with Jesus. We get just a taste of being in HIS presence here on earth. That wonderful feeling will be magnified more than we can even imagine. There will be no more tears, no pain, no grief and death will no longer exist. "Everything will be okay in the end. If it's not okay, it's not the end.". This statement is only true if you are a believer in Christ. If you have not accepted Jesus as your Saviour, then the end will not be okay for you. Hell awaits those who do not accept Jesus. It's not enough to just know about HIM; you must know HIM personally. You must accept HIM as your Lord. That does not mean you will never sin again but it does mean that you will want most of all to please HIM. John 3:16 says "For God so loved the world in this way: He gave His One and Only Son, so that everyone who believes in Him will not perish but have eternal life.". But for Christians, "Everything will be okay in the end. If it's not okay, it's not the end." is a completely true statement!

Notes: _____

_____

_____

_____

_____

_____

The Wisdom Of Gratefulness

Read Psalm 46:10 and Psalm 90.

Verse 12. "Teach us to number our days carefully so that we may develop wisdom in our hearts."

Well, that is a pretty strong clue that our days here on earth will come to an end at some point. What will people say about our days? What will we think when we come to the end of our days? Most importantly, what will God say about the days HE has given us? Have I used the days and resources HE gave me wisely? I catch myself rushing through many days to get to the end of a week. Why? So I can sleep late on Saturday morning, then only to find myself wide awake before 6:30 am. But what is the logic to wish a week of your life away to sleep an extra hour? When I really stop to think about it, rushing through and wishing your life away makes no sense at all. Yet, I, in particular, do that in anticipation of an event or just nothing at all. In reality, the sweetest times of my life are the times I spend with God. Time spent studying his word, singing HIS praises and listening for HIS voice. God has blessed me with many things, which I often fail to enjoy. Things like a warm home, flowers blooming, music, good food, another day on this earth, and the list just goes on. Is my failure to just live in the moment and enjoy His blessings perhaps a form of ungratefulness? Maybe it is. I am not intentionally ungrateful but when I rush through my days with dread and worry, I certainly am displaying a lack of trust in HIM. There are opportunities to be thankful in each day. If I start by just being still and remembering that HE is God, it will provoke the right attitude in me. I don't want to waste HIS blessings. By not enjoying the many blessings HE gives, I am not only displaying a lack of gratitude but probably missing so many of the miracles HE would like to show me every day. I don't want to miss anything HE wants to show me nor one second of HIS great presence!!! I also don't want to waste any of the time HE has given me on this earth. I am here for a reason, a purpose, something HE has for me to do. That is not to say we must work non-stop. Sometimes we influence others more during the time we are relaxing than when we are working at it. It's the unintentional influences for God that are often the most effective. Thank you God for the time you have given me and for the many other blessings. May I always be grateful and make the most of what you have given by listening to your voice.

Notes: _____

_____

_____

_____

_____

_____

Pain and Pearls

Romans 8:28. "We know that all things work together for the good of those who love God: those who are called according to His purpose."

If you consider all the grains of sand together on a beach, it is beautiful to us. It feels good to walk in with our bare feet. We want to lay out on the beach. Sand is a very intricate part of the beauty the beach offers. Yet, one grain inside the oysters shell is constant pain and torment. Pearls are a perfect physical example of Romans 8:28. It's not that we won't have bad things in life. We will. That's a given. We will have hard things in life. Very hard things. We will have very bad things to face. There is no escaping that in this world. When the oyster gets a grain of sand inside its shell, it's bad. A grain of sand is hard, very hard. It rubs on the flesh of the oyster. It irritates the flesh of the oyster. It is painful and a constant difficulty. The oyster has no hands to fling the grain of sand out of its shell. It has no way to be rid of the painful, constant irritation. The difference is in how the oyster deals with the grain of sand. The oyster doesn't give up and die. It begins to coat the painful irritation with something that has sheen and glimmer. It coats it over and over until what once was rough and irritating is now beautiful and smooth. What was once painful, is now a thing of beauty. The oyster grows its pain into something of value. We have hard times in life and painful situations. We can either be bitter, sad and let it ruin us or we can grow from it. We can allow God to grow the painful times into a thing of beauty. The grain of sand doesn't go away. It will always be inside the pearl. But it's covered with growth from the hurt it caused the oyster. We can take our pain and grow closer to God. We can take our difficult times and let God teach us how to comfort others. We, like the oyster, cannot get the pain out of our life. We must, instead, grow something beautiful around the pain so that it has value. If we don't, the pain is just pain and it continues to cause a deeper hurt. The pain will always be there but it will be easier if we grow something of value around it. God will take your pain, your hurt, your irritation, and grow something of value inside your shell, if you will only let Him. The oyster makes the pearl and we must allow God to make something beautiful out of our hurt.

Notes: _____

_____

_____

_____

_____

_____

Mistakes and Do Overs

Luke 14:28-30. "For which of you, wanting to build a tower, doesn't first sit down and calculate the cost to see if he has enough to complete it? Otherwise, after he had laid the foundation and cannot finish it, all the onlookers will begin to make fun of him, saying, 'This man started to build and wasn't able to finish.'"

I'm a crocheter. Beginning any crochet project starts with making a chain stitch. When I make that first stitch, I do it with the understanding that my commitment has to last much longer than that one first stitch. When I start a project, I begin with a ball of yarn and a crochet hook. Two very simple things. That's all I have to begin with. But as I work, something new begins to take shape. Hopefully the work of my hands will become something that will be beautiful and useful to provide a garment or blanket for covering and warmth. Sometimes when I make a mistake, I have to have a 'do over' and ravel the error out and fix it. Sometimes my pattern doesn't come out looking exactly like I have pictured in my mind so I 're-do' and start over with a different stitch or even different thread. Sometimes I don't like the finished product for myself and either give it away or completely ravel it away and wind the yarn back into a ball like I began with. I love to crochet. As a very small child I remember watching my grandmother as she crocheted. She was my inspiration to learn how to crochet. Crocheting is a therapy of the mind and also exercise for my arthritic fingers. It helps keep the joints in my hands loosened and thereby makes them less sore and painful. I love making things for someone else who will get good usage of the item I make. I've made many crocheted hats for ladies who've lost their hair due to chemo treatments while going through cancer. I admit that's a selfish thing on my part because I get so much blessing in doing that. But as I think about crocheting, I think about how God takes us....when we are really nothing of value or use to Him, and IF we allow Him, He can take His hands and work on us and gradually shape and make us into something useful and beautiful in His eyes. How many times He's had to ravel my mess-ups out of my life and perform a 'fix'! How many times He's forgiven my sins and changed the patterns of my life, allowing me to start over! The pattern of our lives may not look like anything much to us or to other people, but when God is finished making us into His image, reflecting His workmanship, we will be as Job 23:10 says: 'Yet He knows the way I have taken; when He has tested me, I will emerge as pure gold.'

Notes: _____

_____

_____

_____

_____

_____

God Knows Before We Ask

Psalm 139:4. "Before a word is on my tongue, You know all about it, Lord."

Can God hear the faintest whisper of our heart? The one thing you feel selfish or foolish for asking? Does HE care when packages deliver? Is HE really into those tiny details? I was expecting a package. It was not anything that I had a pressing need for. But I was excited for it to come. Most of what was in it will be given away at various times but I don't even know when on most of it so I didn't need the box to come today. It was originally tentatively scheduled for tomorrow. But I have been excited about it for some reason. Maybe God has something planned. But for whatever reason, my heart secretly hoped this morning that it would come on today instead of tomorrow. I almost asked God for it to come today, but I stopped myself. I felt guilty to ask for something like that. It didn't matter anyway. It was just a wish for it to arrive today, not a need. Sometimes, I think God gives us things we just want but don't necessarily need, to remind us that HE is present in our lives. He reminds us that HE loves us. And that HE delights in giving us things. The idea that God, who is so awesome, and has so many other people more deserving to bless, but yet does something so particular for me is just amazing. You know my package delivered today! God heard that faint whisper in my heart and HE answered! Thing is, HE arranged that before my heart longed for it. If HE loves me that much, HE will certainly provide all I need. He delights in surprising us just as we delight in surprising our own children!

Notes: _____

_____

_____

_____

_____

_____

_____

Hard Times and Many Blessings

Read Joel 2:18-27.

Verse 20. "I will drive the northerner far from you and banish him to a dry and desolate land, his front ranks into the Dead Sea, and his rear guard into the Mediterranean Sea. His stench will rise; yes, his rotten smell will rise, for he has done catastrophic things."

Wow. After losing my job last August, I have experienced tight budgets and feelings of hurt and almost abandonment by God. I have asked over and over "What did I do?" To make matters worse, I lost my precious Daddy less than two years ago; my son moved to Fort Worth, Texas, to attend seminary; my husband had to close his business one month before I lost my job and he accepted another job four hours away from our home. Yet, even with so much hurt in my life, there is much to be thankful for. My Daddy is in Heaven and thanks to Jesus, I will see Daddy again. My son has an apartment to live in, a great roommate that he already knew, his precious girlfriend moved a drivable distance west, also to attend college, and we have phones to hear from each other. My husband's new job is near a town that we own property in and keep our camper, so he already had a place to stay.

    We do have these and many more things to be thankful for but my life as I knew it has been turned upside down. My dear Mother has had to learn to live alone, without my Daddy. I am thankful she and I have homes only a few steps down the road from each other. But she and I have had to learn how to repair many things. We have had to learn how to live life as women on their own. My husband does come home about once a month and clean up whatever repair messes I have made. But sometimes my life has the feeling of confetti floating in the air, not knowing where it will land and having no control over the same.

    I have sought God's will during this time in my life, probably harder than I have in a while. I have cried. I have questioned. I have experienced anger, hurt, grief and helplessness. I do not hang in limbo very well. I am a planner. A "do-it-in-advance" girl. I have always been that way, but that is not faith. Faith believes what it can't see because God says so! In my devotion reading the other day, this scripture was listed. I read it but I also made a picture of it because I wanted to come back to it. Something about it struck me. It comforted me and brought hope. As I looked back over it again today, I noticed one additional interesting thing. Verse 20. I hold no ill feelings towards the company I worked for that closed down but their home office was in the north. Maybe this scripture, for me, goes all the way back to when our family business closed. Maybe I was never meant to be with this company until I retired anyway. Maybe, just maybe, there are better days ahead for me, just as God Promised for His people here in Joel. God uses different things to speak to us. God promises, here in Joel to give back what the locusts took away. The locusts were sent by God to eat the crops as punishment. Crops meant no food, nothing to sell. That translates to hard times, tight budgets, and some of the same things I have experienced. Giving back what the locusts took sounds like blessings to me. I may not know what blessings God has for me but I do know that God's blessings are good. I may not know what I need but I do know that HE does. His choices for me will work out for my best. So, even though my life is in pieces right now, and where I will land is yet unknown, I know HE is working it out for my good. How do I know? Because HE says so in Romans 8:28 and that's good enough for me.

Notes: _____

_____

_____

_____

_____

_____

_____

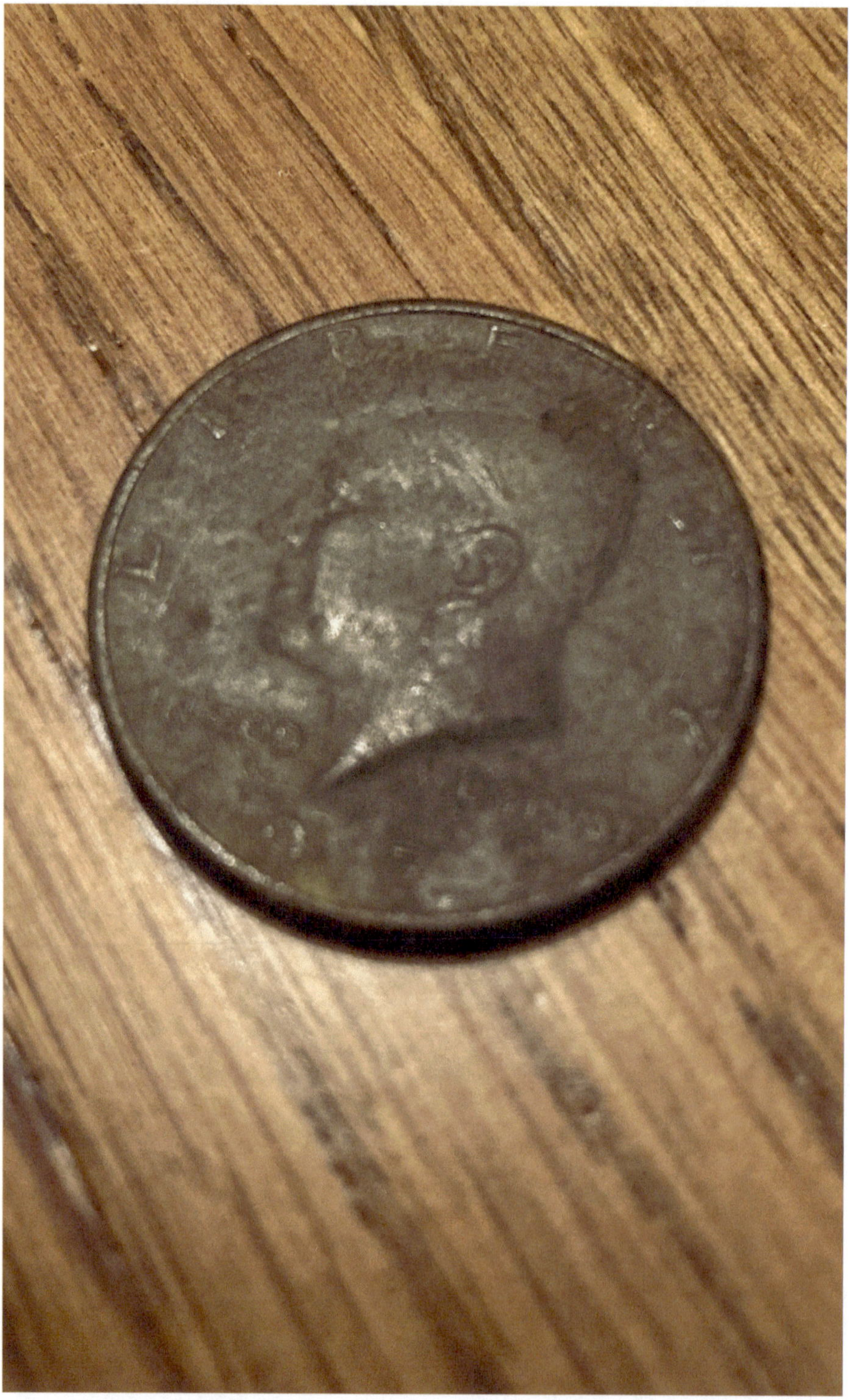

A Half Dollar of Comfort

Psalm 119:76. "May Your faithful love comfort me as You promised Your servant."

Years ago my Daddy built two billboard foundations, each with four faces, to rent. Daddy was a very smart person. He would think things through and come up with different very ingenious ways to test things. Daddy went to Heaven one year and ten months ago. I have missed him terribly. I know he is with Jesus and I know he has no more pain. I know he wouldn't come back if he could, but I just miss my sweet Daddy. It has been that way since the day he died. This week it seems like I have felt the pain of missing him really bad. Mom and I have struggled along dealing with the billboards the best we can. We have had to learn some things about timers and lights. With the recent time change, we needed to set the time on the billboard timers, but we have both been busy. So, being as storms were predicted for tomorrow, we decided to run down tonight after church. We went to the foundation furtherest from the office first and started to work on it. Mom took the locks off of the timer boxes and held the flashlight for me while I started to change the time markers that trigger the lights to go on and off. While she juggled the flashlight, she dropped both locks on the ground. As she turned the light down for me to see to pick the locks up, she spotted something on the ground. I reached down and picked it up. It was a Kennedy half dollar coin. Daddy collected those. It was odd for it to be on top of the ground. It wasn't really covered in dirt but it had rust on one side. It was interesting. I told Mom that Daddy must have dropped it while he was down there sometime. She told me that she wanted me to keep it. When I got home, I realized that Daddy had not dropped the coin out of his pocket, but that Daddy had put the coin up on the cross frame of the billboard years ago when he built it. I am sure of that because the coin has rust on it from laying on the I-beam the billboard is built with. Daddy would have put the coin up there to see how much the billboards shook from the wind. He did little things like that. That billboard foundation was built late in 1998. I think the coin had been up there all that time. I know Daddy didn't come from Heaven and knock the coin off for me to find, but it was a great comfort to me to find it. God has many different ways of comforting His children. He used a half dollar coin that my Daddy placed in a specific place many years before, to show me that He cares about me and is always aware of my needs. God knew I would know how that coin got to be where it was found. This was one way that God comforted me tonight during a very hard week. His timing is always perfect!

Notes: _____

_____

_____

_____

_____

_____

Saltiness and Lighthouses

Matthew 5:10-16. "Those who are persecuted for righteousness are blessed, for the kingdom of heaven is theirs. You are blessed when they insult and persecute you and falsely say every kind of evil against you because of Me. Be glad and rejoice, because your reward is great in heaven. For that is how they persecuted the prophets who were before you. You are the salt of the earth. But if the salt should lose its taste, how can it be made salty? It's no longer good for anything but to be thrown out and trampled on by men. You are the light of the world. A city situated on a hill cannot be hidden. No one lights a lamp and puts it under a basket, but rather on a lampstand, and it gives light for all who are in the house. In the same way, let your light shine before men, so that they may see your good works and give glory to your Father in heaven."

Jesus' words in these two beatitudes (supreme blessings) from His Sermon on the Mount are difficult for me to accept and understand, I admit. How are we to feel blessed and rejoice when we are persecuted or spoken against falsely? We must expect this kind of treatment however, if we are His children. He said that as His followers, these kinds of things will come to us - sometimes just because we claim His name. He experienced these and so much more! John 15:18 says 'If the world hates you, understand that it hated me before it hated you.' And John 15:20a says 'Remember the word I spoke to you: A servant is not greater than his master. If they persecuted me, they will also persecute you.' But the issue is not whether we feel blessed as we go through trials, the verses tell us our reward is not in this life but in Heaven. That indicates to me that we may not enjoy these things here on earth as they come into our lives, but we have to keep our focus on the eternal rewards we will enjoy in God's heavenly kingdom. Jesus tells us in His Sermon on the Mount, how we are to react and respond to trials and persecutions we may experience by saying we are to be salt and light in this unsavory and dark world. Salt was used as a preservative and to give flavor and the salt Jesus wants us to be is that way. We are to preserve, protect and magnify His good name and bring glory to Him. Our lives are supposed to reflect His life in us so that others can see what a wonderful Savior we have. We're not to have any glory; no, not us...the glory belongs to Jesus and Jesus only! That is the kind of salt flavored life He wants us to live. Then He tells us we are to be lights like a city on a hill. I, being a beach lover, immediately think of a lighthouse out on a point of land shining its beacon so that the captains of ships can see the way they need to go. Lighthouses remind me of our Lord, standing out in the dangerous gap in the darkness and storms of life, providing the safe way for us to take. We are to be that kind of light to this dark world also. One that reflects the light Jesus shines and not one that turns our spotlight on ourselves. We are to be Salt and Light examples - even while going through trials and persecutions. Jesus was, and we are to follow our Lord's example!

So I Asked, 'But God, What If.....?'

John 3:16. "For God loved the world in this way. He gave His One and Only Son, so that everyone who believes in Him will not perish but have eternal life."

So I asked. 'But God, What If........?' And He answered, 'My child, I LOVE you; I AM able; I WILL provide...!' John 3:16. ' For God loved the world in this way. He gave His one and only Son, so that everyone who believes in Him will not perish, but have eternal life.' I admit my tendency is to worry. I'm full of 'what if's' and regularly go over them in my mind and talk to God about them. One day recently while I was doing this, God stopped me in mid-prayer sentence and said, 'My child, I LOVE you; I AM able; I WILL provide...!' Let me tell you right now, when you are talking to the Lord and pouring your heart out about your fears, and He puts that kind of answer into your mind, well, there's nothing left to whine to Him about! All the fears and doubts lose their place of importance when compared to that answer! It's the exclamation point at the end of the sentence, replacing the question marks. I still don't know the details of the answers to my 'what if?' questions, but I realize I don't have to know and I don't have to worry because HE knows and HE has assured me that 'My child, I LOVE you; I AM able; I WILL provide...!' John 3:16 proves this also. 'My child, I LOVE you (He gave His only begotten Son who stretched out His arms on the cross willingly where my arms should have been!); I AM able (Because I know He died for me and rose again, He is able to sustain me and I don't have to perish!); I WILL provide (Because He lives and sits on the right hand of the Father as my advocate, I am assured of all I need, including everlasting life!)!' He's the God of answers to ALL my What If's! My part is to trust Him! He's already proved He is able to take care of all our 'What IF?' questions in life.

Notes: _____

_____

_____

_____

_____

_____

Instant Peace

Psalm 118:5. "I called to the Lord in distress; the Lord answered me and put me in a spacious place."

What do you think about it when God answers a prayer for you the moment you finish speaking it? Do you think that is even possible? Why would God bother to answer someone like me so quickly?

My son and daughter-in-law were out at the beach or somewhere enjoying a precious few minutes alone. It was getting late. I was tired. I knew we all had to get up at a particular time the next day and I knew I couldn't sleep until they came in. Yes, they are grown, responsible, sensible, smart people, and they were in a safe area. I think it's just a crazy quirk I have of not being able to sleep if I know somebody's coming in. Whatever the case, I couldn't sleep until they got in.

I prayed to God to let them come on in soon, and as soon as I finished speaking in my heart, I heard a car door. Now some people would say that was a coincidence but I don't believe in those. I know that God knows my thoughts before I even think. He created me, so He knows everything about me, including my strange quirks and ways. God is so amazing and so awesome that He is able to keep up with the largest parts of the Universe at the same time He is coordinating the tiniest of details. That's my God! God has shown me over and over again that He cares deeply for me and that HE has ALL the details covered. Yes, the big details and the tiniest details. Coincidence? No way! God's great love for me? Absolutely!

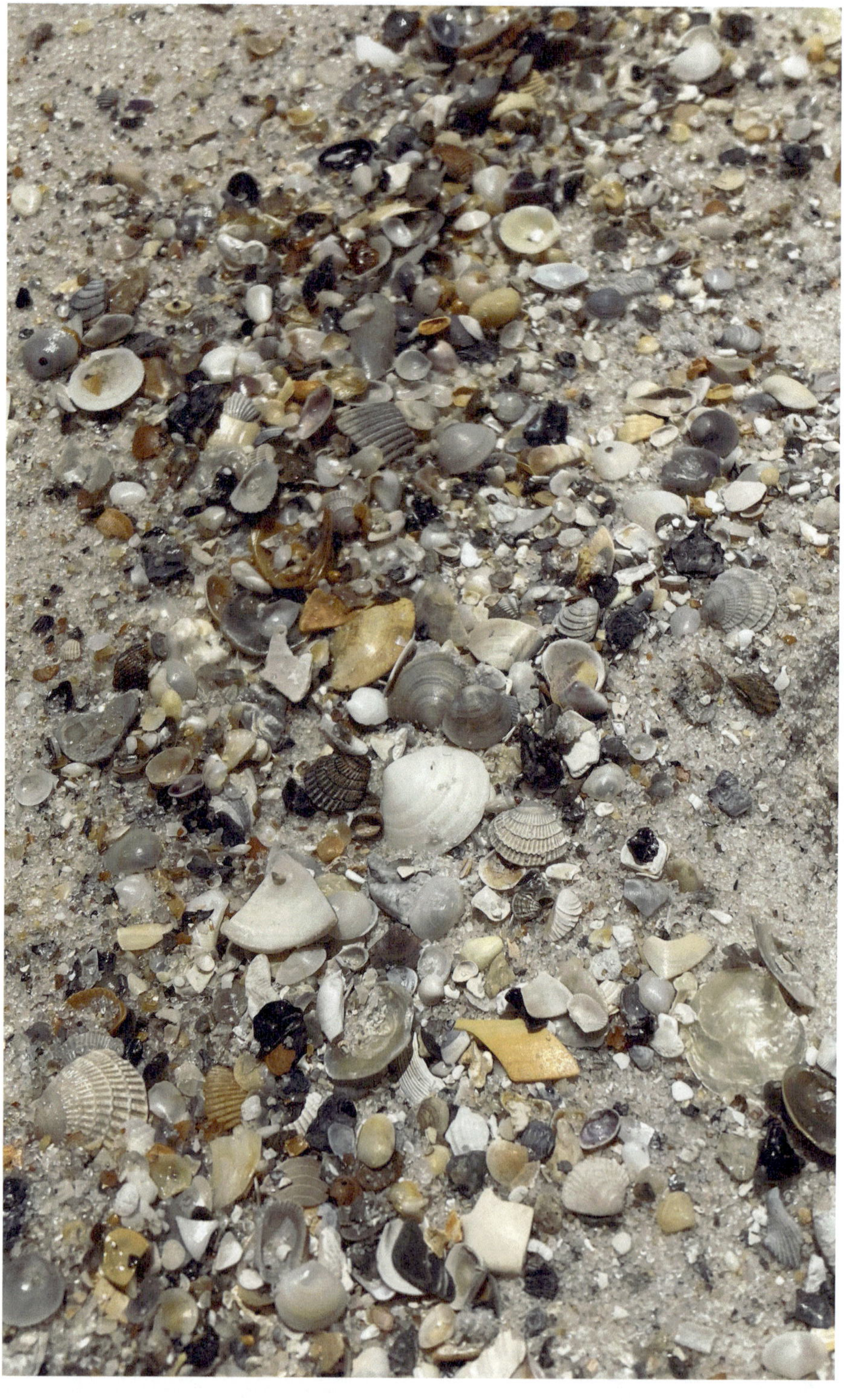

Broken Shells

Jeremiah 18:1-4. "This is the word that came to Jeremiah from the Lord: 'Go down at once to the potter's house; there I will reveal my words to you.' So I went down to the potter's house, and there he was working away at the wheel. But the jar that he was making from the clay became flawed in the potter's hand, so he made it into another jar, as it seemed right for him to do."

Jeremiah 48:38. "'On all the rooftops of Moab and in her public squares, everyone is mourning because I have shattered Moab like a jar no one wants.' This is the Lord's declaration."

Psalm 51:16-17. "You do not want a sacrifice, or I would give it; You are not pleased with a burnt offering. The sacrifice pleasing to God is a broken spirit. You will not despise a broken and humbled heart, God."

Recently while walking on the beautiful white sands on the beach, I noticed areas where many sea shells were washed up along the high tide line. I love the beach: the waves; the beautiful blue-green water sparkling in the sunshine; and the sugar white sand to walk barefoot in. But I think the sea shells I find there hold the most special place in my love of all things coastal. I've always picked up and collected shells. I love all of them...no matter the type, size or coloring. On this particular March outing, while walking a long stretch of beach with few people out, these shell-strewn tide lines caught and held my attention. I scanned each area as I came upon them, looking for that one perfect and unique shell, and as always hoping to find a different kind than I'd collected before. Some of the shells looked perfect and beautiful so it was hard just choosing the ones I liked best since I couldn't pick them all up. But as I looked through each area, I began to realize that most of the shells were broken. Many were shattered and fragmented; some were rough-edged and some had long ago broken edges worn smooth from their movement in the water. But most of what I saw washed up along the tide lines were simply pieces of the shell they used to be. Although some appeared to be perfect, when examined closely, they also had flaws. But God uses the broken shells! Over time, the sun, wind and water, break them down and they become a part of that beautiful sugary-white sand we all love to walk and play in. On that day, God reminded me that His children are like these broken shells. Most of us are broken, have been shattered, and are rough-edged or worn. But God can still use broken things and broken people! As a matter of fact, we have to be broken before we can be made whole again, and God can take our broken selves and use the pieces to create something new. He has regularly shown us how something broken can become useful, valuable and beautiful. He broke the five loaves of bread and fed thousands; He broke Peter's nets with a huge catch; He submitted His own body to be broken by crucifixion unto death so that we could be saved. We are all broken and in need of our Potter's hands to remold our shattered pieces into the beautiful and useful purpose only He knows we can have.

Disgraced But Forgiven By Grace

John 8:2-11. "At dawn He went to the temple complex again, and all the people were coming to Him. He sat down and began to teach them. Then the scribes and the Pharisees brought a woman caught in adultery making her stand in the center. 'Teacher' they said to Him, 'this woman was caught in the act of committing adultery. In the law Moses commanded us to stone such women. So what do you say?' They asked this to trap Him, in order that they might have evidence to accuse Him. Jesus stooped down and started writing on the ground with His finger. When they persisted in questioning Him, He stood up and said to them, 'The one without sin among you should be the first to throw a stone at her.' Then He stooped down again and continued writing on the ground. When they heard this, they left one by one, starting with the older men. Only He was left, with the woman in the center. When Jesus stood up, He said to her, 'Woman, where are they? Has no one condemned you?' 'No one, Lord,' she answered. 'Neither do I condemn you,' said Jesus. 'Go, and from now on do not sin anymore.',"

John 8:36. "Therefore, if the Son sets you free, you really will be free."

FATHER GOD: Please make my life more than just words I speak or words I sing from my favorite hymn! Don't let me voice my commitment and adoration to you and turn and speak condemnation to a fellow pilgrim. Don't let me sing about your amazing grace that saved a wretch like me and not extend grace to others who've stumbled or fallen along the journey! The hurting ones and the ones who are experiencing failure and doubts are ME! I've been where they are. Maybe not just at this moment but in other moments of my life. I am them! Please Lord, keep my mind alert and focused on radiating YOU to those I come in contact with. Some may not read Your Word, but they read my actions and reactions to them loud and clear! I don't ever want to be the cause of anyone stumbling or turning away from You! I don't want to be the one pointing my finger at others and pointing out their sins for rejection; I want to be the one pointing my fingers toward You and pointing them in Your direction for redemption. I call myself a follower of You; help me to live what I say. Jesus, You told the woman caught in adultery, who was dragged to You and pointed out as sinful in a public spotlight, that You didn't condemn her but to go and sin no more. Your forgiveness brings freedom. We all need to have this freedom in You! Help me be the person who gently brings others to You without condemnation from me, so that You can set them free. You never appointed me to be a judge, but you reserved that option for Yourself. Help me to remember that Your mission on earth was to save and offer restoration to those of us who need your salvation and your grace - and that includes every single one of us! AMEN!

One In A Long Line

Read Hebrews 11 and Hebrews 12:1-4 .

Verse 1. "Therefore, since we also have such a large cloud of witnesses surrounding us, let us lay aside every hindrance and the sin that so easily ensnares us. Let us run with endurance the race that lies before us"

Have you ever considered what it might be like to be able to step back in time for an afternoon and have tea with some of your ancestors? Have you ever wondered what they might think of the way things are today or what you might could learn from them? Have you ever wished you could ask one of them for some advice on how to handle something? Hebrews 11 lists many great examples of people who exercised faith in God. It doesn't say their lives were easy. As a matter of fact, it describes some awful things that some of them endured... tortured, cruel mocking, scourging, imprisonment, stoned, sawn asunder, tempted, slain with the sword. But it does say that their faith made a difference. It says the world was not worthy of them. These examples obtained a good report through faith. We must also have faith! We must choose to have faith in Jesus. It is a choice. I would like to be able to step back in time and have tea with my Great Grandmother Maggie. She raised 14 children during an age prior to electric power, running water and indoor plumbing. Perhaps if I could go back and have tea with her, I would get a better grasp on the big picture. Maybe it would help me to realize that I am a part of a plan that lasts longer than my lifetime. It might help me see my place in HIS plan, my purpose and how important it is that I faithfully do my part. Maggie's faithfulness and what she taught her children, one of whom was my grandfather, is part of why I have faith in Jesus today. Because, she taught my grandfather and he taught my mother and she taught me. I, in turn, taught my son, who is now a pastor. Maggie's parents taught her. I wonder if they ever thought about all the generations to come and how many people their words would affect directly and indirectly. I think about my descendants and I pray that they too will one day accept Jesus as their Savior. If I could see the struggles my ancestors went through and how their faithfulness affected my life, it might just give me the courage to stand firm in my faith. That might give me some insight on how my faithfulness, or the lack of, will affect future generations. I believe studying the faithfulness of the many patriarchs in the Bible, and how that has affected us, would encourage us to stand faithful to God and carry out our part of His plan. After all, we are a part of His plan. I have been blessed to be able to trace my Godly heritage back many generations. One day when I get to Heaven, maybe I will see where I fall into the line of people who have fanned the flames of faith for the next generations. It is not all about us. We are only one small lifetime in a long line of lifetimes. And we must do our very best to see that the generations to come know about Jesus.

Notes: _____

_____

_____

_____

His Will Is Best

Mark 14:32-36. "Then they came to a place named Gethsemane, and He told His disciples, 'Sit here while I pray.' He took Peter, James, and John with Him, and He began to be deeply distressed and horrified. Then He said to them, 'My soul is swallowed up in sorrow–to the point of death. Remain here and stay away.' Then He went a little farther, fell to the ground, and began to pray that if it were possible, the hour might pass from Him. And He said, 'Abba, Father! All things are possible for You. Take this cup away from Me. Nevertheless, not what I will, but what You will.'"

Have you ever found yourself praying for what you want? For some, the answer would be, "Well, yes, why would I pray for something I didn't want to happen?" But prayer is not designed to be a time to ask God for the things on our wish list. It's a time for us to bend the knee to hear the almighty Creator of the universe. I mean, really when you think about it, it's amazing that He would even hear us in the first place. We, meaning I, come up with the greatest excuses and reasons for praying for what I want, instead of asking for God's will. I mean, you know, this place I'm asking to live is more familiar to me, so that would be easier. Of course, God wants things to be easier for me right? My house is paid for already. Now that's a good one. God doesn't want us to go into debt. But what if there is someone where God wants to send you that only you can reach for Him? This is just one example of many. Maybe our old car is just fine instead of the shiny new one we are asking God to work out that deal on. There is also the very real possibility that God knows more than we do. Of course, that's not just a possibility but a definite resounding Of Course He Does! I have seen people facing what looked like impossible odds, obey God anyway, only to find out that He had a better blessing worked out when they took the leap of faith. But even if He doesn't work out what appears to us to be a better blessing, His will is still best. I am trying to learn to pray "Thy will be done, not mine" and mean it. Because, even on my best days, I desperately needed Jesus to pray that in the Garden of Gethsemane. On my very best day, I needed a Savior who loved God enough to say "Father, nevertheless, not what I will, but what You will". It sure didn't look like God's plan was best when Jesus went to the cross on Friday but the picture looked a lot different on Sunday when HE rose triumphantly from the grave! Jesus knew what was coming. He knew it would be hard but He knew victory was on the other side. We can't see the future but we have a God who can! His will is best. I am praying for the very best when I pray, "not my will, but Your will be done, Lord". When you leave your life in those Nail Scarred Hands, you are leaving your life in the very best hands!

Notes: _____

_____

_____

_____

_____

God Uses Willing People

Read Matthew 6:33-34, Luke 2:49, and Joshua 6:22-23.

Joshua 2:12. "Now please swear to me by the Lord that you will also show kindness to my family, because I showed kindness to you. Give me a sure sign."

God doesn't just use the people who have always been "good". Look at Abraham, Jacob, Jonah, Rahab and the list goes on. What about me? In reality, there are no "good" people. There are only the saved and the unsaved. As one of the saved, I am so thankful. Thankful that Jesus loved me enough to be beaten for my sins. But the beating wasn't all of it or even the worst of it. Because Jesus loved me so much, I want to serve Him. I want to know Jesus. Not just about Jesus but really know Jesus! I want my heart to follow His heart. I want to pattern my thoughts and my ways after His thoughts and ways. Have I been good all of life? Absolutely not! Am I good now? Absolutely not. But I am forgiven! And being forgiven frees me to concentrate on Jesus, not what I look like to other people. I'm not saying I shouldn't try to keep a good reputation. But I am saying if I put my effort and concentration into following Jesus, into studying His word, into loving Him, then I won't have time to worry about reputation. God didn't call me to worry. He called me to follow Jesus! He called me to love Jesus! As I love

Jesus, I will automatically reach out to others. As I concentrate on Jesus, I will automatically tell others about Him. We generally converse about the things on the top of our mind. The things on our mind, usually control our behavior. So, If I concentrate on Jesus, on knowing Him, on following Him, on patterning my heart after His, then I will be about His business as a way of life. Jesus concentrated on the Father and He was always about His Father's business. As I concentrate on Jesus more, I have found that times with friends more often end up with scripture, prayer and encouragement worked in amongst the coffee and giggles. That has happened, not just because I am concentrating more on Jesus, but because they are too. And as we encounter the waitress in the restaurant and the other patrons in the coffee shop, we tend to reach out to them more. I have found that as I hurt more and go through more hard times, I am comforted more by Jesus. As that takes place, I tend to recognize the hurts of others more and reach out to comfort them. Just as Rahab concentrated on hiding the spies because she had heard about God and knew it was the right thing to do, then God used her to save her whole family. And there she is listed in the lineage of Jesus. It seems to happen more naturally as I concentrate on Him, and before I know it, He has used me. He will use you, too!

Notes: _____

_____

_____

_____

_____

_____

Comforting Scattered Minds

Read 2 Corinthians 1:4-5 and John 16:32-33.

Verse 32. "Look: An hour is coming, and has come, when each of you will be scattered to his own home, and you will leave Me alone."

Trials were coming. Jesus said so. Did the disciples have a clue what was coming? Trials are coming for me, too. If I was told, would I really have a clue what's coming? A resounding "Absolutely not" to both questions. I have known many people who have lost loved ones. I have muttered words in an attempt to comfort them as I passed through the line at the funeral home. I doubt my words held much comfort. Perhaps the fact that I cared and was there offered a little solace but not much. Why? Because until I lost my Daddy two years ago, I didn't know first hand, how they felt. I had not experienced the same kind of pain myself, so I was a pitiful comforter. Now, it's different. Now, I'm different. Now, when I encounter someone who has lost a loved one, I feel a little of their pain. My heart breaks for theirs. I know what comforted me when I was in the same situation, so I can offer more comforting words. I can understand verse 33 now. Jesus was resurrected from the dead. He overcame the world. Now, I finally understand that verse and the comfort it was designed to give the disciples. I doubt they understood it until after Jesus was raised. They spent Friday and Saturday in total fear, confusion and deep hurt. They were scattered. I've been there. That's a good description of the state of my mind and heart after I lost my Daddy. Yes, my Daddy was a strong Christian. I know He is in Heaven. That brought me comfort. But I had to get through the time of feeling scattered, confused, hurt, and fragmented. I thought Jesus would heal Daddy. He did but it wasn't the healing I expected. The disciples thought Jesus would be an earthly king and therefore, they were confused because what happened wasn't what they expected. It took time for trust to replace confusion. It will take time for trust to replace your confusion, also. Read verse 32 and hang on. Think seriously about how the disciples felt. But don't stay there forever. Read on through verse 33 and know that trust will come. In the meantime be courageous! Jesus really has conquered the world!

Notes: _____

_____

_____

_____

_____

_____

My Goal; His Will

John 6:38. "For I have come down from Heaven, not to do My will, but the will of Him who sent me."

Jesus left Heaven and came down to earth as a newborn child. It's amazing that HE chose to be born to someone HE created. HE chose to come to earth as an infant and be subject to a creature that HE created. HE gave up glory to rescue us. Jesus came to earth with the goal of doing the will of His Father. That was always His purpose. It was always on His mind and He never strayed from it. Even at the age of twelve, He was about His father's business. He worked all day every day to do the will of the Father. He prayed late into the evening to spend time with the Father. He rose early in the morning to pray and hear from the Father. The Father and His will were constantly on Jesus' mind. It was His goal. It was His life work. It took complete precedence in every thing He did. If that was the goal of Jesus, how much more should it be ours??? How much thought do I put into knowing the will of my Father? Knowing His will is a start, but how about attempting to carry it out? What would happen if Christians, every Christian, just started each day in prayer asking what the Father's will for that day was and then did their very best to do His will that day? What would our days be like? What would the days of those around us be like? How many unsaved would be reached for Christ? What would our children turn out to be? What could be accomplished? How often during the day do I stop to ask myself what the will of the Father is at this moment? What if making a living was my secondary goal at work? If my goal was to do the will of the Father, would I respond to a long wait in the check out line differently? Maybe, I might see an opportunity to strike up a conversation with the person waiting behind or in front of me, instead of seeing it as an aggravation. Maybe, the person in front of or behind me, might be saved as a result of something Jesus nudged me to say to them. What if I sent the card He nudged me to send? How would listening for the Holy Spirit's nudging change what I do with my time? I am trying hard to learn to listen to the Holy Spirit more. It takes practice and it is a deliberate choice. I have to remind myself often during the day. But every once in a while, I realize that I listened and obeyed. I see more than I could have ever seen, had I not listened. I pray that I become that person who wakes to do His will and keeps that on the top of my mind constantly. I pray that you do also.

Notes: _____

_____

_____

_____

_____

_____

The Importance of Worship

Read 1 Kings 8.

Verse 14. "The king turned around and blessed the entire congregation of Israel while they were standing."

Worship was a big deal to the Israelites. It should be to us. Our society has become fast paced to say the least. I am the queen of multi-tasking . I can be making a list, texting, and thanks to speaker phone, talking to someone all at the same time. But is it really good? I guess, in ways, and at times, it is, but I have to be careful. God has been dealing with me lately about multi-tasking when I am praying or reading His Holy Word, or worshiping. No, I don't text during church, but how often does my mind wander during the singing or preaching. How often does my mind wander when I'm praying? What happens when my phone dings indicating a text while I'm reading my morning devotion? What happens when a call comes in while I am spending time in prayer to my Father? How often do I complain because the temperature in the sanctuary feels cold to me, while my Christian brothers and sisters in other countries fear for their life while they worship?

Worship was serious for the Israelites. They came and stood the entire time Solomon spoke and prayed in Chapter 8. I'm afraid in our modern, casual society, we have lost too much of the awe and reverence we have for our Lord. I think

I am just as guilty as anybody of this. We think "God looks at the heart not the outward appearance", and while that is true, we use that as our excuse not to look our best to come to worship. Could it be that I use this casualness as an excuse not to prepare my heart for worship as well? Ouch! I think that crunching noise is the sound of my toes being stepped on! It's so easy for me to come to worship, that I have forgotten what an awesome privilege it really is. Our persecuted brothers and sisters in Christ treasure that opportunity for worship. Solomon's prayer beginning in Chapter 8 verse 22, starts off praising God. His prayer was humble. He acknowledged God had kept HIS promises. Solomon's prayer was not selfish like most of mine appear to be when compared with his. We complain about two hours at church if the preacher goes five minutes over. The Israelites stayed fourteen days to worship! Then, they left rejoicing because the Ark of the Covenant was in the temple and they could worship there. I think I could learn something about worship from them!

Notes: _____

_____

_____

_____

_____

_____

_____

Conversations About Jesus!

Daniel 4:1-3. "King Nebuchadnezzar, To those of every people, nation, and language, who live in all the earth: May your prosperity increase. I am pleased to tell you about the miracles and wonders the Most High God has done for me. How great are His miracles, and how mighty His wonders! His kingdom is an eternal kingdom, and His dominion is from generation to generation."

How often do we testify about the things God has done for us? What about the things He is doing in our life? Some of us probably tell others about things God has done when we are in Sunday School, or maybe even over lunch with our spouse or best friend. But how often do I say, "I am so excited to tell you how God answered my prayer" ? How often do I tell people who are not saved? Or even the new Christians? How often am I guilty of just muttering a quick thank you to God when He helps me with something and moving right on along to the next big request? Oops. I think I'm guilty of that. I think it is a good idea to keep a journal of prayer requests and then also journal the answers. I think I would be amazed at all the things God does for me if I did that. I also would have a lot more gratitude like I should! If I journaled prayer requests and answers to prayers, what a book that would be. What a wonderful thing to leave my son and one day grandchildren. How much encouragement I would get if I went back and read it again.

God is so good to me. I do not possibly have time to tell all HE does for me. So why not write it down? Share it. Use those stories to encourage others, and pass it down to generations that I might not live to know. Be one to speak up and say "I am pleased to tell you about the miracles and wonders the Most High God has done for me." I need to speak up more whether it be to my family, my friends or to Kings. We have something worth sharing!

Notes: _____

_____

_____

_____

_____

_____

_____

Praying for Others!

Ephesians 6:18-20. "Pray at all times in the Spirit with every prayer and request and stay alert in this with all perseverance and intercession for all the saints. Pray also for me, that the message may be given to me when I open my mouth to make known with boldness the mystery of the gospel. For this I am an ambassador in chains. Pray that I might be bold enough in Him to speak as I should."

I used to work at a church. One of my tasks was to keep the prayer list updated and put copies out for Wednesday night and Sunday morning. I updated the prayer list every time I was made aware of a need or received an update on a need already listed. I imagine that most churches have a prayer list that is kept updated. There are many people hurting for a variety of reasons so the prayer list is often long. Each name on the list represents a need that most likely affects not only that person but a family. We all know this is true. Often, we know at least some of the people on the list or someone in their family.

My question is.... why don't we pray more for these needs? I put our prayers lists in the church I worked at. I don't put out many copies of the printed list because it is also sent out electronically. But usually, when I pick up the left over lists, much of the stack remains. Why? Do God's people just not pray for each other any more? Have we gotten so busy surviving in our own life that we forget our brothers and sisters in Christ who also struggle? And what about the unsaved? If we as Christians, do not pray for them, who will? Colossians 4:2 says to devote yourselves to prayer. That says to me that prayer is important. I am sure that some people pray for the needs from the electronic copy of the prayer list, but I am convinced that many simply don't give it a thought after it's mentioned. Could it be that's why the list is so long? 2 Chronicles 7:14 says "If My people who are called by My name. will humble themselves and pray and seek My face, and turn from their evil ways, then I will hear from Heaven, forgive their sin, and heal their land" (NKJV). Pray...and then, Pray even more!

Notes: _____

_____

_____

_____

_____

_____

_____

Trusting God

Read Genesis 37-45, the book of Daniel and Psalm 27:11-14.

Psalm 27:13-14. "I am certain that I will see the Lord's goodness in the land of the living. Wait for the Lord; be strong, and let your heart be courageous. Wait for the Lord."

Verse 13 is an expression of trust; Verse 14 is living the expression of trust.

Do you trust God? If so, you are sure you will see God's goodness. Do you trust God? If so, wait for the Lord. Not just wait but wait while being strong. Courageously wait. Is it easy? Most of the time, absolutely not! Was it easy for Joseph (Genesis 37-45)? I seriously doubt it. He faced being sold into slavery, imprisonment for a false accusation, and the complete loss of communication with his family, just to name a few things. Was it easy for Daniel as he waited during his time of exile in Babylon? It couldn't have been, yet he chose to remain faithful to the Lord even though it made certain things harder for him. God rewarded both Joseph's and Daniel's faithfulness. We can read through both of those stories in the Bible in just a few minutes but we often forget that years passed during those stories. Not just days, or months but years! I think at least fifteen years passed between Joseph being sold into slavery and his brothers bowing before him to purchase food. Yet he remained faithful to God. Daniel lived in captivity for seventy years! That's most of a lifetime. He was about 15 years old when he was exiled in captivity and in his early eighties when he was thrown in the lion's den. Yet he had kept his faith in God in a foreign country for all of those years. Joseph and Daniel are just two examples out of many, many in the Bible who suffered, yet continued to trust in the Lord. When you are tempted to give up, don't! Wait for the Lord. Go back to your Bible and read about some of the many faithful servants of God. It will encourage you. Study their stories and see what they did. Don't act on your own. Wait for His action. He's got this. And He's got you. He's got your back. Wait for the Lord. You can trust Him. Be strong. Let your heart be strong.

Notes: _____

_____

_____

_____

_____

_____

_____

Facing Grief

Read Nehemiah 1:4-11.

Verse 4. "When I heard these words, I sat down and wept. I mourned for a number of days, fasting and praying before the God of heaven."

When you have days of deep hurt, mourning, discouragement, heartbrokenness and despair (as we all do sometimes), it is ok to just sit down and weep as Nehemiah did, but don't let that be all you do. Nehemiah also fasted and prayed for a number of days. He took his deep hurts and despair to the one who could help - God! The God over all the universe. Nehemiah's prayer is a great example of how to pray also. He starts by acknowledging who God is. Sometimes, it is good for us to be reminded of just who God is. We let that get to the back of our thoughts as we are weighted down with the burdens and stresses of life. We need to remember that healing for a heavy heart is often found in worship of the One who created it. Nehemiah also confesses sin. That is something we should never forget our need to do. We must continually repent of and confess our sin. He then moves to remind God of His promises. God has not forgotten His promises but we need the reminder. Reminding God of the promises He has made to His children is seen in numerous prayers in the Bible. We will all face deep hurts and even despair at some point in our lives. The road of life is long and hard to walk. Being a Christian does not exempt us from troubles and trials in this world, just as Christ was not exempt from difficulties. But, we have a Hope. We have a God who loves us and is able. It is most important during our times of the deepest despair, to lift our eyes and hearts to Him. He alone is worthy and He alone has the power to take care of our every need.

Notes: _____

_____

_____

_____

_____

_____

Local Missionaries Needed!

Read Isaiah 6:8.

Matthew 5:15-16. "No one lights a lamp and puts it under a basket, but rather on a lampstand, and it gives light for all who are in the house. In the same way, let your light shine before others, so that they may see your good works and give glory to your Father in heaven."

What comes to your mind, when you hear the word missionary? Most people think of Isaiah 6:8, and think about going to a foreign country to tell people about Jesus. There is a great need for people to go to foreign countries and tell people. I greatly admire those people who are called and go. I often wonder how they survive. I wonder how they deal with leaving their parents behind and everything they have known. I am pretty much a coward when it comes to that. But not all of us are called to go somewhere else and tell. What about the people in your hometown? What about the cashier at the local grocery store? What about the nurse who takes your temperature in the doctor's office? What about your mail carrier? What about those people that we encounter as we "go" about our daily lives right here at home? Those people also need to hear about Jesus. We tend to assume the people around home have heard about Jesus. We assume they all have a Bible in their home. We know everyone is not saved but we just pass off the possibility that nobody has ever taken the time to just talk to them about Jesus. We need to take Matthew 5:15-16 to heart. The lampstand in verse 15 gives off light for everyone in the house. I know our lights need to shine in foreign countries but it needs to shine at home, too. Let your light shine in your house first. Start with your family and move out from there. Instead of assuming the people you are standing in line with at the dollar store have all heard about Jesus, assume they have not. Look at the Mama struggling with three kids. Assume she has never heard of Jesus. Assume that man waiting to check out with something he picked up on the way has never heard. And then tell them! Strike up a conversation. You are going to spend the same amount of time waiting anyway. Use it for Jesus. Keep an extra Bible in the car to give to someone who might not have one. It doesn't matter if they could afford one or not. If they don't have a Bible, give them one. You might not ever know on this earth if they get saved or not, but plant the seed anyway. Sometimes, the "go" in the "Who will go for US?", is just down the street to the store. Be willing to respond like Isaiah did by saying "Here I am. Send me." If you listen to the gentle nudge of the Holy Spirit, you will know who to talk to. Here I am. Send me–to the store to tell someone, to the mailbox to talk to the carrier, to wait in line at the fast food restaurant to tell the person behind you. Just start by telling one person you encounter every day. And pretty soon, the light of Jesus will cover the world!

Notes: _____

_____

_____

_____

Just Call Him

Jeremiah 33:2-3. "The Lord who made the earth, the Lord who forms it to establish it, Yahweh is His name, says this: Call to Me and I will answer you and tell you great and incomprehensible things you do not know."

The Word of the Lord came to Jeremiah a second time. God doesn't quit on His servants. HE alone is God. There are things that are incomprehensible to us that we do not know. God is able to share these things with us, if HE chooses. The Lord goes on to explain the outcome of a future battle to Jeremiah. HE explains that the enemies of Judah will be struck down in HIS (God's) wrath and rage. Things looked impossible from Jeremiah's vantage point. There is this one thing to be considered in this scene: God can do the impossible! In verse 2, God says "Call to ME, and I will answer you and tell you great and incomprehensible things you do not know.". Personally, there is a lot that I don't know. There are many things that I have never even fathomed, but there are a lot more things that are just plain incomprehensible to me. I do not have the knowledge or education to know many things. Yet, God knows all things. Nothing is too hard for HIM to understand. And, nothing is too hard for HIM to reveal it to me. That's not because of anything to do with me. It's because of HIM. You would think a message like this might have been given to Jeremiah when things were going great in his life, but that is not the case. The Lord gave this message to Jeremiah while he was still confined (imprisoned) in the guard's courtyard. He was in jail! Things were pretty bad, not only for Jeremiah, but for all of Judah. When things look bleak, and you feel like you are at your worst, listen for a message from God. HE has not abandoned you. HE gave Jeremiah a message that was incomprehensible. BUT, HIS first instruction to get the message was "Call to ME". God will not give up on you, but you also, must not give up on God. Pray to HIM! There are many times, we do not have words to explain our feelings or needs. During those times, the Holy Spirit will put our feelings and needs into words for us. But we must make the effort to pray. When you feel like praying, pray. When you don't feel like praying, pray anyway. That is where faith comes in. Jeremiah 32:27 reminds us that nothing is too difficult for God. That, my friend, is comforting to me.

Notes: _____

God Cares When We Mourn

Read Daniel 10:2-9.

Verse 2. "In those days, I, Daniel, was mourning for three full weeks."

Daniel was about 81 years old in Chapter 9. In Chapter 10, he is about 85 years old. He was mourning. He was discouraged and hurting. Sound familiar? Have you ever been down, ever been discouraged, ever hurt deeply, ever mourned??? We all think of Daniel as some super hero that was incredibly strong and always just walked with God. Well, he was strong and he did walk with God. He was about 15 years old when he was captured and taken to Babylon in exile. He was of noble or royal blood, so this was not the life he was accustomed to or expected. But his parents or somebody had taught him about God, for he did have a great faith. Yes, he walked with God his whole life. He walked with God through many trials. We forget when we read the book of Daniel that he was exiled his whole life basically. Oh, they tried to wipe out his faith. They even changed his name (see Daniel chapter 1). But instead, Daniel remained true to God and even influenced some of them. If you don't believe me, just ask the wise men who came years later looking for Jesus who their ancestors learned from. The wise men were after all, Persian. But back to today's text. Daniel was mourning, when he saw someone spectacular. Or something. It scared him bad enough that he passed out face down on the ground (verse 8). But this angel he saw was sent to help and encourage him. The first thing he said to Daniel was (verse 11) "you are a man treasured by God.". He brings a message that God heard Daniel's prayers and sent an angel. Verse 19 reiterates the same message. "Don't be afraid, you who are treasured by God. Peace to you; be very strong.". Daniel was about 85 years old by now. He had seen God do some amazing things during his 70 years in exile. But he still needed encouragement. And God still treasured him enough to send it. I think the KJV says "greatly beloved". I love that! We are no better than Daniel, nor are we any less treasured by God. Let me repeat that. We are not better than Daniel, nor are we any less treasured by God. We hurt, we get discouraged and we mourn. We have in the past and most likely, we will again. We are human, just as Daniel was. But we are also treasured by God, just as Daniel was. You don't know who is watching your walk through life. We look at Daniel and think "super hero". But verse 2 proves that he didn't feel like a super hero. You may not feel like a super hero either but somebody else may look at your walk with Christ and think that about you. Peace to you. Be very strong.

Notes: _____

_____

_____

_____

_____

_____

Our Helplessness, God's Provision

Read John 5.

John 5:5-6. "One man was there who had been sick for 38 years. When Jesus saw him lying there and knew he had already been there a long time, He said to him, 'Do you want to get well?'"

Jesus always noticed the most needy people. The paralyzed man caught His attention that Sabbath day. Jesus knew him and knew he'd been an invalid for 38 years. The man, although still hopeful enough to get someone to help him get to the pool, had pretty much given up on being able to get in the water first and receive healing. He was so weak, he couldn't get up and walk fast enough to be first. Jesus knew he'd just about lost the determination to even try. He waited for someone else to come and help him. "He said to him, 'Do you want to get well?' And then, 'Get up,' Jesus told him, 'pick up your mat and walk!'" (HCSB). In that instant Jesus restored the man's will and determination to be healed. Scripture says 'immediately' he was made well, stood up, picked up his mat and walked away with it. Proof to us that even when we are at the lowest, most vulnerable point in our lives, when we can't possibly do anything for ourselves, if we have faith in what Jesus says and obey what He tells us, we will be given the strength and ability to do what He says do. Any time that Jesus is working so that it is obvious to people around us, there will be criticisms and doubt - people looking to find fault. It's, of course, the work of the devil in the hearts of people doing that. We already know that the religious leaders and political leaders of that time were violently opposed to Jesus and His ministry. That continued and some still are today! I am sure that some people today would be like them even if they witnessed a miracle like that! Satan is still roaring and roaming, looking to cause doubt. One little shred of doubt is all the encouragement he needs to get inside our hearts and minds. Then, what comes from us...words, actions, etc....reflect him and not Jesus. Jesus says in verse 41 that He knows He doesn't receive honor from men. HE knows Who He is but He knows also that many do not believe Him and accept His Father. He's known from the beginning Who He is and it is the colossal failure of mankind that we don't recognize, worship and honor Him and the sacrifice He made for us. I think sometimes, that if only I could have been there in person and seen these miracles with my own eyes, how much faith I'd have with no doubts whatsoever; but then, I realize I'm so weak in my faith that I'd probably have questioned and wondered also. Woe is me!

Notes: _____

_____

_____

_____

_____

Star Gazing

Genesis 15:5-7. "He took him outside and said, 'Look at the sky and count the stars, if you are able to count them.' Then He said to him, 'Your offspring will be that numerous.' Abram believed the Lord, and He credited it to him as righteousness. He also said to him, 'I am Yahweh who brought you from Ur of the Chaldeans to give you this land to possess.'"

Have you ever paid any attention to the stars and the moon? I haven't until maybe a year ago. Mom started talking about seeing the stars at night when she takes her little dog Josey out. So, I started looking at them deliberately. My Daddy passed away two and a half years ago. I miss him terribly. I don't look at the sky to predict events. I'm Christian, so I don't believe in that. But I started looking up at the stars and the moon. God put those all in place. The sky seems to have a depth that goes forever. It certainly goes deeper than my human eyes can see. But not God. His vision sees deeper (or higher) than the sky's limit. I started looking up, thinking about Heaven. I know you can't see it from here. But I guess I was looking anyway. I was thinking about where my Daddy is, and missing him. I was looking for comfort. A strange thing happened. The more I look up at the night sky, with the moon and stars, the more I realize how awesome God is. It's interesting to me that God used something He created to point me back to Him for comfort.

He did that with Abram (aka Abraham, later) also. In verse 5 of Genesis chapter 15, God took Abraham outside and told him to look at the sky and count the stars. The stars are impossible to count. There are too many. Abram had no children. He and Sarai were both already old. God made a promise to Abram to make his descendants as numerous as the stars in the sky. This promise was humanly impossible, but Abram believed God. You see, with God, the impossible suddenly becomes possible. Now Abraham's descendants are too numerous to count, and the number continues to grow. God is a keeper of promises. I have wondered if Daddy can see the top side of the sky from Heaven. I guess I won't know the answer to that question until I get to Heaven myself. But I know God is there. He's also here. I know He hung more stars than I can count or imagine. I know He's in control of the details both great and small. I know HE promised I can be with Him in Heaven one day. And I know He's a keeper of His promises. So, I go out to look at the stars at night fairly often. And I remember that God IS and I am comforted. Give it a try! God took Abram out star gazing one night. And he believed the great I AM! You can too!

Notes: _____

_____

_____

_____

_____

_____

I Am Not Home

John 14:1-3. "Your heart must not be troubled. Believe in God; believe also in Me. In My Father's house are many dwelling places; if not, I would have told you. I am going away to prepare a place for you. If I go away and prepare a place for you, I will come back and receive you to Myself, so that where I am you may be also.

Some days, I miss my Daddy so bad, I want to scream, begging him to come home. Today was one of those days. I thought I was ok. I was fine, and then out of the blue, I was not fine. Grief is like that. The times when you suddenly are not fine, are random and unpredictable. It becomes your new normal. And it has become mine. So today was one of those days. It was during this time of not being "fine" and just wanting Daddy to come home, that Jesus gently reminded me that I am the one who is not home. HE reminded me that Daddy is the one who is home, not me. This place called Earth, is temporary. Daddy is home and I am the one who is still the weary traveler. I am weary, today in particular. I am tired. But Jesus reminded me that I will be home one day. Jesus walked this earth. I am sure HE knew what it was to be weary. During HIS ministry, the Pharisees constantly tried to trap Him into saying something they could use against Him and people were always begging Him to heal them. And HE compassionately healed many of them. They were weary too. We are all weary from something or the other. We should expect to be, but somehow we don't. When I am away from home, I can never quite relax, like I can at home. The same is true of us about being on this earth, compared to Heaven. We just haven't been to Heaven yet, so we haven't managed to grasp the difference. But I will be home one day. Really home. And HOME will be better than I have ever imagined. Jesus reminds me of this ever so quietly and sweetly. He uses it to dry my hot tears and soothe my aching heart. He's like that you know. Instead of condemning my misunderstanding, HE gently holds my hurting heart until I can hear His soft whispers of comfort. HE has compassion for me just like HE had for the crowd all those years ago. Daddy is home. He's home with Jesus. For Christians, it's a reward to die, not punishment. Heaven is the only place we will ever truly be home. That home will never be taken away from us, nor will the comfort HE gives us there. But until we get there, HE sends the Holy Spirit to bring our hearts comfort when they are full of pain. It's a strange thing that we would forget that we are travelers, temporary residents in this imperfect world. You would think all the pain and sadness here would be a constant reminder that here is not home, but sometimes I forget when I am weary from traveling. I feel His comfort most of all when I am weary and pained. Yet as bad as the pain is it is all worth it to feel the closeness of my Jesus. Instead of deserting this slow moving weary soul, He sends the Holy Spirit alongside me and helps me limp along on my journey towards home, with a quiet joy that only He can give.

Notes: _____

_____

_____

_____

Two Sides Of Gossip

Psalm 10:2. "In arrogance the wicked relentlessly pursue the afflicted; let them be caught in the schemes they have devised."

As I read Psalm 10 this morning, my thoughts turned to a touchy subject - slander. There are two sides to gossip. The first side is the one of the person doing the gossip. Often, it starts out when someone decides they will add a person to the prayer list. That's a noble thing to do. You can add someone to a prayer list without telling a whole story to go with it. But the temptation to tell what you know, or what you think you know, is great. You know, if you tell what you "know", then people can pray more accurately, right? Wrong! Oh, if it's an illness or something, that's one thing. But it's the "juicy" parts, that you really want to tell. Suzy has to go to doctor because she's having stomach issues....I have wondered if she might be pregnant. Or, elderly Mrs. Jones, needs prayer... you know her only son died and his family has completely abandoned her. She says they tried to take everything she has. Really? Suzy might not be pregnant and Mrs. Jones' family may not be guilty as accused. And then there is that preacher's wife. We need to pray for her. She's the most unfriendly person I have every seen. She's probably a great pastor's wife. It may be more accurate that she's soft spoken, stays out of the spot light and quietly checks on people, keeping in confidence the things they share with her. So, back to our two sides of gossip. I think we covered the first side pretty well - the person doing the gossiping. Now the second side—the person being slandered in all of this. I have been on the second side of gossip, and God forgive me, I'm sure I've been on the first side sometimes also. But after being on the second side, I'm a lot more conscious of not being on the first side anymore. Verse 10 says the oppressed is beaten down. Verse 2 says in arrogance the wicked relentlessly pursue the afflicted. Slander usually takes place about someone who already had troubles. So, they are already afflicted. Gossip just further beats them down. I don't think it would be any more painful, if they were physically beaten. It destroys a person's self esteem, and it makes them want to stay away from people. Well, that may not sound so bad.... but wait. You have to be around people to go to church and corporately worship as God wants us to. The person spreading the gossip, doesn't give a thought to God holding them accountable. They are just "sharing". This same person would go on later to say, "I don't know why Susy no longer comes to church." If gossip was exposed for what it really is, and if we could see a physical picture of the hurt it causes, I think we would be stopped in our tracks. God sees this hurt. Jesus experienced slander. HE was accused of refusing to pay taxes, for one thing. If you have been spreading gossip, know that it is listed in the same verse with murderers. It is not pleasing at all to God. And HE knows the difference in your heart between praying for someone and spreading the juicy details. If you have been the object of gossip, know that Jesus knows how you feel. HE knows the truth. More people than you realize, probably know the truth too, but the only one who really matters is Jesus.

Notes: _____

_____

_____

Just A Lump Of Clay

Read 2 Corinthians 4:7.

Isaiah 64:8. "Yet Lord, You are our Father, we are the clay and You are our potter; we all are the work of Your hands."

I bought a bowl in an art store in Foley, Alabama. It is beautiful to look at it but it is also useful. It would hold all kinds of things, and it can also be put in the oven and the dishwasher.

It was not always a beautiful bowl though. It started off as clay that was dug in Bay Minette, Alabama. The potter dug the clay. Then he took his hands and formed the bowl. The clay in it's original form would not hold water. It was not beautiful. After the potter found the clay and used his hands to shape it, the clay became a beautiful bowl that is useful for all kinds of things. It became more valuable.

We too are just clay. The only difference between us and the bowl is God's breath in us. Without His breath, we become as hard as the clay bowl. Like the clay is just dirt dug from the ground until the potter makes it into something beautiful, we are just dust from the ground without the Potter's hand making us into something beautiful and useful.

If the clay hadn't submitted to the potter, it would still be just clay shaped like a lump. With the potter's touch, the clay was made into a beautiful, useful bowl. Then, the potter placed it in the fire. It had to go through the extreme heat process to retain the shape and be useful. Sometimes the Master Potter has to be put us through the fire to make us useful, too. That's often a painful process, but the end result is something beautiful and useful to the Potter.

With the Holy Spirit living inside us, we can be most useful to God, the Master Potter. We can be the most beautiful things when we submit to the Potter. When we die, our spirits leave our clay bodies, and our bodies go back to being just clay. So, we really are a lot like the clay bowl that I bought. Let's not fight against the Master Potter when He wants to shape and form us into something beautiful and useful for His work!

Notes: _____

_____

_____

_____

_____

_____

_____

Boundary Limits

Jeremiah 5:22. "Do you not fear Me? This is the Lord's declaration. Do you not tremble before Me, the One who set the sand as the boundary of the sea, an enduring barrier that it cannot cross? The waves surge, but they cannot prevail. They roar but cannot pass over it."

As I sit here at my desk listening to the rain pouring down, my mind drifts back to days spent sitting in the warm sunshine on the white sandy beach watching the waves roll in. Each wave rolls in one after another, after another, in a continuous cycle. Each one is different from the last and the next. They all stop at different places in the sand, some almost reaching my chair. Some waves quietly, almost timidly roll in. Some waves roll in big and boastful as if they want to crash over you. Some roll in with spray in the air. Some roll in bringing sea shells or small fish in the curl. They roll in with such beauty and such strength. Even the smaller timid waves show determination to make it ashore. Some wash down sand castles left behind. Some waves make the little shore birds run. They all come ashore with different speeds. They all roll in with one thing in common. They all stop. There is a limit to how far on the sand they can come. Even during a hurricane, when the tide reaches into the towns and sometimes into buildings, there's a limit they must adhere to. Who sets that limit? Who could have the power to control those beautiful, powerful waves? It's Yahweh God that limits the waves. After all, HE created the waves and the sand. When I have the privilege of sitting on the beach, watching the endless waves, my mind goes to Yahweh, our great God. He limits the waves. HE alone has that kind of power. I am filled with awe at His might. I am filled with wonder that God, who is so amazing, would love me, but that's exactly what HE does. HE loves me. HE loved me so much that HE came to this earth that HE created and allowed people that HE created to nail Him to a cross. HE died for my sins. HE took my place. But it didn't end there! HE rose again on the third day to live forever! And because HE did, I can live forever. And THAT Jesus, MY Jesus, MY friend, is the One who sets the boundaries for the waves!

Notes: _____

_____

_____

_____

_____

_____

_____

Just Do What He Says!

Read Luke 5:1-11.

Verse 5. "'Master,' Simon replied, 'we've worked hard all night long and caught nothing! But at Your word, I'll let down the nets.'"

Jesus was standing on the edge of the Sea of Galilee teaching. The people were getting closer and closer. The crowd was hungry to hear what Jesus had to say. We do that now when a famous person is speaking. So, why are there any open pews on the front in church now? Let me repeat that for those in the back... So, why are there any open pews on the front in church now???

    Jesus got into Peter's boat and asked him to put out a little way into the water. This gave Him some space from the crowd which allowed everyone to see. It also allowed everyone to hear because your voice carries better on the water. Peter was tired. He had fished all night, but he obeyed Jesus, expecting nothing in return. But Jesus had other plans to show Peter who HE was. HE wasn't trying to reach only the crowd. After HE finished speaking, Jesus told Peter to put out into the deep water and let down the nets. Jesus had been raised by a carpenter - not a fisherman. Every good fisherman on the Sea of Galilee knew you fished at night in the shallow waters. It's still true today that bigger fish come to the more shallow water to eat the smaller fish who have come in to feed. That's why you don't get in the water on the beach at dawn or at night. You could become supper for one of the big guys who is hungry! But again, even though he was tired and thought it a waste of time, Peter obeyed. And like every other time, Jesus was right! What a catch! Peter had to have James and John bring their boat to help get this catch to shore.

    We see three things from these eleven verses; (1) Jesus paid Peter back for the use of the boat and Peter's time as captain. Obeying Jesus will cost you, but His rewards are far greater than your cost. (2) He came to get Peter where he was. Jesus showed Peter who HE was in a way that Peter understood with no doubts. Jesus comes to seek us where we are also. HE comes to seek the lost. HE comes to find us just as HE came for Peter. (3) By doing that, He also showed Peter his own sinfulness. When we start to get a grasp of who Jesus really is, we too will see our own sinful nature. When Jesus asks you to do something that seems senseless to you, trust Him and do it anyway. The "catch" will be amazing!

Notes: _____

_____

_____

_____

_____

_____

Be Deliberate About Worship

Psalm 30:4. "Sing to Yahweh, you His faithful ones, and praise His holy name."

God has been dealing with me on a few things lately during all this time with the corona virus keeping us from going to the church building.

We, as Christians are sometimes deliberate about Bible study. Maybe, we have a study we are doing with a group of other people, or maybe we are reading through the Bible. Maybe we just have a specific time each day that we read a few verses. If you don't, let me definitely encourage you to do that.

Probably as a Christian, it's the same thing with a prayer time. We have a specific time each day that we pray. I mean, we have a long prayer list filled with requests for others and ourselves. That's good, but may I say that prayer should be more than just a list of requests? Prayer is a two way conversation, or it should be. A two way conversation involves listening. We must be deliberate about that. We must choose to spend some time in prayer being quiet before God.

The last thing I want to mention that we must be deliberate about may catch you by surprise. It did me when God laid it on my heart. And I must say, I am convicted. We must be deliberate about our worship. When the Lord laid those words on my heart, my response was yeah, yeah, yeah, I need to watch out for that while the corona virus is keeping us away from church. But actually, I needed this reminder for regular time also. So, I thought about what being deliberate to worship might be. Well, when I worship, I praise. There are several ways to praise the Lord. Now, I'm not talking about listening to somebody else praise Jesus, I mean me doing it! You can say your own words of praise to God, you can read a Psalm of praise to God or you can sing a song (or sing along with someone else) in praise to God. You may be thinking, "Well, I go to church." And so we should. But God laid it on my heart that I must still be deliberate to worship when I go to church. Ouch! Toes stepped on. I must choose to set my heart to worship even when I go to church. Otherwise, I may just go through the motion of sitting in church. For those of us who lead busy lives, it's so easy to just go sit in church and check that off your to-do list while your mind races on to the other million things you have to do. Wow! Surely not. But yet I realized I have been guilty. To worship, I must choose to set aside my problems, to-do list and other things on my mind, and deliberately concentrate on worshiping Him! Sometimes we have to be deliberate in choosing to worship even when we don't feel like it. It's always a choice for us. It's hard sometimes though, to set aside all the things that burden and overwhelm us, but we need to always think, yes, I have all these cares worrying me, but....Jesus ... and I need to focus on Him, not my troubles. That deliberate attitude will always push the devil out of my way and allow me to worship and praise the Lord! But it is like most everything else, a choice we make.

    I realized that God was telling me that I need to choose some time every day to deliberately worship Him. Oh, I don't mean you have to go to church every day. You can sing (or sing along) to a song and praise Him, or speak words of praise. You can look at His creation and acknowledge how very awesome He is! When I look up at the stars and moon in the night sky, I cannot help but give Him praise for being so awesome. He is awesome and oh , He is so worthy of our deliberate worship!!

Don't Waste The Wait!

Psalm 27:14. "Wait for the Lord; be strong and courageous. Wait for the Lord."

I don't know of anyone who likes to wait. We are so blessed during this time in history that we rarely wait for anything. We have fast food, microwaves that heat food almost instantly, cell phones to call each other immediately wherever we are, automobiles and airplanes to travel quickly wherever we want to go, and the list goes on. Abraham and Sarah knew what it was to wait on the Lord as they waited for the child HE promised, yet even they did not wait patiently, and so Ishmael was born. Waiting in the doctor's office, or the drive-up line gives us a feeling that we are wasting time, not accomplishing anything… and sometimes that is true. The time spent in waiting in line, or the doctor's office, or wherever doesn't have to be wasted. But waiting on the Lord is far different from those times. When we are waiting on the Lord, we are waiting for Him to act. While we wait, HE is preparing us for what HE wants us to do. During this pandemic, we may feel just like we do when we are waiting in the drive-up line, accomplishing nothing. That could be true, but it doesn't have to be. Don't waste your waiting time. We could take this time to wait on the Lord. We can use this time of waiting at home to study His Word, pray, listen for His voice, deliberately worship Him and let Him mold us into what He wants. If we choose to do those things with the extra time at home, HE will accomplish much during our wait!

The Comfort Of Christ Through Suffering

Philippians 3:10. "My goal is to know Him and the power of His resurrection and the fellowship of His suffering, being conformed to His death."

I am going to bed soon but first I want to re-read one of my devotions today. Philippians 3:10 is the scripture referenced in the devotion. I have not thought a huge amount about knowing Christ so well that I know the fellowship of His suffering. I have thought about trying to know the will of Christ for my life. I have thought about knowing my Bible better and I actually study every day to pursue that goal. I have prayed and tried to listen for God's voice and guidance. Many times I believe I have received His guidance - sometimes I have listened and sometimes I have not. But to know the fellowship of His sufferings....To know His sufferings will mean feeling pain and sorrow. Do I want to know Jesus so well that I even know the fellowship of His sufferings? Do I long to be so close to Jesus that it's worth experiencing pain? Sorrow? Suffering? Do I truly seek Christ that deeply? Suffering is not on anyone's bucket list. But it seems life is full of sorrow and suffering for all of us at some point in some way. It just seems to be unavoidable. So, if I have determined that I will suffer...indeed, we all will suffer, then maybe the difference is what I allow the suffering to change in me. How do I respond to the suffering? What is my attitude towards it? Will I spend my energy trying to avoid the unavoidable? Or will I embrace the suffering and spend my energy seeking Christ's way of responding to it? Will I use the suffering to learn more of Him? If I can only convince myself not to waste the sorrow; To embrace it instead of fighting it; To keep the bigger picture in mind; Then I might truly learn more of Christ and His ways. With that, I am convinced, will come a closer relationship and a much deeper trust in Him. That would seem a much better response than wasting energy fighting the unavoidable and what do you know? Having a purpose for the pain seems to make it more bearable. This can be the comfort of Christ through suffering.

Notes: _____

_____

_____

_____

_____

_____

_____

Jesus Makes The Impossible, Possible

Read Acts 12:4-18.

Verse 15. "'You're crazy!' they told her. But she kept insisting that it was true. Then they said, 'It's his angel!'"

This will speak more to those of us who are already Christians. Do we pray to God for what seems impossible expecting Him to answer making the impossible, possible? When we need something, we pray. That's what Christians do. We ask, beg, plead with God to answer. Please change my request to reality. But do we believe HE really will? Or that HE can? The church was praying for Peter. These were the Christians. Many of these people had watched Jesus perform many miracles. One of the people praying was Mark's mother. Surely they were without excuse for not expecting a miraculous answer because they had been witness to so much. But haven't we also witnessed many miracles? I personally have witnessed God work miracles and answer seemingly impossible prayers. Sometimes, it has been seeing a person healed from cancer. But I have witnessed God do other things too. I think we all have, if we have paid attention. Peter trusted God with his outcome. How do we know that? He was sleeping on the night before Herod planned to execute him. When the angel tapped Peter on the side, he immediately obeyed. Peter wasn't sure if he was seeing a vision or if what he saw was reality. But he still obeyed. When he was free and the angel had left him, he went by to tell the church what Jesus had done. Their prayers had been answered. Even with him standing at the door knocking, the prayer warriors did not believe their prayers had been answered. I saw myself in these prayer warriors. Today's question is - Are we more like Peter (sleeping in peace, trusting God with our outcome), or more like the prayer warriors (praying but not really expecting the answer)? We need to learn to expect the impossible from our mighty God!

Notes: _____

_____

_____

_____

_____

_____

_____

Trust, Follow, and Obey

Read John 21.

Verse 12. "'Come and have breakfast,' Jesus told them. None of the disciples dared ask him 'Who are you?' because they knew it was the Lord."

The disciples had left everything to follow Him. They thought HE was going to be king. Then the awful crucifixion took place. The ONE they thought would be king died. They watched HIM be buried. They had seen HIM twice since HIS burial. They didn't know what to think or do, so they went back to do what they had done before HE came into their lives - fishing. They went back to the familiar. They needed to do something. Isn't that what we do? We don't know what to do, but we feel we have to do something. We are not a people with patience. They fished all night but caught nothing. Doesn't that happen to us also? Our greatest efforts produce nothing on our own. But when Jesus showed up and told them to cast on the right side of the boat....They hadn't even recognized HIM yet! This man on the shore who said something to them. Perhaps HE could see something from the shore they could not. Why not try it? What did they have to lose but a little more time? But oh the catch they caught on that right side! This catch brought back a memory for John. A memory of a previous unexpected catch. "It is the Lord!", he said. Jesus met them where they were. HE met their need. In his excitement, Peter swam to shore. He had denied Jesus. Would HE take him back? How could HE forgive him? They were exhausted and hungry. Jesus greeted them with a warm fire and breakfast. This is exactly the comfort they needed at the moment. The catch of fish that HE blessed their obedience and provided was what they needed to produce some income. Then HE restored Peter. "Feed my sheep," Going forward, Peter would preach. Jesus provided a plan for the future. Jesus met them where they were. HE provided for all of their needs. HE was enough for the disciples. HE will meet us where we are too. And HE will provide for all our needs–physical and emotional. And HE is enough for us, just as HE was for them. HE will and always does! We are just fearful because we want to be able to see and know in advance the "hows" and "whats" of HIS provisions, but we are supposed to believe even when we cannot see any way ourselves. I need to be reminded that HE sees and HE knows and my part is to trust, follow, and obey. HE's going to take care of the rest because WHEN we trust, follow, and obey, HE accepts responsibility to provide HIS best for our lives. It may not be what WE think it should be, but it will always be what's best!

Notes: _____

_____

_____

_____

_____

_____

_____

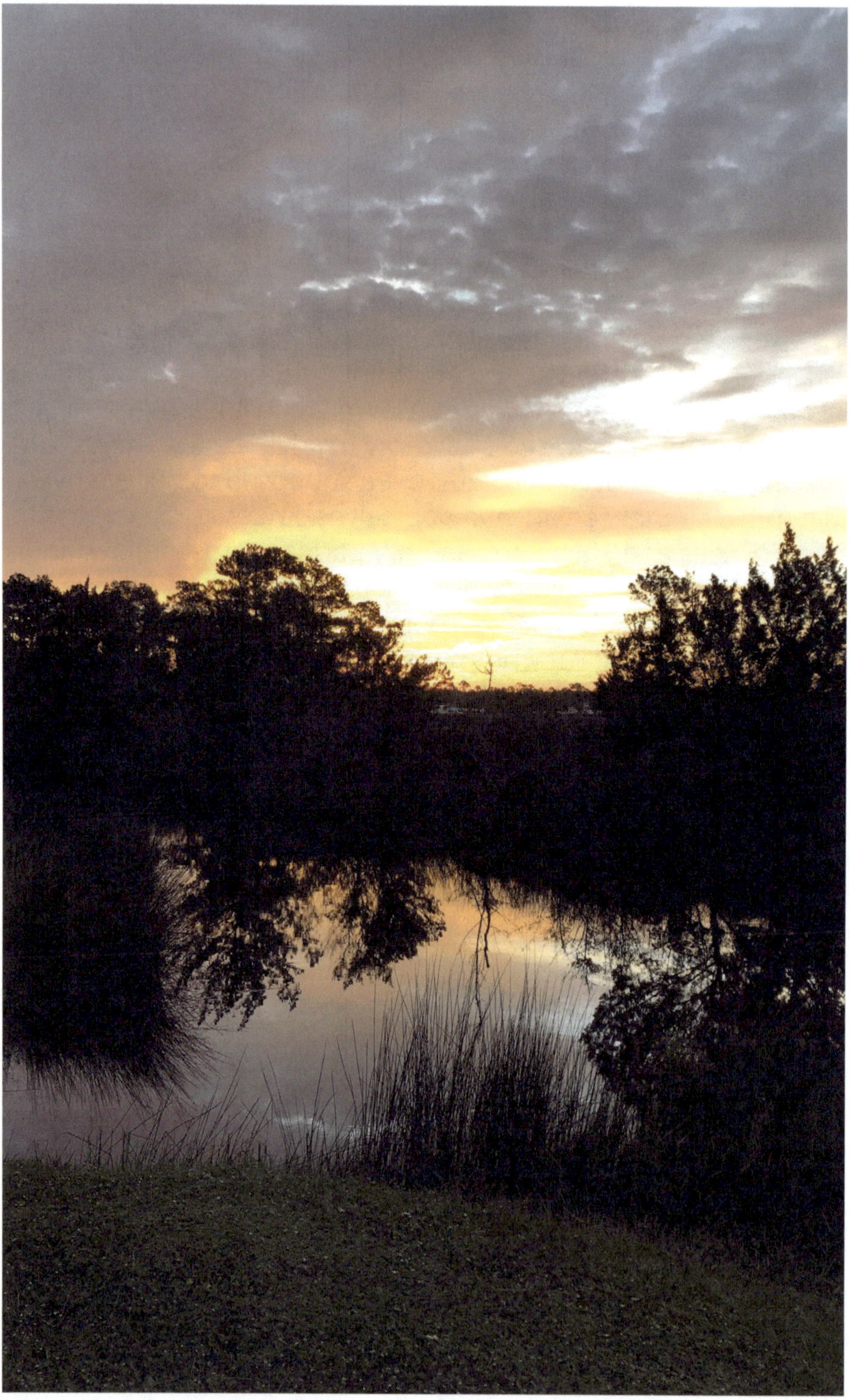

Blessings, Even In Loss

Hebrews 10:24. "And let us be concerned about one another in order to promote love and good works,"

Hurricane Sally came ashore at Gulf Shores, Alabama, on Wednesday, September 16, 2020, about 12:30 a.m. The hurricane was predicted to go in on the Louisiana shore but changed directions. It was also predicted to be a strong tropical storm or low level hurricane, however, it strengthened to an almost category three hurricane off the Alabama coast within about an hour of coming ashore. There was really no time to prepare. We did not have time to go get our camper out, nor warn the two renters with campers in our small campground. The eye of hurricane Sally came right across our happy place in Gulf Shores. We left home at 3:00 a.m., on Friday morning to go see what was left. We had received differing reports and several pictures. The destruction to the whole area was difficult to see and it increased in severity as we traveled further South. We arrived at our campground just in time to watch the sunrise. The sunrise was beautiful, full of hope that God was not finished with this area. On the campground, we had eleven trees and two buildings damaged. Seven of the trees were hanging over one camper, with one of those trees resting on it. One building was beyond any hope of repair. One was laid partially over on a camper and a vehicle. How would we even begin to get these two campers out? We were not the only ones with damage. Our friends and neighbors had similar issues. Our hearts were hurting, not just for us, but for our friends. It was an emotional sight. Our own camper, sitting on a different lot, appeared untouched, even though it had been surrounded by water during the storm. Amazingly, we had nothing but clean up to do there even though we had two trees down. We would have much rather had our own things damaged, than see our renters with damage, but you don't get to choose what happens during a hurricane. Mom's camper appeared untouched as well. There was damage to the awning covering it, but amazingly nothing on her camper. There was a huge pine tree down from the neighbors lot that fell in about a ten foot triangle area behind her camper. Only God could have placed that tall tree where it lay, barely brushing the back of her camper but not damaging it. Our campground is now closed due to the damage. This is hard for us but I will say there were some amazing positives through those three days of clean up. We had no power but we did have running water. As we begin the daunting task of trying to clean up, some of our neighbors appeared. There began to be a team spirit. What none of us could accomplish alone working on our own properties, we accomplished even more as a team going from place to place helping each other. We all pooled together with what we had to offer and worked tirelessly together. When darkness fell, we joined together, bringing the food we had and enjoyed the fellowship of a meal. The spirit of love and friendship was beyond words. We counted our blessings and laughed about what we could. We had all suffered, but we concentrated on the blessings. Together, our spirits were lifted. I have to say that weekend was some of the sweetest fellowship I have ever experienced. It was a fellowship of suffering but it was also a great fellowship of God's love. New friends were even made that weekend. Romans 8:28 played out before our eyes as we experienced God's grace, mercy and blessings while also experiencing damage and loss. We could truly see and say... Even with all this, our God is a good, good God!

Why Worry?

Read Matthew 6:28-31.

Verse 28. "And why do you worry about clothes? Learn how the wildflowers of the field grow: they don't labor or spin thread."

God has some interesting and unique ways to encourage us all. This morning, while I was at our camper down on the coast, HE chose to remind me of HIS care. We have had a major hurricane there and just a few weeks later a serious tropical storm. We didn't get finished making repairs from the hurricane before we had flooding from the tropical storm surge which left flood debris. We have been working there trying to clean up and make repairs every other weekend since the hurricane. Damage from the hurricane also forced the closure of our small campground. This loss of income comes on the heels of job shake ups for both myself and my husband over the past two years. Thankfully, we are both working but our new jobs do not produce the income we had grown accustomed to. This has presented a few challenges. Of course, we have also faced many challenges as a nation from COVID. Yesterday, we found out that my brother is sick and awaiting test results from his COVID test. We also found out just a few hours later that our son is sick and has also been tested for COVID. Things tend to get to me more when I'm tired and worn down. I got up this morning still tired and sore from yesterday's storm clean up efforts. I was down. I've been wrestling discouragement through the job changes, storm damage, business closure and overwhelming amount of work we need to get done on our property but the news of my brother and son being sick, coupled with my exhaustion, just got the best of me. Discouragement won out. I got up pulled some clothes on while my coffee made. Determined to fight the tears that wanted to run down my cheeks, I took my Bible, devotion books and coffee out to my rocking chair on the porch. It was a beautiful morning. The temperature was perfect and the birds were chirping. But I was still moving slow. As I begin to read my devotions and sip, okay slurp, my coffee, I noticed my Hibiscus bush. It had three big beautiful blooms fully opened up. Those were new this morning. Yesterday, much to my disappointment, I had noticed that it had small buds on it but not one single flower opened up. But this morning, there were three big mature red flowers staring at me. I couldn't help but smile and feel a little better. God is still handling things. And HE loves me so much that HE reminded me that HE is with me. HE's here even when things are tough. This showed me that God is working even when I can't see it. HE has plans that I don't know about, just like HE had plans for those flowers to bloom out and put a smile on my face again just when I needed it!

Notes: _____

_____

_____

_____

_____

_____

Rejoice, Rejoice!

Read Philippians 4:4-9.

Verse 4. "Rejoice in the Lord always. I will say it again: Rejoice!"

What do you do when life is hard? When work is stressful, the whole family is sick, money is tight and the car needs tires? And on top of that, your best friend just received a bad diagnosis? When your heart wants to comfort your friends, your neighbor and several people in the church who are facing awful things but you are overwhelmed with hard stuff yourself, what can you do? Most likely, you can't change one hard thing someone else is facing. You can't change most hard things you have to face yourself. What should you do when you, your family and almost everyone you know is going through a "winter" season in life? This life is hard way more often than I would like for it to be. Actually, it's hard a lot for most of us. We live in an imperfect world. How are we to deal with our problems? If I concentrate on my problems, it can become overwhelming. If you are like me, you have no control over most of your problems. After all, if it was something we could control, we would take care of it and there would be no problem. So, what are we to do? The Bible doesn't say we won't have problems. Actually, it says just the opposite. But thankfully, it provides instructions for coping with life. Here are some thoughts I have on how to deal with life. Well, actually, these are instructions from Paul, not me: (1) Paul says to rejoice in the Lord. I have so much to rejoice about because Jesus saved me from my sins. That's reason enough to be shouting. I'm not going to die and get the eternal punishment that I deserve. Before you mumble under your breath about that advice, just know that Paul was in prison for sharing the gospel when he wrote this very encouraging letter to the Philippians. (2) Be gracious. That should be my Christian example. Christ lives inside me and I need to let that show. (3) Don't worry. It's a command, not a suggestion. Pray instead. But pray with thankfulness that your prayers will be heard. (4) Concentrate on the true, honorable, just, pure, lovely commendable and moral things. It doesn't do any good to concentrate on the negative things anyway. So, think about the things worthy of praise. I can start with the fact that I'm saved. That's worth praising Jesus for if there is never anything else. (5) Obey what I've learned. I may not understand absolutely everything in the Bible and I may be unsure of what to do about some things but I can obey what I know now and trust God for the rest. We rejoice in the Lord. HE is always reason to rejoice. Our only hope is Jesus. Things are bad on earth sometimes, but we are only here temporarily. No matter how it feels right now, this life on earth is temporary. I'm not making light of my problems. I need to pray about those and then let God be God. I can relax. I don't have to be God. That lets me off the hook for knowing and handling a lot of things. I feel my headache easing up already. And that knot in my stomach is not nearly as tight.

Notes: _____

_____

_____

_____

Prayer... Not Worry!

Philippians 4:6. "Don't worry about anything, but in everything, through prayer and petition with thanksgiving, let your requests be made known to God."

I have read this verse many times through the years. Most of us have. We often quote it when times are tough and we are anxious about something. It has certainly been a good verse to read this year. I don't know about you, but I'm TOO OFTEN guilty of reading the verse and rushing by the words WITH THANKSGIVING. I am not thankful for hurts, or hard times, but I can be thankful (and should be thankful) for the lessons learned through those times. I also don't want to be guilty of being so anxious over one thing, that I fail to concentrate on the TREMENDOUS number of blessings that God has provided. I have salvation through Jesus. That is the greatest blessing that I can ever receive. If I have no other blessing, I am still greatly blessed because I have Jesus. All of my family are saved. I have the hope of being with Jesus from now through eternity. I certainly have more blessings than I can count if I started listing blessings and typed the rest of my life. I have food, clothes, a warm home, a vehicle to get around in, freedom to worship the Lord, the privilege of owning a Bible, and the ability to read it. I am blessed with many other things that I enjoy, not just needs. I could go on and on but you get the point. You are blessed too. May my prayers (and yours) include thanksgiving to God, not just today, but every day. Thank you Lord for your blessings on me.

Notes: _____

_____

_____

_____

_____

_____

God's Not Finished Yet!

Jeremiah 18:4. "But the jar that he was making from the clay became flawed in the potter's hand, so he made it into another jar, as it seemed right for him to do."

God gives us all a ministry if we are willing to obey Him. It may not look like what we planned for our lives originally or what we thought, but that's okay. We all have plans for our lives when we are young. Sometimes (often times), things in our lives don't go as we had planned. We become broken for one reason or another. I'm not digging on you for that. I understand you know. I'm broken too. I have felt the pain of thinking that God would never be able to use me. But I want to encourage you this morning and remind you, that God can and will use the broken if we are willing. And we are ALL broken. Some of us know we are broken and some don't recognize it in themselves. It seems that as humans, it's easier to see others' supposed flaws at a distance than to see the flaws in the mirror. But don't let that ever slow your ministry down. You work for God. He sees your work and your value. Others do also, even if you don't realize it. But the main thing is that GOD sees your work and your value. HE sees your heart. I will never forget the lady who asked me to teach a children's Sunday School class after I was divorced. So much had been said about me. Much of it was untrue, but I didn't know who believed what. I will never forget what she did for me when she asked me to teach that class. It showed me that God wasn't finished with me yet. And HE isn't finished with you either. Please never ever forget that God isn't finished with you until you are in Heaven. Then our work will be to constantly praise HIM. Those of us who have been judged harshly by people who did not know our stories learn the lesson of not judging others better, I think. At least I hope we learn. Our job as Christians is to restore people to fellowship with Jesus, not push them farther away. I pray I never forget that. If you are doing the job God has assigned to you, thank you. Your work is invaluable. You may never know how many you've had a hand in reaching on this earth. If you have hesitated about doing the job God has called you to do, then take the leap of faith. God has a work for you that only you can do.

Notes: _____

Humble Sinner or Arrogant Hypocrite?

Read Luke 18:9-14.

Psalm 51:1-4. "Be gracious to me, God, according to Your faithful love; according to Your abundant compassion, blot out my rebellion. Wash away my guilt and cleanse me from my sin. For I am conscious of my rebellion, and my sin is always before me. Against You - You alone - I have sinned and done evil in Your sight. So You are right when You pass sentence ; You are blameless when You judge."

The story in Luke 18 of the self-righteous Pharisee and the sinful, but repentant, tax collector...both praying...really struck a chord in my heart today while reading it. How much more God listens to, honors, and answers the humble prayers of one who acknowledges their unworthiness, in contrast to one who dares to come before the Lord with an attitude of bragging about their own righteousness!

I've been a self-righteous thinking hypocrite like this Pharisee before God revealed to me how totally unworthy I am of His love. I am so thankful that He showed me the error in my thinking of myself as better than others and I pray I never fall into that sinful attitude again.

The pure repentance of the tax collector, acknowledging his sin and unworthiness, is so revealing and has a huge lesson for me. God looked upon him with love, forgiveness and mercy, gave him peace and he was cleansed. In stark contrast, the haughty religious leader didn't consider himself to be in need of forgiveness or mercy, but instead elevated himself to a pedestal equal to God and walked away self-righteously satisfied, but completely lost.

I've seen this kind of thing happen in life. I've seen this exact encounter happen in a church sanctuary between people I know personally: a religious leader and someone who acknowledges they've made many mistakes but has repented of their sins and is now walking with the Lord. God used this to show me how wrong I've been to have such an attitude toward others. To witness it openly happening to a friend, hurt my heart deeply, and so far as I know, there has been no remorse for the hurt and damage it caused. But my humble friend who experienced this, rose above the intended slight and extended graciousness and forgiveness...a true example of how Jesus treats us when we sin and misrepresent His name in our conduct to others.

I'm not glad that the ugly incident happened, and I'm still wounded over the intended hurt it caused, but I'm so grateful that God used it to open my own eyes to how those of us who call ourselves Christ-followers should never behave. I know we all fail and falter but we must always be aware that how we act to others will tell them how closely we actually follow the Lord. We must never deliberately do or say anything in a self-righteous attitude that would cause someone else to stumble in their walk with God. Father please forgive us when we misrepresent you by thinking ourselves more righteous than our fellow believers.

Walking In Faith

2 Corinthians 5:7. "For we walk by faith, not by sight."

I should start by saying I am not a fan of heights. Actually, I'm very afraid of being in high places. I've always had this fear as long as I can remember. This includes bridges. I know bridges are helpful and necessary to get from one side to the other. And honestly, I don't give most bridges a lot of thought as I drive my normal route to work and back. But there are a few bridges that I drive over quite often that still make me uneasy. One of those is the Bay Bridge over the river near the State Docks at Mobile, Alabama. I don't know much about that tall bridge that crosses the water even though I've driven and ridden over it many times. I don't know who designed it or who managed its construction. I don't know what year it was built or how often it is inspected. This evening as I drove down to Gulf Shores I happened to be alone. I also happened to be driving straight into a terrible thunderstorm. It was one of the worst storms that I've driven in lately. It was raining so hard that you could not even see one third of the way across the bridge as I got onto it. Traffic was slowed way down. Well we were actually all just creeping. Now did I mention that I don't like bridges, especially tall bridges across water… Oh right. I think I mentioned that already. It was difficult to make myself continue moving forward across the bridge because I could not see very far out in front of me at all. My practical mind knew the bridge was still there but my heart was fearful because I couldn't SEE the bridge. Isn't that how a lot of life is? I KNOW that Jesus is going to take care of me, but my heart is still fearful because I can't see the end result. Romans 8:28 promises that He will work all things together for the good of those that love the Lord. I've seen Him work things out for me many times in the past, just as I've safely driven across this same bridge many times before. Just because I could not see much of the bridge this evening did not make the bridge any less there. It didn't lessen its strength at all. My inability to see very far out in front of my vehicle did not change anything about the bridge that was holding my weight. My inability to physically see Jesus doesn't change His faithfulness either. My inabilities do not have any bearing on His strength or ability to take care of me. It also doesn't mean He is not present holding me up through every storm. HE is just as much with me through the storms as He is in the sunshine. I made it across the river because the bridge held me up, and I will make it through life because Jesus holds me up. I crossed the bridge on faith this evening even though I could not see much of it at a time. I will walk through life on faith because Jesus is with me. For we walk by faith, not by sight! Thank You Jesus, for Your faithfulness to me!

Notes: _____

_____

_____

_____

_____

_____

Get Behind Me Satan!

Luke 22:31-32. "Simon, Simon, look out. Satan has asked to sift you like wheat. But I have prayed for you that your faith may not fail. And you, when you have turned back, strengthen your brothers."

Doubt. Just one little doubt that edges into my thoughts and finds a spot to settle in. That's all it takes to make me stumble on my daily walk with the Lord. That's all Satan wants to accomplish because he knows if he can get me to entertain one tiny doubt about the sovereignty and goodness of God, he's turned me to head in a direction away from where God wants me. That's his goal every day.

One tiny doubt provokes one tiny question, and then the first tiny step away from complete trust in God. Satan is very content to just get the separation process started. He knows if he can get his foot in the door, he can stop me from slamming that door in his face. Oh, of course he loves causing me to make a huge misstep and fall on my face in a big way, but he's also glad to accept the success of causing just that tiny doubt to raise its head in my thoughts or my heart.

He's a sly demon, but a patient one also. He knows how to bide his time and catch me down and out, or tired or not feeling great, and he knows the exact moment to attack - just at my weakest point. He loves it when I feel lonely and alone and sorry for myself, also. If I think those thoughts, he agrees with me and tells me I'm right, nobody cares, and I don't count for anything. He reminds me that I'm too old to be useful or fun to be around and that everyone is too busy to have time for me. I have to fight off his advances and be wary of his tactics because he's persistent and very smart. Just think about what happened to Eve when he planted that tiny doubt in her mind with his insidious little question about God. So I have to be alert and cautious and aware to keep him from tripping me up and causing me to fall. I have to keep my armor on and my sword of the Spirit polished and ready for use. I have to order him to get behind me, not allowing him to come near me, lest I fall and he pounces. I know I can't fight him and win on my own so I must stay close to my Protector, my Redeemer and my Rock. In the shelter of His arms I am safe and secure and He fights my battles and destroys my enemies for me. Satan cannot stand before my Savior. When God says Go! he has to flee. I'm so grateful I don't have to fight that demon alone, aren't you?

Notes: _____

_____

_____

_____

_____

_____

_____

A Heart Of Flesh

Read Ezekiel 11:16-21.

Verse 19. "And I will give them one heart and put a new spirit within them; I will remove their heart of stone from their bodies and give them a heart of flesh,"

God is speaking to Ezekiel telling him what to say to the children of Israel and their leaders who have become corrupt. The leaders have strayed from obedience to God, and in their own disobedience, are also leading the people into following the ways of other nations and their false gods. God doesn't ever condone disobedience in His children.

    I admit I have a hard time understanding some of Ezekiel's prophecies but this particular one seems to speak clearly to me about my own straying from obedience. It's so easy to just take notice of worldly things and worldly ways. But when I do, it's also easy to look at them with tolerance and sometimes even acceptance. God does not allow this in His followers. We are to keep our eyes and focus on Him, following only His leadership. This is true even if government leaders are not following God's directions. He will deal with them as He sees fit, but that's not an excuse for us to stray from Him. Verses 16-18 and verse 21, tell us what God may allow to happen when we need His reminder to get back on the path He wants us on.

    Studying more in these scriptures, we see that even though

Jerusalem was about to be destroyed, the people remained blind to their own disobedience and rebellion against God. I'm afraid I often do the same. Sometimes I can't see the forest for the trees! They didn't really believe that God's warnings applied to them, and they resented Ezekiel's messages to them. Sometimes I'm blind to the truth of God's words too, and often I'm guilty of resenting His discipline.

But then, verses 19 and 20 are the ones that give me so much hope in His forgiveness and redemption. 'I will give them integrity of heart and put a new spirit within them. I will remove their heart of stone from their bodies and give them a heart of flesh, so that they will follow My statues, keep My ordinances, and practice them. They will be My people, and I will be their God.' These are goals I want to have...integrity, and a new spirit within. Stone is dead but flesh has life. I want a heart that is living and on fire for God, not a hardened and cold piece of stone. There's nothing better than 'being God's people' and He being committed to be my God.

Notes: _____

_____

_____

_____

_____

_____

_____

God Is Faithful To Finish

Lamentations 3:21-23. "Yet I call this to mind, and therefore I have hope. Because of the Lord's faithful love we do not perish, for His mercies never end. They are new every morning; great is Your faithfulness!"

I've already mentioned that I am a crocheter. It gives me a great feeling of satisfaction to take a skein of yarn and a crochet hook and make something that is useful with those two things. Of course it takes me using my hands and a certain amount of 'thinking' and focus, along with dedicating the time needed to complete a project, but it can be a feeling of real accomplishment. It's also satisfying to see the blankets, socks or sweaters being used and fulfilling the purpose for which they were made.

I have on occasion, made a complete mess on my crochet project and felt the need to ravel the entire thing out and start over with the first chain stitch. It is especially frustrating to have to do that after discovering a 'mess-up' that is several rows back but will affect the finished product. Amazingly, when that happens, the piece is new, the error is gone and cannot be seen again.

I've learned over the years that these mistakes that require starting over from the beginning, are a lot like my life. How many times over the years I've recognized errors I made and had to go back and ask for forgiveness! God has been faithful and shown me so much grace and mercy in these times. When I've asked for a second chance, He forgets about the mistake I made and no longer sees it. His love for me and His faithfulness is unending.

I've taught several people how to crochet and one of the most important things I always stress to them is that mistakes happen, and not to get discouraged, because it's not etched in stone. I remind them that they can always ravel the thread and start again. Actually, practice is good and it helps train us to have to correct mistakes and sometimes go back to the beginning.

How like life crochet work is! I read an article about crocheting being a kind of spiritual discipline. I think that's true. It's a creative process which results in something beautiful. I've seen a meme which said, 'Only a crocheter can take some string and a stick and make something to wear!'

With God's help, IF I make all the right stitches and rows, I can end up with something beautiful and useful. But, our Heavenly Father did that first when He created this world from nothing and made us in His image from dust. He made everything beautiful and saw that it was all good. IF we are closely following our Creator, He can make us into beautiful and useful beings, bringing glory and honor to Him. I hope you learn to crochet, and in that process, I hope your life becomes what God created you to be! Just remember to keep your focus on the finish!

Notes: _____

_____

_____

_____

Hope Grows

Read Lamentations 3:17-26.

Verse 17. "My soul has been deprived of peace; I have forgotten what happiness is."

Have you been hurting so long that you have forgotten what happiness is? Jeremiah says in verse 17 that he has . Many of us can relate to that feeling. We don't have any tears left to cry. We've struggled. We've carried a heavy load–one that is too heavy to bear. We've walked through fire and rain - but neither seem to stop. There seems to be no end to the long road of sorrow. Jeremiah suffered from affliction, homelessness, wormwood and poison! He had become depressed. Life is hard for all of us and it's easier to become depressed than not. But, we can have this one thing that causes a small glow in our hearts as it comes to mind– The Lord's faithful love. It has an amazing effect. The more we concentrate on the Lord and His faithfulness the more our hope begins to grow. We will still have problems in this life but we don't have to be overcome by those problems. The Lord's mercies are new every morning. Great is HIS faithfulness!

As I think on His great love and faithfulness, my hope grows. As my hope grows, I gain the strength to wait on Him! It is a good thing to wait on the Lord. Wait for His answer! His answer is always the best. And He will deliver us. Help me, Lord, to wait for your answer and Your direction! And please help me to concentrate on You as I wait.

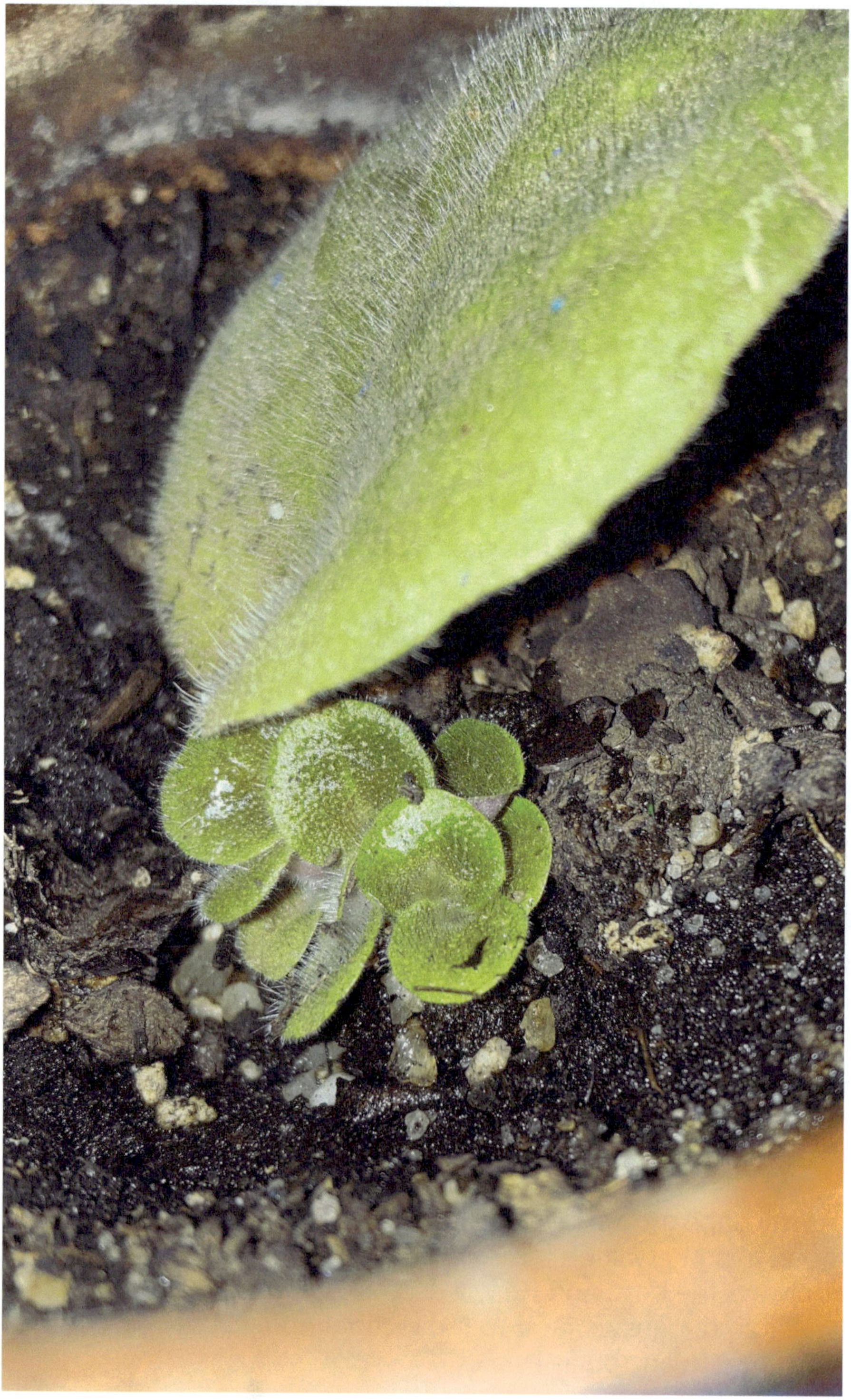

Hope's Fulfillment

Hebrews 11:1. "Now faith is the reality of what is hoped for, the proof of what is not seen."

I have a couple of pots of African Violet flowers. I enjoy seeing them bloom, and I enjoy rooting them for friends. I typically pinch a leave off the plant and put it in a clear glass of water on the windowsill to root them. It takes a few days but pretty soon, I usually see tiny little roots coming out of the bottom of the stem. I have a pot that my son painted for me when he was in kindergarten. I needed a flower to put in it, so one day I pinched a leaf off an African violet plant and instead of sticking it in a glass of water like I normally do, I stuck it straight in the dirt in this pot. I had the pot on the kitchen counter where I would see it every day. I watered the leaf and went my way.

I gave this leaf a small drink of water almost every day for two, or maybe three, months. Nothing seemed to be happening. The leaf appeared to be just as it was when I had stuck it down into the dirt. Even though I was careful not to let it dry out but not to over water it, nothing seemed to be happening. The leaf didn't turn brown, nor did it grow. I began to doubt that it would root and grow this way. I couldn't see anything happening. I couldn't see any change in the leaf. But the thing is, something was happening. Jesus was working under the soil where I couldn't see. Yesterday morning, I saw the leaves. The tiny little baby leaves. Several of them! They have been above the dirt apparently for several days but I was so used to nothing changing that I didn't notice. Just a quick water and off I would go. I had considered not watering the leaf anymore. It didn't appear to be changing. Nothing seemed to be happening. It hadn't turned brown, but was it worth it to keep watering a leaf that didn't grow? Jesus showed me something through those tiny leaves. Today HE told me that my watering that leaf those months was like faith, and that HE worked under the soil in ways that I can't see. Just because I can't see it, doesn't mean things are not happening or changing. In time, in HIS time, I will see a difference, just like these tiny little leaves.

Keep sharing the gospel. Keep encouraging that friend or acquaintance. Keep teaching that class. Keep PRAYING! Whatever you do, keep on praying for people. Even if you can't see a difference. Jesus is working in the soil of hearts. HE's working in ways that we can't see.

Notes: _____

_____

_____

_____

_____

_____

_____

Are You Shy or Bold?

Read Luke 8:40-48

Verse 48. "'Daughter,' He said to her, 'your faith has made you well. Go in peace.'"

I saw a video posted on social media a couple of days ago. The video was of a cat, who's owner had passed away. The cat was healthy looking and well cared for. The interesting part was the cat was watching a video of the deceased owner on someone's cell phone. The cat was staring intently at the cell phone, as the image of it's deceased owner played in a video. I don't know who played this video for the cat, but they must have known how much this poor cat missed its owner. The cat watched for a few seconds, then suddenly started trying to rub against the image on the cell phone. I am not so much a cat person, but I do know that cats tend to rub against the legs of people they love. Watching that video, it really struck me that this cat was trying to show its love in the only way it could. I feel sure the cat didn't understand where the owner was or how they were in the cell phone. The cat only knew that it missed the owner and wanted to show love. The video of this cat has been on my mind for the last couple of days and as I have thought about it, God showed me some things that I needed to think about. Just as the woman in today's verses did not necessarily approach Jesus in a way you would expect someone to approach our King, she approached Him in the only way she could muster up the courage for. Timidly, and from behind. She was afraid, no doubt. Her ailment made her a social outcast in that day, and she was not supposed to touch anyone. But her faith (and the desire to be well) overcame her fears, even just enough for her to timidly touch the hem of His garment from behind in the huge crowd. Our cat often approaches me while I am sitting in my chair and rubs against my feet. She does not approach me the same way my dog does. Our cat is much more fearful than our dog. She runs at the slightest sign (to her) of rejection, whether intended by me or not. The dog, on the other hand, continues to wag his tail and nudge my hand for petting. His personality includes being sure enough of himself to demand my attention. Even though both animals show their request for attention in very different ways, for each individual one, it is the best they can do. People are the same way. Each person is unique. Each person has a different way of approaching others. Some are bold and just come right up to you, hugging you or talking as they walk up. Others come quietly hoping you will say something to them first. And yet others, may wave at you from a distance. I am certainly all for showing love to others. Sometimes, I am bold enough to walk right up to somebody and just start talking. Other times, I am the quiet one who simply waves with a smile from across the room, hoping someone smiles in return. Does that mean I love each person any less? I have realized that I need to appreciate my cat for shyly rubbing my foot, just as much as I appreciate my dog nudging my hand for petting. Just because their way of approaching me to show their love is different, it doesn't mean that one loves me more than the other. Couldn't this be true of people too? Couldn't it be true that the shy person who simply eases up to me and smiles, while waiting for me to speak first, is just as glad to visit with me as the person who has the courage to walk up talking? I need to remember that both made an effort. And that likely, the effort was just as great for the shy one (maybe more) as the more courageous one. But both made an effort to communicate with me. I need to look at the example Jesus gave us. HE considered the heart of the woman who approached Him from behind. I need to slow down and remember that I can't see the heart of others. But then maybe, if I look more carefully, I can see the love behind each gesture. Jesus showed grace and mercy. I need to do that too!

Notes: _____

How Do I Respond To Troubles, My Own and Others?

Read Acts 8:4-8.

Verse 4. "So those who were scattered went on their way preaching the message of good news."

As I read this scripture, I tended to jump over the persecuted part and skip straight to the preaching in their towns. But this morning, the fact that they were persecuted and scattered really jumped out at me. The preaching was their RESPONSE to the persecution. I usually respond to persecution and hurt feelings with tears, a sour face and a poor attitude, not with joyful witnessing about Jesus. But what would happen if I kept my focus on Jesus? What would happen if I responded by keeping my thoughts on HIS saving grace? I mean, HIS message of salvation is absolutely, hands down the best message I could ever share. It's the best thing that has ever happened to me. And it's the best thing that can ever happen to anyone else.

Philip was one of the ones persecuted for telling others about Jesus. Stephen had just been stoned for it. The others were forced to leave their homes and basically run for their lives to other areas. Start over. Move. Live somewhere else. They were scattered. They didn't all go to the same areas. They started over, alone. Philip went to Samaria. Samaria wasn't known for being a necessarily Godly place. He didn't go with friends.

Verse 4 says, "So those who were scattered went on their way preaching the message of good news.". Have you ever been persecuted? We can be persecuted for various reasons—looks, abilities, possessions, and a number of other reasons. Persecution looks different for different people. Someone may be jealous of you for having friends, and treat you poorly. Someone else may not like you because of your cheery personality. Yet another person may be angry because you got the promotion at work. Or maybe you have the nicest home, or the newest car. It could be the success of your children. There are any number of reasons you are treated poorly, snubbed, left off the invitation list or given the stink eye. There are people in others countries and in this country, who are beaten for various reasons. Some are just random targets of violence for no reason at all. All of these things hurt, either physically, emotionally or both.

If you are a strong Christian, I imagine if you think carefully back over your life, there are invitations you didn't receive because of your stand for Christ. Maybe you knew the reason and maybe you didn't. I am sure we can all list times that we suffered certain consequences because of our stand for Jesus. We don't compare those times to what the early Christians suffered and we don't always recognize those things as persecution. Of course, I haven't been murdered for being a Christian like many of the early Christians were. But back to the persecutions we have suffered. Let's think on those for a minute. How did it make you feel? How did it affect your mood? Did you recognize it for what it was? Did you feel joy for being persecuted? Did you retreat to lick your wounds? It's okay if you took time to sort through your hurt feelings and heal some. I have done that also. Just don't camp out in that bad mood.

Philip (and the others) went on their way preaching the good news of Jesus. They kept reaching out to people they didn't know instead of sticking to themselves or with friends they knew were Christians. They kept sharing the gospel with others. And they must have done it with joy and excitement because people believed them. I know there are times that we do everything right when we share Jesus with people, yet the person we are sharing with still does not accept our message with joy. There are many times like that. But there are times when we share the message of Jesus and people do respond with belief! There are times that people do respond with joy. Verse 8 says there was great joy in the city! This was the result of people being scattered due to persecution. The ones persecuted didn't let persecution define the rest of their life. They didn't let persecution stop them from sharing the message.

Notes: _____

_____

_____

_____

_____

_____

Encourage One Another In Christ

Read First Thessalonians 4:9-18 and 5:16-24.

Verse 9. "About brotherly love: You don't need me to write you because you yourselves are taught by God to love one another."

Persecution is just one of many problems in life. We all have troubles and most of the time we would not trade our troubles with each other. I think it is important to encourage our Christian sisters in their walk with Christ. We need to sympathize and pray for each other over our hurts. We need encouragement from each other. The Scriptures are the best thing that we can use to encourage each other. Jesus has given us everything we need to survive this life. We need to share that information with the ones who don't know Him and with the ones who do! I forget just how very much I have to be joyful about. The best way I can be reminded is to spend time in the Scriptures. We have such a treasure in the Holy Spirit who will help us. We just have to listen. And we need to remind each other.

We have all lost loved ones to death. Grief is a very real part of life and to say it's hard is putting it mildly. But it's not the end. At least not for the Christians. Death is not the end for Christians or non-Christians. The question is which end will you face?

In verse 13, Paul offers encouragement for the loved ones of Christians. He wants us to understand what will happen and where our deceased loved ones are. Isn't that our greatest fear anyway? Losing someone we love dearly. If we walk with Jesus in life on this earth, then we will be with Him when we die. There is no greater joy than to be with Jesus. As Christians, we need not fear death. We also need not fear HIS return if it takes place prior to our death. Either way, we will be with HIM! Make it a point to remind someone today of all that we have in Christ. And do it with joy! (First Thessalonians 5:16-24) How do we do this?

    Paul gives instructions on how Christians are to live in a few simple verses. Rejoice always! Why is that hard for me? I think it's because I take my eyes off of Jesus sometimes. When I concentrate more on my problems than I do on Jesus, I forget that HE is bigger than any problem I face. HE created the world and everything in it. HE can solve my problems or take me through them. That"s something to rejoice about! Pray constantly. During this life, we will have troubles. That's a guarantee. It takes prayer to walk closely with Jesus and not be distracted by the world around us. The Holy Spirit is here to help us. Sometimes, my prayer feels like the route the little boy in the comic strip Family Circle took. But that's okay. The Holy Spirit was sent to help us and that includes with prayer. HE's all we need. HE understands our hearts, even when we ourselves don't. Give thanks in everything, for that is God's will for you. We may not know exactly what God's will is for everything in our life, but this is one thing we do know. Give thanks! A grateful heart will worship God every time. We may not be thankful that we broke our leg, but we can be thankful for the extra time to study our Bible while we recover in our recliner. We can be thankful for the kindness of whoever took care of us, or the opportunity to witness to the nurse in the emergency room. There is always, always a reason to be thankful. As Christians, we have more to be thankful for than anybody else. I need to work on this in my life. Don't stifle the Spirit. This is the Holy Spirit we are not to stifle. Listening to the Holy Spirit takes practice sometimes. But HE is with us as Christians and HE wants us to hear His voice. Obedience is a choice. Sometimes, we can't see how what HE wants us to do will work out or do us any good. Obey anyway. We used to have a Captain when we reenacted. When we would have to join in with other groups, and have a different captain over us, Captain B would tell us, "Just do what he say; just do what he say." Regarding the Holy Spirit, it's simple.... just do what HE say.

Don't despise the prophecies, but test all things. Listen to what the pastor preaches, but read and study your Bible for yourself also. Check what he preaches against what the Bible says. This goes for Sunday School teachers, TV preachers, devotion books and double for Facebook. This new motto of "Do what makes you happy" is unchristian. Do what makes God happy should be the motto of Christians. As Charles Stanley says, "Obey God and leave all the consequences to Him.". Sometimes, we have to just plain obey. Stay away from every kind of evil. Christians are not to engage in evil. We are sanctified. That means we are set apart for God's work. HE has work for each of us to do. The time to do it is now. We should all be about HIS business. We are not exempt from doing God's work at any point in our life. May the God of peace Himself sanctify you completely. Sanctification is a lifelong process. God isn't finished with us yet. We are to be set apart for Him. But we don't just get saved and immediately know what we are to do. We must read and study our Bibles, pray, listen to Godly sermons and fellowship with other believers who will tell us the truth when we are wrong. It's a life long process. I can't stress the need to read and study your Bible enough. The more you read, the more you learn. The more you learn, the more you want to learn. The Bible is the most exciting book ever written. I've seen a picture of a person that looks like she has just run and jumped straight into the arms of Jesus. Jesus is holding her in the picture. Our goal needs to be to run as straight towards Jesus as we possibly can. The only thing that should slow us down, is to stop and point others towards Him. We are so loved by Him. We must encourage each other with this news.

Pray For Opportunities

Read Colossians 4:2-4

Verses 3-4. "At the same time, pray also for us that God may open a door to us for the word, to speak the mystery of Christ, for which I am in chains, so that I may make it known as I should."

Paul prayed for opportunities to tell people about Jesus. He was in prison at the time for sharing the gospel. I've never been to prison for sharing the gospel. Well, I've never been to prison for anything. I wonder how bold I would be if I was put in prison for telling people about Jesus. There are many around the world today who are put in prison for sharing the gospel. Paul is suffering in prison for sharing the gospel and yet he's still looking for opportunities to tell people about Jesus. And he's even praying for those opportunities to come. My Daddy used to pray for opportunities to witness. And he watched for and often made opportunities in conversations to talk to people about Jesus. There is no other name so important. There is no other news more important than that Jesus died and rose again to save us from our sins. We tell people about our kids, grandkids, yesterday's ball game, what we had for supper last night, a new TV show and any number of other things. Let it be our normal conversation to tell others about Jesus. Let me be found praying for opportunities and then using those opportunities to reach others. You can't make anybody accept what you are saying. It's not our responsibility to try to force anyone to be saved, but it is our job to tell them. Let me be found telling others what Jesus has done for me. Let my speech be seasoned with the salt of Jesus!

Notes: _____

When Things Don't Go Your Way, Obey Anyway

Daniel 1:8. "Daniel determined that he would not defile himself with the king's food or with the wine he drank."

Daniel was about 15 when he was taken captive to a foreign land to be a slave. Up until then, he had been of noble background. Daniel, being a young Jewish man, had grown up being taught about the God of Abraham. When his country was overcome by an enemy, he, along with several others, were taken captive at the order of the foreign king who wanted the best of the young men as slaves. The foreign king took these young men far from home and family. His plan was to saturate them with the Chaldean way of life. This king worshiped pagan gods. So he ordered the process of teaching them the Chaldean language and literature. They were to be fed the same food the king ate. The Jewish young men had always kept a strict diet as part of their obedience to God. The food the king ate had been offered to idols. The king even ordered their names changed to Chaldean names. These Hebrews were young, and they were prisoners of war. Who would have blamed them for going along with the pagan king's orders? The king could have easily ordered them killed for disobeying him. But Daniel and his friends were serious about their relationship with God. Their commitment to Him was strong. Strong enough to risk their life to obey God. They were being saturated with the pagan way of life but they continued in their strong commitment to serve God. How easy it is for us today to become saturated with the ways of the world. If we do not keep serving the Lord at the top of our hearts and minds, it will be so easy to let the ways of the world become our ways. How easy it is to watch that TV show instead of studying our Bibles? Will you listen to the dirty joke being told or will you walk away? One compromise leads to another, and it's a slippery slope after the first compromise. It's hard. There is no doubt that it's hard. We work hard every day. The house needs cleaning. We have to cook supper and help the kids with homework. We are already late from working overtime and stopping at the store. It's hard. We are tired. We are exhausted. But compromise is not the answer. Jesus didn't compromise instead of going to the cross to save us from our sins. He is absolutely worth our devotion. How long would our devotion last if we were taken captive to a foreign land like Daniel? May our commitment to honor Him and share the good news of the gospel grow stronger and stronger.

Notes: _____

_____

_____

_____

_____

_____

Time

2 Peter 3:8. "Dear friends, don't let this one thing escape you: With the Lord one day is like a thousand years, and a thousand years like one day."

Time is no more in Heaven. That doesn't mean you don't exist anymore. It means you don't have to count time anymore. "Time is no more" has kind of always had a sad ring to it for me. But I think it's because I've been wrongly interpreting it. Time is just not COUNTED in Heaven. Time doesn't matter. You don't have to keep up with what time it is there. Where are you waiting to go that is better than in the presence of Jesus? There is no better place to be.

Your time in Heaven is not limited. Our days here on earth are numbered. Job 14:5 says "Since man's days are determined and the number of his months depends on You, and since You have set limits he cannot pass." We tick off time when we are on earth from the moment we are born, before we even understand time, until the day we die. But after we die, if we are saved, time doesn't matter. Because in Heaven, we are there forever. For eternity!

Remember those moments when you feel the presence of the Lord? (This is only if you are saved.). Sometimes those moments are in church but also when you are praying or reading the Bible. Or sometimes when you just worship privately. For me, sometimes it is when I'm on the beach watching the waves roll in because I'm always reminded that the Lord CREATED this beautiful world for us to be in. And HE is incredibly AWESOME! Those times, where ever you are, that you feel the presence of the Lord, are just a tiny sampling of what Heaven will be like! And the bonus part about Heaven, is that we don't have to worry about our time in the presence of the Lord running out! We don't have to be watching the clock or setting an alarm because we have to leave. We don't have anywhere else to go or anything else to do. We don't have to worry about pulling ourselves away from Jesus to run the vacuum, scrub the bathroom, go to the store, take the dog to the vet or get to work. How many times are you really enjoying your devotion and prayer time, only to have to stop and rush off to work? Or how many times are you really enjoying the pastor's message at church, only for him to finish up and suddenly Sunday morning worship is over?

    I don't know about you, but my life here on earth is hectic. It's full of rushing around and hurrying to get things done. I very rarely get to simply just lose track of time. Heaven won't be that way because we won't run out of time with Jesus!

    Time on earth is definitely a gift. Time spent in worship. Time with loved ones. Time spent reading your Bible, in prayer and time spent just listening for God's guidance. I'm not down playing the precious gift of time on earth that God has so graciously given us. But the thing about time on earth, is that we only have so much of it and we never know how much time we have left. Never forget that we are spending our time faster than a kid spends a dollar bill in the toy store. We need to make sure we spend our time on things that are valuable because we will be held accountable for how we spent our time. I'm so very thankful that when I get to Heaven with Jesus and take my place around the throne to worship Him, time (ticking off) will be no more!

The End Result

Read Genesis 37-50 and Matthew 16:21-23.

Verse 21. "From then on Jesus began to point out to His disciples that He must go to Jerusalem and suffer many things from the elders, chief priests, and scribes, be killed, and be raised the third day."

When Jesus was explaining to the disciples how HE was going to suffer, Peter took Jesus aside and said "Oh no, Lord! This will never happen to you!". Why would Peter do such a thing? Why would he dare to argue with Jesus? I'm not defending Peter for arguing with Jesus, but as a human I can see what caused Peter to do this. It was three things: (1) Love; (2) Lack of sight; (3) Lack of trust. The first one, love, sounds pretty noble. We can surely relate to that. Peter loved Jesus. He truly did. Peter was willing to defend Jesus with his life. After all, he proved that in the Garden of Gethsemane when he drew his sword and cut off Malchus' ear. Malchus was the servant of the high priest, in case you have forgotten who he was. The disciples were certainly outnumbered in the Garden of Gethsemane, or so they would have thought. They would have been no match for the Temple Police and soldiers. So, at that moment, Peter was brave and willing to die for Jesus. He simply just couldn't understand what Jesus had told them. Jesus was going to die on the cross for their sins and ours, and HE was going to rise again. Peter couldn't understand or envision that.

Peter couldn't see the end results, although he had witnessed Jesus raising Lazarus from the dead. He had been with Jesus and witnessed miracle after miracle. Surely, someone who calms the wind and seas could do anything. Peter SAW those things with his own eyes. Peter walked on the water at Jesus' bidding to come. When Peter took his eyes off of Jesus, he sank, only to have Jesus save him, but Peter still couldn't see the end results of the crucifixion.

This brings us to the last reason Peter argued with Jesus, lack of trust. We would never lack trust in Jesus. I mean, after all, we have trusted Him with our salvation. That is eternal. Forever. That is the biggest thing we could have, so why would we not trust Him with everything else? Surely, we can trust Jesus with everything because we have the entire Bible. If you have lived any time at all since being saved, Jesus has done other things for you. HE has for each of us. So, why do we have issues trusting Jesus with the day to day things, and the bigger things? Things that we fear will hurt. And honestly, things that do hurt. Things with our children. That's not fair, you say. I have a son too, so I understand. Do you think Jacob would have chosen Joseph to be sold into slavery and sent off to Egypt, so the family could be saved from starvation later? I seriously doubt he would have allowed that if he had seen that coming. See Genesis 37. Peter loved Jesus, so if he could have prevented Jesus' death on the cross, I believe he would have. We love our children, spouse, family and friends, as well as ourselves. If we think we might can prevent hurt, we do it, or try to. That is a natural response of love. And in most cases, I think it is the right response. But when the hurt comes anyway, we have to remember that Jesus can see the end that we can't. HE doesn't have the lack of sight that we have. HE loves us. Love wants the very best. And that is where our trust in Jesus comes in. See Romans 8:28. If we are saved, Romans 8:28 applies. The thing is this... sometimes Jesus uses the hurt for our very best. Or for our children's very best. The truth is that Jesus knows way more about what is the very best than we do. Our idea of what is best is not always what is actually the very best. Sometimes the lesson we learn through the hurt is more valuable than avoiding the hurt, but our lack of sight prevents us from seeing this at first. If we trust Jesus for our salvation (and the salvation of our children if they are saved), then surely we can trust HIM with ANYTHING else in this life. Because salvation matters more than anything else. That doesn't mean we don't hurt. And it doesn't mean the hurt is not real. It is. And we can certainly talk to Jesus about it. HE knows anyway. But we need to choose to trust HIM. It's hard. And I can't say that I'm good at it. But, HE is trustworthy. Oh, and God used the hurt and hardships that Joseph went through to save his entire family from starvation. In the process of saving Joseph's family, HE saved his brother Judah. Do you remember who the Lion of Judah is? Jesus! Jesus' earthly descent was through Judah. Jesus died on the cross to save us from our sins, and rose the third day! And that my friend, was for our best!

Notes: _____

_____

_____

_____

_____

_____

_____

God Cares

Read Exodus 3.

Exodus 3:12. "He answered, 'I will certainly be with you, and this will be the sign to you that I have sent you: when you bring the people out of Egypt, you will all worship God at this mountain.'"

This morning, I am getting ready to go to work, like a lot of people in the world. Like most everyone I know, I have problems on my mind. Things I am facing, things other people are facing, and things I and others have been through in my life. Have you ever noticed that when you concentrate on your problems and hurts, they just seem to grow until they loom over your whole life like a huge black storm cloud? That's how it feels anyway. In Exodus chapter 3, God gave Moses an assignment to go help the Isrealites with what I would call a very real problem. Not that my problems are not real, but mine are certainly not the same as what Moses was being assigned to deal with. God told Moses in verse 12, "I will certainly be with you, and this will be the sign to you that I have sent you: when you bring the people out of Egypt, you will all worship God at this mountain.". God doesn't change. HE loves us just like HE loved Moses. HE will certainly be with you and HE will certainly be with me. God is not blind to our lives and the things we face. HE is GOD! HE knows all things. HE says in verse 16, "I have paid close attention to you and to what has been done to you in Egypt.". We all have Egypt experiences. Some last longer than others, but we all have those. The Israelites' Egypt time was 400 years. Their experience was tough with no way out, or so it seemed. But then God said, I have paid close attention to you and to what has been done to you in Egypt.". God pays attention to HIS people. HE did then and HE does now! I am humbled and awestruck thinking about the God of all the universe paying attention to me and what has been done to me. But HE does! And HE pays attention to you too! God will work these difficult days for your good, somehow, someway. And HE will for me too. Romans 8:28 promises that. HE promises to bring us up from the misery. He promises to bring them up from the misery in verse 17. HE keeps HIS promises.

Notes: _____

_____

_____

_____

_____

_____

Enemies

Read Psalm 27.

Verse 3. "Though an army deploys against me, my heart will not be afraid; though a war breaks out against me, still I am confident."

As I read this Psalm today, my first thoughts were about King David fleeing from his enemies. His enemies included whole armies that were searching for him. He must have been terrified more than once as he hid in caves and wherever he could. I know that still happens for some people, even now. We have soldiers deployed who have very real enemies. Those are very real and very serious problems and what I face pales to zero quickly in comparison with what they face. So, does this Psalm still apply for me? What about the "enemies" and things that I face daily? What about the challenges you face daily? I work a full time job in an office, and in another state, there is a corporate office. Issues in the office on every level are very real these days. This may seem petty and again, compared to what our military faces when deployed, it is not worth mentioning. But, when we are at work trying to do our job to the best of our ability, it is very real. It feels real anyway. In today's office world, this department handles one portion of responsibilities, while another department handles something else. We forget to see each other as humans, much less friends on the same team to accomplish a common goal. Something that makes one person's job easier, makes ours harder and vice versa. And then we become enemies. I think this happens mostly because we don't understand the whole picture and what we each need to do to accomplish the tasks the boss has given us. And then, there's the boss, or multiples of bosses in most corporate worlds today. They appear to be looking at reports that have unsatisfactory figures and searching for someone to blame, so they can just "crack the whip" on someone. Do you ever feel discouraged by someone's comments about you? Do they feel like a modern day enemy out to get you? Well, for me, sometimes the answer is yes! And as a Christian, it just might be true in the world we live. Throughout the Bible, the people of God faced enemies who persecuted them in various ways, mostly because they were, well, the people of God. We tend to make light of the things we face now and think these comforting Psalms don't apply to things going on in the office. But the truth of the matter is, oft times they do apply. Maybe on a smaller level, as I don't think anyone from corporate is looking to actually kill me. But, I certainly do feel singled out sometimes. Maybe, I can face the hard days in the office, if I keep my perspective accurate and remember that King David, King Hezekiah, and the apostle Paul, all had "bad days in the office". I am not running for my life, but my life is certainly made more stressful by those days. The "enemy" is not necessarily the people but maybe the devil who is doing all he can to cause me to stumble. People are certainly unknowingly used by the devil. That happened in the Bible times and it still happens now. I'm so thankful that I can still pray Psalm 27 and it still applies to me, just as it did to King David. "Because of my adversaries, show me Your way, Lord, and lead me on a level path." (verse 11). Sometimes the level path can be as simple as a level "headed" path. "Hold my tongue, Lord.". "Please give me a response that honors You.". I hope I can keep this in mind at work on the days the "enemies" are out to get me. I hope it helps you too.

Christians Need Each Other

Read Ephesians 6:10-24.

Verse 18. "Pray at all times in the Spirit with every prayer and request, and stay alert in this with all perseverance and intercession for all the saints."

Paul wrote this letter to the church at Ephesus while a prisoner in Rome. Paul's letter starts off with a normal greeting and then moves to praise of God. Throughout the letter, he gives much needed instruction, which benefits us all. One thing of note fairly early on in the letter, is his statement of giving thanks for the Ephesian Christians when he prays for them. Paul was a very strong Christian himself. He had been through many trials and tribulations and yet kept his strong faith. I believe the Ephesian Christians would have found the knowledge that Paul is not only thankful for them, but that he also prays for them quite encouraging. We all tend to look at Paul as some kind of superhero of the faith, who would not become discouraged or feel the need to ask to be remembered in prayer by another Christian brother. But what we see in verses 18 - 24 is Paul asking the Ephesians to pray for him. In verses 10 - 18, Paul explained Christian Warfare to the Ephesians. I'm so thankful he explained this to them, so that we also have this information. Sister, this life is full of battles. If it were not, why would God have put instructions for fighting, in the Bible for us? The part that is so easy to forget, is that these battles are spiritual battles, not just physical ones. Part of fighting that battle is praying for each other. Verse 18 instructs us to "Pray at all times in the Spirit with every prayer and request, and stay alert in this with all perseverance, and intercession for all the saints.". Paul asks them to pray for him in the very next verse. Paul, of all people, asks them for pray that he will have boldness to share the gospel. PAUL! Now if Paul needed Christian brothers and sisters to pray for him to have boldness, there is no doubt that I need someone to pray for ME to have boldness. I don't know about you, but I don't often feel very bold about sharing the gospel. I should be, but I just don't always feel bold. He goes on to say he is sending Tychicus to give them news about how he is doing and to encourage them. Sisters, we NEED EACH OTHER. Every person I know right now is fighting some kind of battle. Even the battles that appear to be physical, are also spiritual battles. Every Christian is fighting a battle. Not one of us is exempt from that. As soon as we are saved, the devil starts attacking. I know Jesus has already won the war, but we face some fierce battles while we are still on this earth. I think I have tended to concentrate on the armor listed in verses 14-17, and not paid enough attention to these last few verses. I cannot stress enough the need to pray for and encourage each other. Make a commitment today to pray for your Christian brothers and sisters... and then encourage them. We have so many different ways of communicating in this time era. Call, text, email, write a note or visit someone who you think needs encouragement. Boldly share the gospel with someone.

Notes: _____

_____

_____

_____

God Listens

Read Jeremiah 29:11-13.

Verse 12. "You will call to Me and come and pray to Me, and I will listen to you."

We all love Jeremiah 29:11. I almost dare to say you quoted it in your memory as soon as you read the words "Jeremiah 29:11". And it's true. God does have plans for each of us. Plans for a future and a hope. He loves each one of us so much that He gave His only Son to die an awful death on the cross to pay for our sins—mine and yours—so that we could be reconciled to Him. (John 3:16). His plan for every one of us is salvation: a restored fellowship with Him. Verse 12 speaks to that relationship. "You will call to Me and come and pray to Me, and I will listen to you." I don't know about you, but I find it completely amazing that the God of all the universe would even consider listening to anything that I have to say. It seems to me there would be a lot of people with more important things to say than me. People who are more obedient to Him, people who speak more eloquently, you know, people who just seem like they would be a whole lot more important than a middle aged woman who was born in Bessemer, Alabama. But that's not what verse 12 says. It says "You will call to Me and come and pray to Me, and I will listen to you.". There's no 'might, maybe or if I feel like it at the time', in the verse. That's humbling and amazing all at once. It is amazing grace!

Grace given by God who reaches down to me, because I can't possibly reach high enough to get to Him if He doesn't reach for me first. That's love, real love. Verse 13 says "You will seek Me and find Me when you search for Me with all your heart.". God is giving us the key to a relationship with Him in this verse also. Seek Him with all your (and my) heart. He is God and I am not. It's up to me to give Him all of me! Not a partial commitment but all of my heart. There is no one better to trust your whole heart with than God! He's the same one who will listen to you when you pray, even if you are like me—just a regular everyday person with nothing in particular to impress Him with. But then honestly, what human could possibly have anything to impress God with? It's a good thing He just accepts the gift of ourselves! Thank you Father, for this reminder that You will hear my prayers, even the ones I stumble through that might not make sense.

Notes: _____

_____

_____

_____

_____

_____

_____

How Should We Respond To Our Fears?

Isaiah 43:5a. "Do not fear, for I am with you;"

Fear is no stranger to any of us. We are all afraid at different times in our life. If you are afraid, you are in good company. People throughout the Bible were afraid. What are we to do with our fear? Is it a sin to be afraid? How did the people in the Bible respond to their fears? Let's look at how God responded to people's fears. Joshua 1:9 says "Haven't I commanded you: be strong and courageous? Do not be afraid or discouraged, for the Lord your God is with you wherever you go.". In Judges 6:15, we see Gideon ask "Please, Lord, how can I deliver Israel? Look, my family is the weakest in Manasseh, and I am the youngest in my father's house." In Judges 6:16, we see these words: "But I will be with you" the Lord said to him. What about in the New Testament? Let's look at Jesus' response to the disciples' fear in John 6:19-21. "After they had rowed about three or four miles, they saw Jesus walking on the sea. He was coming near the boat, and they were afraid. But He said to them, "It is I. Don't be afraid!" Then they were willing to take Him on board, and at once the boat was at the shore where they were heading.". In each example above, we see God give comfort in response to fear and then He goes with the fearful! We can surely face anything if God is with us and He definitely is!

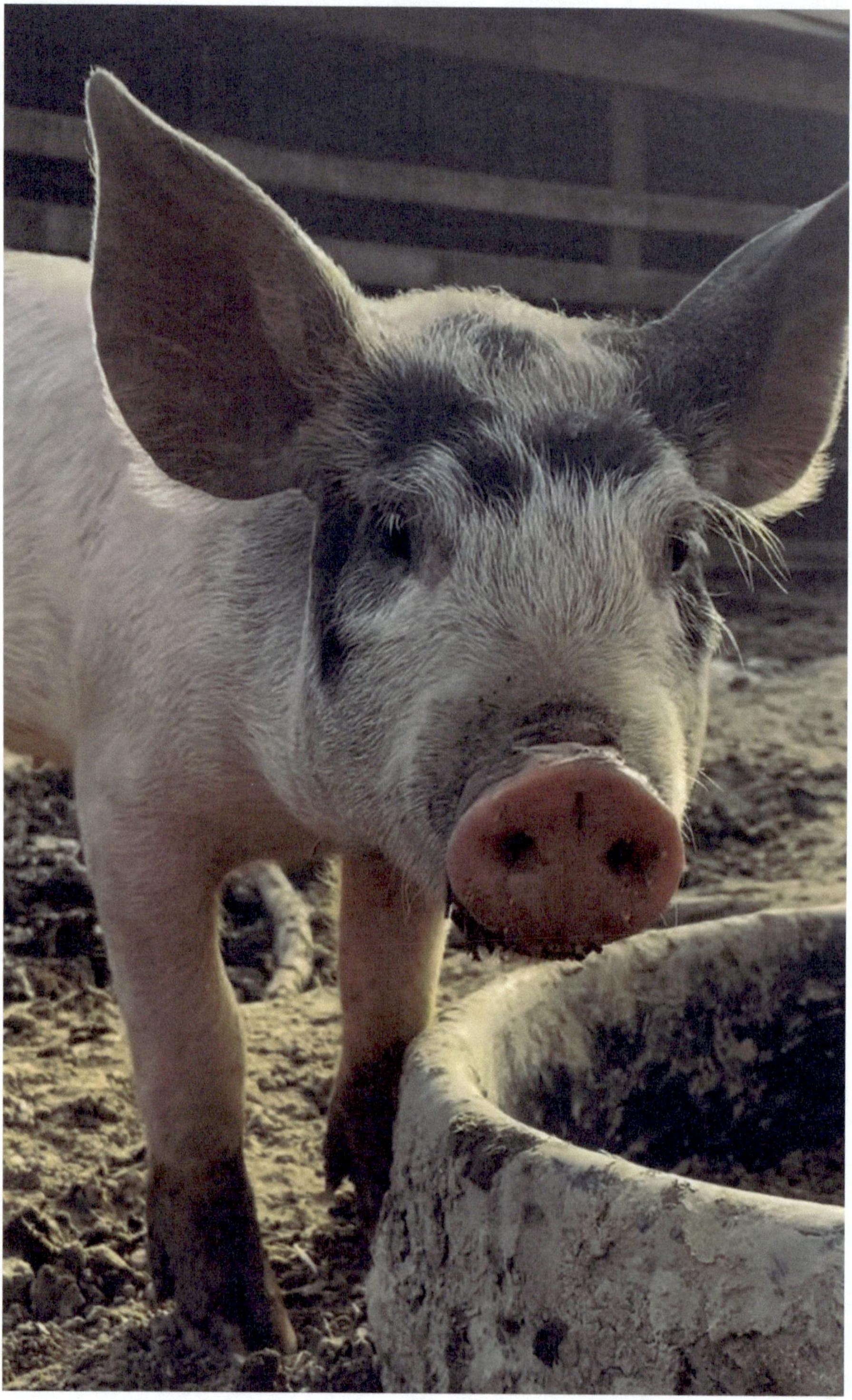

Of Pigs and Prodigals!

Read Luke 15:11-32.

Verse 21. "The son said to him, 'Father, I have sinned against heaven and in your sight. I'm no longer worthy to be called your son.'"

Over the weekend we enjoyed a visit with my oldest grandson and his sweet wife. They have a farm and have numerous animals, including cows, goats, chickens, geese and pigs. When my grandson first told me he was going to get some pigs, I remember asking him...'Are you really sure you want pigs'? Goats are cute and friendly...natural acrobats and always curious; chickens are great...laying eggs and eating bugs in the grass when out of their coop. Cows are okay too, and their baby calves are cute. But pigs! My Daddy had pigs when I was growing up and I guess I've just never liked pigs. They love mud and muddy water holes to wallow in. They don't care if they have it stuck all over them; in fact, they seem to be happiest if they are muddy. I know pigs have their place, and I enjoy bacon and pork chops as much as anybody, but I just don't really care much for pigs.

I was reminded of Jesus' Parable of the Prodigal Son by something my grandson said about his pigs while we were there. He said that he really likes having pigs and now there are babies also, so he has two pens of pigs to tend. He said he enjoys them and is glad he got them, but....they sure do smell bad when the weather gets really warm. That was one of the memories I had about pigs when I was a child, the smell at the pig pen! Probably one reason I never liked them. But then my grandson went on to say that IF you have to go inside the pen and walk around, you cannot get the smell off your boots. He said he had noticed that even when he'd cleaned his boots afterwards, the smell was still there and he would still smell it when riding in his truck later. He had to get something really strong to finally get the smell off his boots.

    I think the stinky pig pen is a good reminder of what walking in this evil world is like for us. We have to go back and read the scripture in Luke where Jesus is talking about the Prodigal Son and pigs. There's a great lesson for us all in those verses. Sometimes even if there are good points about something, it is not meant for us as Christians to walk around in. We need to stay close to and abide with our Father God and stay out of the pig pens of the world. When we leave the safety and security of our Home in God's courts, we risk getting the mud and smell of the world on us and we can't get it off by ourselves. We should never want to risk getting comfortable wallowing in the mud! We have to go back to the Father for help and His deep cleansing. He is the strength we need to combat the stinky smell of our sins and He is our only hope of being clean again because we can't clean our own selves up!

Notes: _____

_____

_____

_____

_____

The True Light

Genesis 1:15. "They will be lights in the expanse of the sky to provide light on the earth."

John 1:9. "The true light, who gives light to everyone, was coming into the world."

Revelation 21:23. "The city does not need the sun or the moon to shine in it, because God's glory illuminates it, and its lamp is the Lamb."

Why are we drawn to light? We are drawn to Christmas lights, white lights on a string under a covered porch, the late evening light of sunsets, the light of the moon, the stars in a night sky, a candle burning, an oil lamp burning, a porch light, a light in the window at night, a fire and warm sunshine. As you read these, you probably had a mental picture of the glow of each one, just like I did. It made you feel just a tiny bit warmer inside and maybe you even smiled. It's just something about driving up to a home that has the porch light on that makes you feel welcome. You are glad when you drive up at Mom's house late at night to see a light on in the window. We have a fascination with sunsets, the moon and the stars. We light tall tapered candles and put them on the dinner table for special occasions. Before we had electricity, people lit oil lamps to read by. If you want to draw an impromptu crowd from your neighborhood, just light a bonfire in the evening. People bring chairs and gather around. I personally love to be outside on a warm sunny day. But why the draw to light? God knew we would need light when HE created the earth. That's why HE put lights "in the expanse of the sky to provide light on the earth.". HE created us to need light. HE could have just as easily created us not to need light, but HE didn't. HE created the light we would need before HE even created Adam. John refers to Jesus as the true Light. Perhaps, somewhere deep inside us, our need for light is a reminder that we need the true Light, Jesus. HE is the Light that draws us to Himself. On this earth, we need the sun, moon, stars, and numerous other lights to dispel the darkness. We also need the warmth of the sun and sometimes the warmth of a fire. One day, the ones who are saved, will not need the light and warmth of the sun, because we will be with Jesus! HE will be all the Light we need. His light will be brighter and more comforting than any light on this earth. In the meantime, when you are drawn to a light or the warmth of a fire, let it remind you of your need for Jesus. HE will provide all the light and comfort you need.

Notes: _____

_____

_____

_____

_____

_____

God's Order

Read Genesis chapter 1.

Romans 1:20. "For His invisible attributes, that is, His eternal power and divine nature, have been clearly seen since the creation of the world, being understood through what He has made. As a result, people are without excuse."

Everything in creation points to God because HE created it all. Nothing was created randomly or by chance. Genesis 1:1 says "In the beginning God created the heavens and the earth.". HE started with nothing and created something. HE created huge, unmeasurable heavens, and HE created the earth. We find the order in which HE created everything in Genesis chapter one. Nothing was created randomly or by chance. If you randomly toss a handful of jelly beans in the air, they do not land in two straight lines with like colors together. Chance does not create order. The rotation of the earth is orderly. The sun does not rise in a zig zag pattern until it's finally up. The rising and setting of the sun and moon are orderly, so much so, that you can look on a weather app on your phone to get the predicted time for each day in advance. Many people, myself included, love to watch the sun rise and set. It has a calming effect on me. It reminds me that God has set everything in order and He is in charge. I love to sit on the beach and watch the waves roll in. At times, waves appear to crash ashore and at other times, they seem to gently roll in. But always, it is one after another, after another. I cannot control the timing of the waves or how far ashore they roll in. God does that. Job 38:8-11 says so. "Who enclosed the sea behind doors when it burst from the womb, when I made the clouds its garment and thick darkness its blanket, when I determined its boundaries and put its bars and doors in place, when I declared: "You may come this far, but not farther; your proud waves stop here"?". At times, those waves are rough enough to destroy buildings and at other times, those waves are so gentle that even a toddler is not overpowered. God uses the moon to set the rising and lowering of the tides, which is also orderly and predictable. Flowers grow in the Spring, and bloom with the most intricately detailed petals. Trees bud out with tiny green leaves, that grow to maturity and turn amazing deep colors in the Fall, only to drop off in the winter. This process happens every year, in the same order. God is so powerful and yet so interested in the details that even the ants march in line. Only man dares to disobey Him. Our amazing God, who loves us so much that He gave His only son to die for our sins, is worthy of our praise and worship. And His creation reminds me of Him in every direction I look. Oh, let me always be found worshiping Him.

Notes: _____

_____

_____

_____

_____

_____

Encourage One Another In Love

First Thessalonians 5:11. "Therefore encourage one another and build each other up as you are already doing."

After Christmas, I put all of the Christmas cards my husband and I received on the coffee table. As I did that, I took the time to look at each one. Each person who took the time to write out a note in a Christmas card for us. I thought about each of those people as I read the cards. I was humbled, honored and felt so loved. I appreciated the time and effort (not to mention the expense) that each person went to providing the card or note to us and it made me really think.

As Christians, we are called to love and encourage each other. Paul wrote to the Thessalonian church. He was writing to Christians. He reminded them in chapter one verse 2 that he was constantly praying for them. And in 4:18 and 5:11, he told them to encourage each other. There are many ways to encourage each other, but two of the best are praying for someone and telling them you have prayed for them. Timothy had told Paul the Thessalonians were suffering but they were holding onto their faith. Could that be reported of me? What about you? You may say "Well, I am surely suffering.". Couldn't we all say that? Almost all of us suffer with something. It may be from different things, but we still suffer. Given that, shouldn't we pray for and encourage each other? Absolutely! I know that I often pray for many different people. And in my heart, I want the best for them. But how often do I TELL them? There are many people who are praying for somebody. They wish for and want the best for that person. They probably even smile when they think of them. I know there are many people that I could make the following statements to: "Somebody somewhere is praying for you and wishing the best for you. Somebody somewhere smiles when they think of you.". We would probably be surprised if we knew who thought of us with love and friendship if we just knew. I think it would be such an encouragement to people if we shared those thoughts more, instead of assuming they knew. I ran out of Christmas cards this year (and couldn't find anymore to purchase) long before I got to the end of my Christmas card list. It's great to send Christmas cards, and I truly appreciated every card we received, but I also love those cards, texts, emails and phone calls I get at random times. We all need encouragement to keep walking with Christ. Honestly, sometimes I just don't know what to say to someone. When that happens, I pray and open my Bible to look for a scripture to encourage someone. I know I can't possibly come up with better words than what God has already given us in His Word. I know a lot of people who have faced and are facing very difficult things. I see you. My heart hurts for you. I pray for you. I am amazed at how bravely you carry on with your strong faith. Even though you don't feel like one, (or wear the cape), you are superheroes in my humble opinion. Oh Father, please help me obey those nudges from you to tell these precious ones of yours who are hurting, how much they are loved and prayed for. I want the best for you. God always wants the best for each of us and HE actually knows what that best is! We don't have to wonder about that. We can rest on HIS love for us. He came to earth to reconcile us to HIM. He reached out to us first. Now, let us reach out to each other and encourage each other through this journey of life!

Dress For Success!

Ephesians 6:11-18. "Put on the full armor of God, so that you can stand against the tactics of the Devil. For our battle is not against flesh and blood, but against the rulers, against the authorities, against the world powers of this darkness, against spiritual forces of evil in the heavens. This is why you must take up the full armor of God, so that you may be able to resist in the evil day and having prepared everything, to take your stand. Stand therefore, with truth like a belt around your waist, righteousness like armor on your chest, and your feet sandaled with readiness for the gospel of peace. In every situation take the shield of faith and with it you will be able to extinguish all the flaming arrows of the evil one. Take the helmet of salvation and the sword of the Spirit, which is God's word. Pray at all times in the Spirit with every prayer and request, and stay alert with all perseverance and intercession for all the saints."

These verses are good reminders of how we need to be 'dressed' as we go out into this world daily.

(1) Wear the Belt of Truth... displaying honesty and trustworthiness in your daily life;

(2) Our Breastplate (covering) protecting our hearts against temptations of the evil one, should be the Righteousness of

Jesus so that everyone sees Him not us. (Romans 3:23 When we accept Jesus as our Savior, His Righteousness is imputed to us; we have no righteousness of our own.)

(3) Shoes of peace - Walking in peace and showing the love of God to all we encounter; not allowing bitterness or prejudice to affect our witness that we belong to and represent God.

(4) Shield of faith - Always knowing Who we have our trust in and Who is the trustworthy One, knowing He will not leave us nor forsake us.

(5) Helmet of salvation - protecting our minds against the worlds enticements to sin and trusting God's salvation to help us stay strong.

(6) Sword of the Spirit - The Holy Spirit living within us is our weapon against the evils of this world - always guiding us with the wisdom of God if we listen. The Bible, God's Word is 'sharper than a two-edged sword'.

(7) Praying and always covering our day ahead with prayer for God's direction and guidance so we don't fall.

Paul tells the Ephesian church (and us!) how to dress each morning as we wake and start our day. We'd be wise to heed his instructions and dress accordingly.

Notes: _____

_____

_____

_____

_____

_____

It Is Personal

Read John 4:3-24.

Verse 4. "He had to travel through Samaria."

Verse 4 says "He had to travel through Samaria." Is it possible that Jesus changed his route and went through Samaria to meet up with this Samaritan woman who needed salvation? Would Jesus go out of His way for someone society would consider worthless? Would He do it then? Would He do it now? Sure He will! He left Heaven and went out of His way to go to the cross to provide salvation for us all. He also goes out of His way to reach down and touch us; for us to know Him better; for us to see how very much He loves us. For us to have a relationship with someone, we must get to know each other. He already knows us; all about us because He created us. We must get to know Him to truly enjoy sweet fellowship and worship Him. The better we get to know Him, the deeper and truer we will worship Him. To get to know Him, we must humbly reach up towards Him in faith and He will reach down to us, revealing His great love for us. We cannot choose how He reveals Himself to us. If we could, we would never choose any way as wonderful and amazing as He chooses. His ways are so much higher than ours. When He reaches down to us, it is the sweetest, most tender fellowship ever possible. Lift your heart to Him today. Ask Him to reveal Himself today and watch, expecting to see Jesus! You will see something that you cannot put into words.

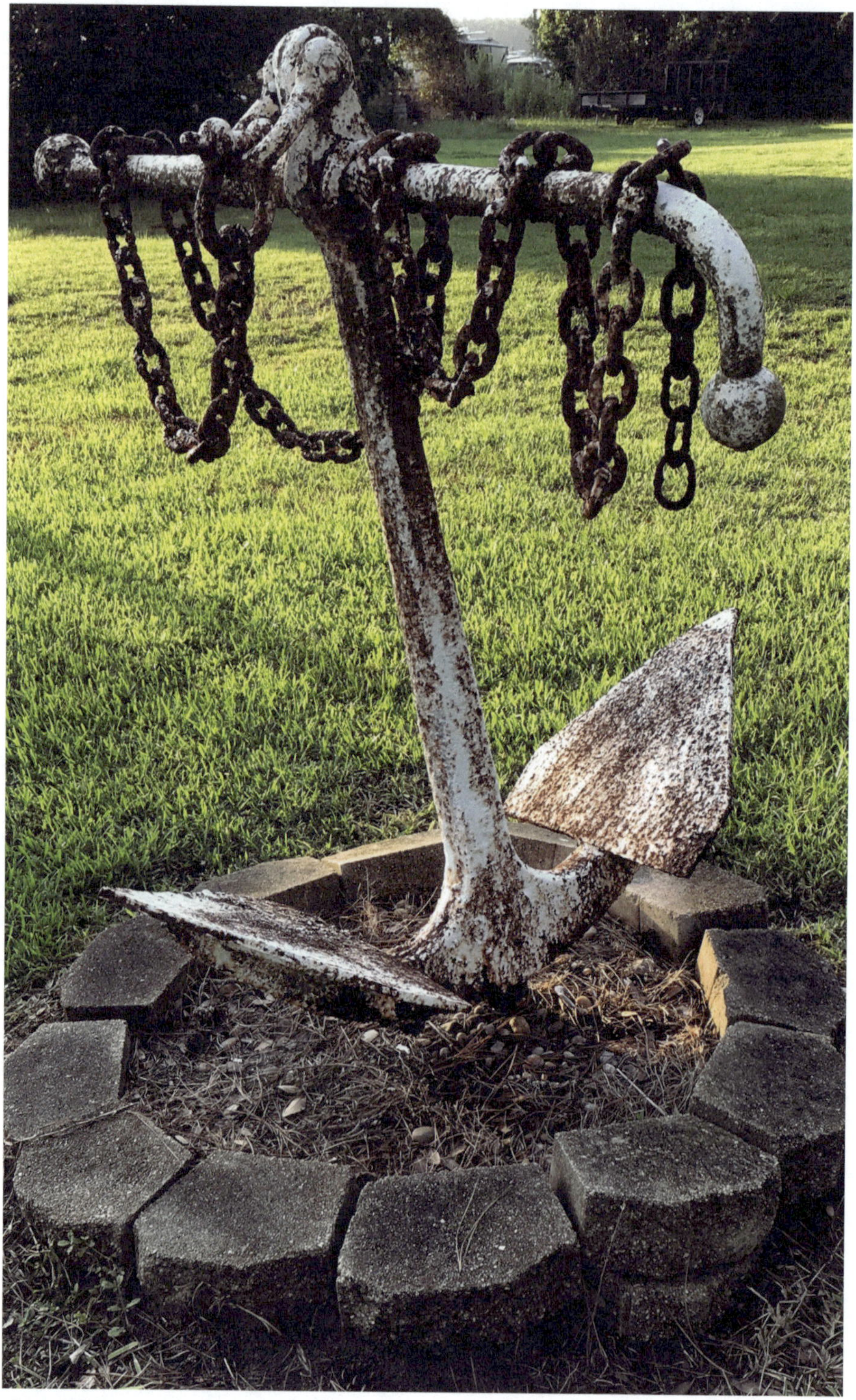

Anchored In Hope

Hebrews 6:19a. "We have this hope as an anchor for our lives, safe and secure."

My late husband gave me an old ship's anchor for our 50th anniversary. It is huge and even though it is over 100 years old, and was lost from a ship and lay on the floor of Mobile Bay for a lot of years, it is still strong and sturdy. I researched a little about it and found that it was purchased by a friend who has a boatyard. He bought it from a shrimper who had pulled it up from the bottom tangled in his shrimp netting. Needless to say, the shrimper was not happy because it had torn his net and caused him trouble. But I love it and was so happy with my gift. It's 'anchoring' my front yard now and every time I see it, I am reminded of its strength and tenacity to hold on through rough waters and adversity. Hope is that Anchor that keeps us close to a protected and safe harbor; the Anchor which keeps us from drifting without direction; the Anchor Who keeps us from being battered by the storms of life. Our Hope is in God our Father, and His Son, Jesus, our Savior. Without Hope, we drift through life aimlessly without direction and purpose. We have nothing to look forward to. Without our Anchor of Hope, we can't truly know the joy that comes with putting our trust in God and yielding our life and future into His hands. Like a giant anchor on a ship, He keeps us from being battered by the winds of life and from being wrecked upon the rocks of life. We still have hardships, pains, hurts and losses, and sometimes our journey takes us through rough seas, but our Anchor stays strong and steady through all these things and keeps us safe.

"We wait for Yahweh; He is our help and shield. For our hearts rejoice in Him because we trust in His holy name. May Your faithful love rest on us, Yahweh, for we put our hope in You" (Psalms 33:20-22).

Notes: _____

_____

_____

_____

_____

_____

_____

_____

Peace With God Produces The Peace Of God

Philippians 4:7. "And the peace of God, which surpasses every thought, will guard your hearts and minds in Christ Jesus."

The peace God can give to us to guarantee the results in this Scripture can only come when we have peace WITH God. We cannot have peace with God unless we come to Him with a humble heart of repentance asking Him to forgive us. Our hearts and our hands need to be open and freely given to Him in gratitude for Jesus' sacrifice for our salvation.

We can't hold onto this world with our hands nor hold back a portion of our heart's dedication. We have to come wanting nothing but Jesus and a living, life-long relationship with Him. God accepts us and adopts us into His family as joint-heirs with His Son and we share in the family inheritance. Only then can we have the peace He gives and peace with Him which produces the result of guarding our hearts and minds as promised in this verse. We miss all this as long as we're at war against God. You may think 'I'm not at war against God!', but you are if you have not accepted His Son, Jesus as your Savior. The choice has to be made. No one comes to the Father, except through the Son. Don't wait...come to Him today, and experience the ultimate peace of God within. You wont regret your decision to trust Him!

He Is Seeking. Am I Hiding?

Genesis 3:9. "So the Lord God called out to the man and said to him, 'Where are you?'"

Luke 19:10. "For the Son of Man has come to seek and to save the lost."

If you read Luke 19:10, you see that God, the Father, sent Jesus, His Son, to seek those who are lost. That includes all of us until we've accepted Jesus' offer of salvation.

In thinking more about this, I realized that from man's creation, God, the Father, has been seeking fellowship with mankind. He deliberately sought a relationship with the first couple, Adam and Eve, and wanted to spend time in fellowship with them (Gen 3:8a 'And they heard the voice of the LORD God walking in the garden in the cool of the day:').

They lived in the Garden He created for them where everything was beautiful and good. Yet, they chose to give in to temptation and risk it all...including fellowship with God, their creator. We can easily see how bad their decision was!

I was convicted to wonder how many times I've done the same thing as they did! (Gen 3:8b..."and Adam and his wife hid themselves from the presence of the Lord God among the trees of the garden."). They damaged the fellowship they had with the Father and we, today, still live with the consequences of that disobedience. And yet, have I really learned what I should have from this lesson? We know sin can cause broken relationships in our daily lives with family and friends, but do I also consider what it does to hurt my Father and His Son? My Creator and My Savior? The Ones Who love me most of all and Who are continually seeking fellowship with me? When I see the Father always seeking and realize the Son is seeking also, it causes me to humble my unworthy self in gratitude that They didn't give up on me! I'm so glad They both still seek, in order to save, those who are lost. That was me! Thank you Father God, and Jesus, for not giving up on me! If you're hiding from God, now is the best time to run back to Him! He loves you and is seeking you today. Don't wait, answer His call today!

Notes: _____

_____

_____

_____

_____

_____

_____

_____

Job: Patient Or Faithful?

Job 1:9. "Satan answered the Lord, 'Does Job fear God for nothing?'"

Have you ever heard someone mention having 'the patience of Job'? I have heard that comment often over the years. But, Scripture never really says Job had unlimited patience through his suffering, does it?

Job's friends came as soon as they heard of his trials and in the first days they were with him, they did a good thing. They sat quietly with him in his suffering and grief and didn't really try to analyze or explain what the problem was. They just sat and sympathized with him in his sorrow and pain. But that eventually gave way to unsolicited advice, and even accusations, judgment, and condemnation, rather than heartfelt sympathy.

Doing a Bible study on the book of Job, opened my eyes to how I probably have sometimes taken the same path as Job's friends. I can be caring and sympathetic but at some point, I might start 'analyzing' the situation with a judgmental attitude and trying to dig into the cause of someone's problems! God says have compassion, show love and judge not! He's the One who has the power and authority to restore or discipline if that's what's needed. My job as a Christian is to represent Him and treat others with love and compassion as He does.

Job's 'unending patience' toward his friends, ended at a point of exasperation and hurt. Job stopped them cold with his declaration, 'Even if He kills me, I will hope in Him.' (Job 13:15). He was strong in His trust in God even though he had no idea why he was going through all the trials. The reason for Job's faith and strength is in verse 9 where God declares Job's perfect integrity and fear of God. Job knew that God was in control and no matter what God allowed to come his way, his God would take care of him. Having the 'patience of Job' would be good, but, having the kind of faith Job had in God, would be even better! Just remember, Jesus said in Matthew 17:20, it's not the amount of our faith that's important, it's Who our faith is in that makes the difference. Job understood that, and his story is presented in the Bible as one of our best examples of how to live our lives in complete trust in God.

Notes: _____

_____

_____

_____

_____

_____

Surrender Of The Will

Luke 22:42. "Father, if You are willing, take this cup away from Me—nevertheless, not My will, but Yours be done."

God has been dealing with me this morning on the question of surrendering my own will to His will. When HE gives me something, I have to write it down or I'll lose it. Maybe that's because I am scatter brained or maybe it's because HE gives me something with the intent that I share it to help someone else too. When HE gives us something, it's not to be wasted.

HE gave His life willingly to love the people HE created. What did that really look like? What should my response to that be? What should your response be?

Most people can easily produce an answer to the question "What did it look like for Jesus to give up His life for us?". What would you answer? The obvious and most likely to be given answer is that Jesus died on the cross for our sins, and that is definitely true. HE died an awful death on the cross for my sins and for yours, but that's not all HE gave up.

Most people in the United States have heard the gospel. (That's no excuse for us not sharing it again and again by the way.) On any Sunday morning, you can turn on the TV and hear the gospel preached for several hours by numerous different preachers. You can turn on the radio to a Christian station any day of the week and hear the gospel in music of various styles. You can also hear some good preachers on Christian radio.

A number of people from my generation grew up in church on Sunday mornings. I'm sad to say the number of people in church on Sunday mornings now seems to have decreased from when I grew up, but that's another devotion. Most hotel rooms and hospital rooms have a Bible in the bedside table drawer. So, why have we missed understanding what all Jesus gave up for us?

Back to my original questions. The first response should be to ask Him for forgiveness of your sins and accept Him as your Savior. We are taught to follow that up with baptism as the outward sign of having accepted Jesus into our hearts. Baptism is the first act of obedience after salvation. That is the correct first response to understanding that HE died on the cross for our sins. But this should only be the beginning of a lifetime of devotion. I'm not sure how many of us (me included) really can grasp how much Jesus gave up when He came to walk on this earth to the cross. Honestly, I am not sure we will ever manage to grasp this side of Heaven just what HE gave up. We can read about Heaven in the Bible, but we can't begin to even imagine what Heaven will be like for ourselves, much less what it was/is like for Jesus.

Jesus had such a close fellowship with the Father and HE gave that up on the cross. Mark 15:34 "And at three Jesus cried out with a loud voice, "Eloi, Eloi, lema sabachthani?" which is translated, "My God, My God, why have You forsaken Me?".

Jesus gave up the splendor of Heaven, while He was here on earth. He came as a baby and walked here for 33 years. We shouldn't take that sacrifice lightly because HE deserves glory, praise, honor and worship, all of which He received in Heaven before He came to earth and He is now receiving in Heaven again. He willingly surrendered that time in Heaven to come rescue the people He created that had rejected Him. That's me and you folks.

Being as Jesus surrendered His will to the Father, in order for me to be saved, can I not possibly surrender wanting my own way, for the few short years I am on earth to bring Him honor? He loves me. He also loves the other 7.888 billion people on the earth just as much as He loves me. I forget that part sometimes when I am being aggravated by one or two of those people over something petty that doesn't amount to anything for eternity. Everything that doesn't amount to importance in eternity, is petty when it compares to what Jesus did for me. So my response to what Jesus did for me should start with worship! Heartfelt worship. The fun part of worship is singing the praise songs to Him in church, but there's way more to worship than that. Obedience to Him is worship. Ouch that was my own toes that I just crushed. Loving the people He created is worship. Sharing His story is worship. Studying His word is worship. And somehow, when I think about all He has done for me, having my own way instead of obeying His will for me doesn't seem so important anymore. I hope I meet you surrendering your will to His somewhere on this earth, as we walk this path of life, but if not, I hope to join with you as we worship Him in Heaven for eternity to come.

Notes: _____

_____

_____

_____

_____

_____

God Is Faithful

Read 1 Corinthians 12:7-11.

Verse 7. "A demonstration of the Spirit is given to each person to produce what is beneficial."

Are you facing something that you are afraid of today? Are you starting a new job? Maybe you are getting married? Are you moving to a new community, or town or state? Or are you beginning a new stage in life—maybe you've lost a spouse, or a child or a parent. Or maybe it's just the beginning of a new year for you and you don't know what it may hold. Honestly, none of us know what tomorrow may bring and it is often scary.

Has God called you to a new task? God calls each of us to something. 1 Corinthians 12:7

A manifestation of the Spirit is given to each person for the common good. You can know for sure God has work for you to do using your God given talent. And, yes, we ALL have some God given talent, even if you are not sure what it is yet.

Does it mean we won't be afraid just because we are starting something HE has called us to do? Absolutely not! Matter of fact, you are in good company if you are afraid. Joshua was called by God to step into Moses' role and lead the Israelites on into the Promised Land. He had been Moses' assistant for a long time, so you might think he had received "training" and wouldn't be afraid. If leading all the people across the Jordan River, and distributing the land to each family wasn't enough, he had to lead them in battle to take their inheritance from the people currently occupying the land! Talk about a scary task! I can certainly understand Joshua feeling overwhelmed and incapable. God said "Haven't I commanded you: be strong and courageous? Do not be afraid or discouraged, for the Lord your God is with you wherever you go." Joshua 1:9. Being strong and courageous wasn't just a suggestion, it was a command! But God gave Joshua exactly what he needed to complete this daunting task—God, Himself going with him! God plus one is always a majority because God alone is a majority! God promised to be with Joshua every step of the way.

God gave Joshua instructions on how to lead the people and do HIS will. Joshua 1:6-8 "Be strong and courageous, for you will distribute the land I swore to their fathers to give them as an inheritance. Above all, be strong and very courageous to carefully observe the whole instruction My servant Moses commanded you. Do not turn from it to the right or the left, so that you will have success wherever you go. This book of instruction must not depart from your mouth; you are to recite it day and night so that you may carefully observe everything written in it. For then you will prosper and succeed in whatever you do."

Just as Moses and Joshua had done, Daniel applied those instructions (verse 8) to his life when he was taken captive to Babylon as a young teen years later. He continued to obey God's commands his entire life into his eighties, even though he was cast into the lion's den for doing so. Daniel believed God could shut the mouths of the lions and guess what?? HE did!! Because of Daniel's obedience, a king was influenced. Those same instructions still apply to us today. The same God who closed the mouths of hungry lions, can guide you as you seek to obey HIM today.

We aren't the first ones to wade into the waters of seeing God is faithful. Hebrews 10:23-25 "Let us hold on to the confession of our hope without wavering, for HE who promised is faithful. And let us be concerned about one another in order to promote love and good works, not staying away from our worship meetings, as some habitually do, but encouraging each other, and all the more as you see the day drawing near." God is faithful! HIS word is true. HE will be with you. Hebrews chapter 11 is full of people who obeyed God and experienced HIS faithfulness. (By the way, that chapter is a good read, especially when you are afraid). Stay on course. Be faithful to what HE has called you to do. Trust God. Take HIM, who is faithful, at HIS word. The proof comes AFTER you believe, not before. But, it DOES come! Heaven is the joyous proof of what we've believed on earth. If God is telling you to jump off the cliff of faith in Him, then run as fast as you can to the edge and leap with both feet! HE will catch you!

Notes: _____

_____

_____

_____

_____

_____

_____

_____

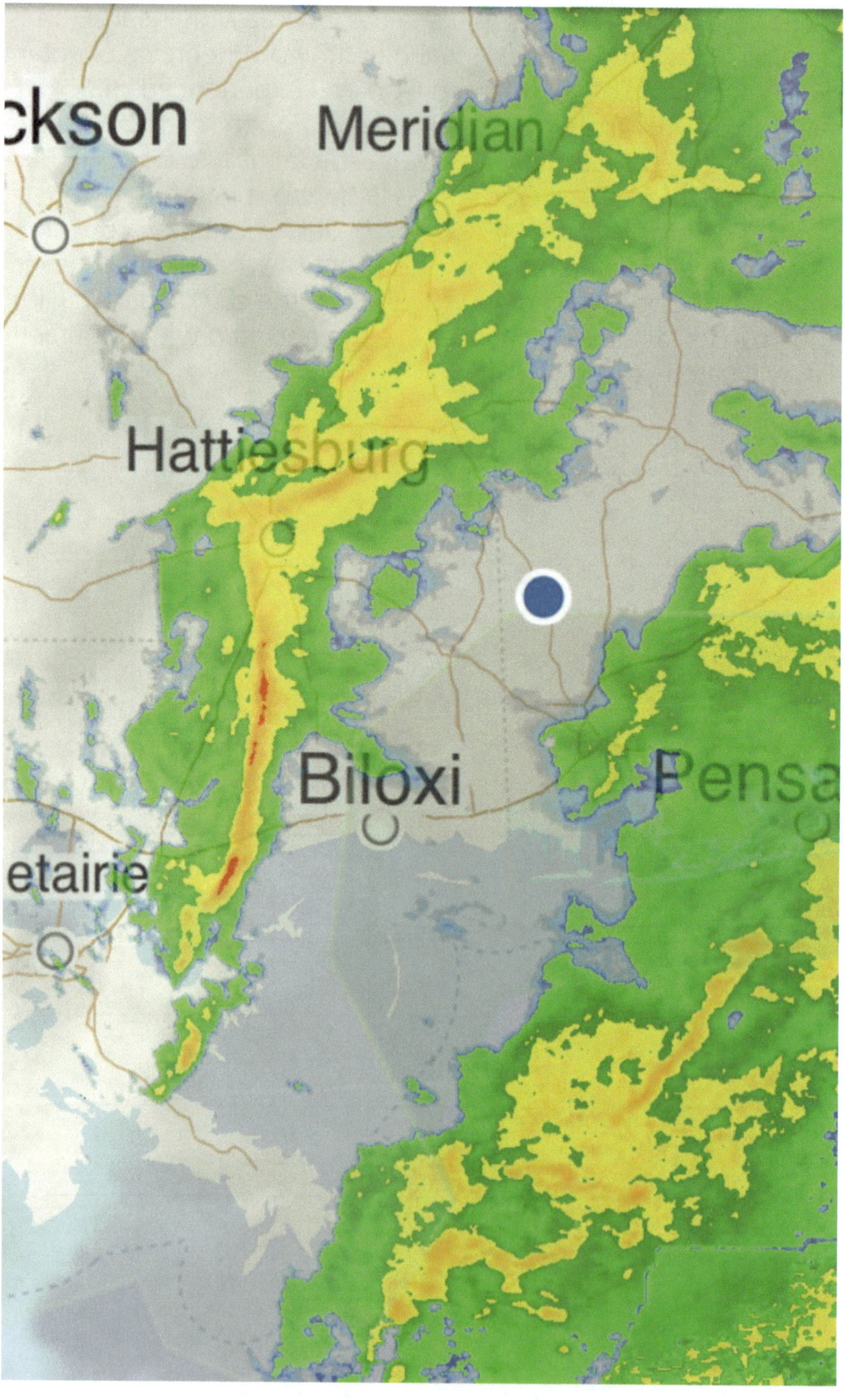
ckson
Meridian
Hattiesburg
Biloxi
Pensa
etairie

Sheltered Through The Storms

Psalm 57:1. "Be gracious to me, God, be gracious to me, for I take refuge in You. I will seek refuge in the shadow of Your wings until danger passes."

Psalm 57:10-11. "For Your faithful love is as high as the heavens; Your faithfulness reaches the clouds. God, be exalted above the heavens; let Your glory be over the whole earth."

My daughter and I had recently planned a trip to coastal Alabama for my birthday weekend. We were leaving after her Friday workday was finished and driving mostly at night. We knew the weather forecast was for rain and sometimes heavy thunderstorms all along our route and most of the weekend. We'd planned this trip and wanted to go in spite of the not so great weather forecasts.

Before we left home, I prayed for a safe trip and asked God to go with us. Then I looked at the radar app on my phone to see what kind of weather to expect ahead. It was night and we couldn't see the sky to have any idea about what we were heading toward.

The screenshot radar photo from my phone showed that indeed rain was on each side of us as we traveled southward, and closed in behind us. It immediately reminded me of the

Angel of the Lord hovering over us and sheltering us with His wings. At first, I didn't mention it to my daughter, but I was so intrigued with what I was seeing on the radar screen that I began to check it more often. To our amazement and delight, as we traveled the 200 miles southward, the radar stayed the same over us. We had a clear path along the highway while the thunderstorms remained behind and on each side of us. As we moved along toward the southeast, so also did the storms, so that we were always in the clear area between the bad weather. We made our trip sheltered in between a lot of heavy rain and stormy weather.

    This was a delightful, eye opening reminder to me that God does care about even the seemingly trivial things in our lives, and that He, who created all the elements of weather, still has control of it all. Plus, He delights in answering our heartfelt prayers and does not want us to be anxious, but wants us to rely on Him for our care. He wants to be involved in every aspect of our lives, and will be, IF we let Him. There's a popular contemporary Christian song that says God 'REALLY' does love us, and it's true, He does. Much more than we can ever begin to imagine. I'm so, so grateful that He loves us and shows us that love continuously. And yes, my birthday weekend was great fun! How could it not be a success when it was so blessed by God!!

Notes: _____

_____

_____

_____

_____

Tell Somebody About It!

Read 2 Peter 1:16-18.

Verse 18. "And we heard this voice when it came from heaven while we were with Him on the holy mountain."

When something exiting or good happens to me, and even when I survive something not so good, I tend to tell others about it. If I experienced it with at least one other person, I discuss it with that person. It strengthens my memories to discuss what I've experienced. If whatever I experienced was positive, it makes me happy again every time I talk about it.

Peter, along with James and John, personally saw Jesus transfigured on the mountain. They also heard the voice of God while they were there. That was pretty awesome if you ask me! They never forgot what they saw and heard. They could not unsee what they had witnessed. I can't even imagine how many times after Jesus ascended back to Heaven, that one of them said to the other two, "Hey do you remember when Jesus took us up on that mountain with Him and we saw Him transfigured?". And the other two would chime in "Yea, I'll never forget that. That was sure something.", as they all three began to have a far away look of memory in their eyes. You just don't ever forget some things. And nobody, not anybody, can ever convince you that it didn't happen. You are permanently changed for the better.

That's what Peter is writing to these Christians about. Clearly these intended readers have heard this story before, but Peter knows his time left on earth is short and he doesn't want them to forget what he's told them. Jesus is real and He's alive!

Peter felt an urgent need to remind them of what he had told them. And honestly, Peter probably enjoyed telling this story again. He enjoyed the memories of his time with Christ. Don't you enjoy feeling HIS Presence yourself? Don't we all enjoy remembering the miraculous things HE has done for us? And HE's done things for all of us, at least for those of us who are saved.

Tell others about the things you have witnessed. Tell what HE's done for you personally. When you have an experience with Jesus, you will never be the same, just like those disciples from long ago. Nobody can ever convince you that Jesus is not who HE says HE is! I know nobody can ever convince me that HE's not my Savior!

Notes: _____

_____

_____

_____

_____

_____

_____

Building Only With The Spirit's Strength

Read Zechariah 4:1-14.

Verses 6-7. "So he answered me, 'This is the word of the Lord to Zerubbabel: 'Not by strength or by might, but by My Spirit, says the Lord of Hosts: What are you, great mountain? Before Zerubbabel you will become a plain. And he will bring out the capstone accompanied by shouts of: Grace, grace to it!'"

In this scripture, the Jews were trying to rebuild the Temple. It was a noble but seemingly impossible task. And, honestly, without God's help, it was impossible. They faced a lot of opposition and were just plain downtrodden.

Have you ever been there? Do you ever feel overwhelmed? What impossible situation are you facing? I don't know about you, but I face lots of things that I can't accomplish, deal with, do, fix, or handle. There are lots of little things that I might can work towards fixing... burnt toast, bicycle tires that go flat, garbage that spills out of the can, flowers that need water, you know, the small things. But what do we do with the big things? My child's learning disability or their struggle to make friends at school. Those times when there is more month left than money for groceries. Or when I lose my job altogether. What about when the doctor shakes his head sadly, as he tells your loved one there is nothing else he can do and the end is near? How do you survive burying your loved one? And the biggest one, convincing a lost loved one that Jesus is the answer. Those are the mountains that you can't climb alone I haven't faced everything listed here but I can tell you that I have faced several of those things. Those are the things that completely drain every ounce of strength out of you when just trying to think about what you are going to do. I can tell you that you don't survive those types of things without Jesus. Those are the things that will send you to your knees. When we come to those things that make us realize we are completely helpless, the ones that knock the breath completely out of us, we find help in the only One who can truly give help.

On your knees is where you get your strength renewed. Oh friend, on your knees at the throne is where HE provides the answers you so desperately need. It's there that HE says, "Not by your strength or your might, but by My Spirit." It's there that you surrender your will to HIS way. It's on your knees that you realize you are not alone. You can't flatten the mountain in front of you, but oh, I know the one who can move that mountain or help you climb it! The task of rebuilding the Temple overwhelmed Zerubbabel just like some of the things we face today. We may not understand what he faced but we know how he felt. Why? Because most of us have been there over something. Let the same God who comforted and strengthened Zerubbabel, comfort and strengthen you. He is just as strong now as HE was then. When I rest in His strength, I find His peace.

Notes: _____

_____

_____

In The Twinkling of An Eye

1 Corinthians 15:51-52. "Listen! I am telling you a mystery: We will not all fall asleep, but we will all be changed, in a moment, in the blink of an eye, at the last trumpet. For the trumpet will sound, and the dead will be raised incorruptible, and we will all be changed."

I miss a lot of sunrises. Even though I'm up at sunrise more days than not, I don't often get to watch. I'm usually getting ready for my day.

Today is different. Today my husband and I are traveling a little over two hours away to get some roofing material for our home. Today is Saturday and although I enjoy my husband's company, neither of us really wanted to get up and leave home at 6:00 am, in the dark. This time of year, 6:00 am is before sunrise.

As I was riding along in the dark, waiting on the sun to rise, I admit I was feeling a little sorry for myself about having to be up and dressed so early on a Saturday. But then my thoughts began to change. I began to silently thank God for another day. I thought about how many people did not get this day to rise.

Now, the sunrise takes a few minutes. It's beautiful and kind of one of those things that slowly sneaks up on you. While you watch one spot (the sun) daylight slowly creeps across the sky. The sky changes colors from black, to dark blue with orange, to the blue of a day time sky. This whole process takes time. It's not instant. Though we live in an instant world of microwaves and finger snap answers on the Internet, the process of the sun rising still invites us to take a few deep breaths and enjoy a few minutes of watching another one of God's miracles take place. I do not often get this privilege in my rushed life. The sunset also takes a few minutes. It is not rushed or hurried no matter where we need to be or what we need to do.

As we rode along and I watched, I thought of something. When Jesus comes back, it won't be this way. I won't just carry on with the day to day activities. I also won't just sit back and watch while I enjoy a cup of coffee. No matter where I am or what I'm doing, I won't miss it! Whether I'm dead or still here on earth, it will take place in an instant. If I am still on earth, my body will change in the twinkling of an eye! Faster than an Internet response. I know I won't miss Jesus coming back because I am saved. I'm going to hear the trumpet sound. This old body is going to be changed to one that won't decay. As beautiful as the sunrise was, I know that day is going to be even better!! The next time you watch the sunrise, remember there's coming a day that we will see THE SON in the sky! That will be worth being up for any time.

Notes: _____

_____

_____

_____

_____

Rest Easy

Psalm 139:16. "Your eyes saw me when I was formless; all my days were written in Your book and planned before a single one of them began."

I am a planner by nature. I think that might be because I want to know everything before it happens. I am a "be prepared" kind of person. If I know what is going to happen before it happens, my mind somehow thinks I can be ready to handle it. That's simply not true. I can't know much of anything really that is actually for sure going to happen. Sometimes I think I do, with all my planning. Often, things don't turn out like I had planned or even like I (gulp) had worried that they would. That's because I can't see the future nor can I control it.

Could my need to know what's going to happen be a lack of faith on my part? It sure has some characteristics of a lack of faith.

Verse 16 says "all my days were written in Your book and planned before a single one of them began." That means God planned my life before I was thought of on earth.

If God planned my entire life before I was born and HE knows what is going to happen before it takes place, why should I worry about anything? Psalm 139:5 says "You have encircled me; You have placed Your hand on me." God is so good to me. HE has encircled me. HE is protecting me. HE will be with me, and HE knows what is going to happen in advance. Who could better protect you than God? There is nobody more qualified than HE is. Rest easy encircled in His great love!

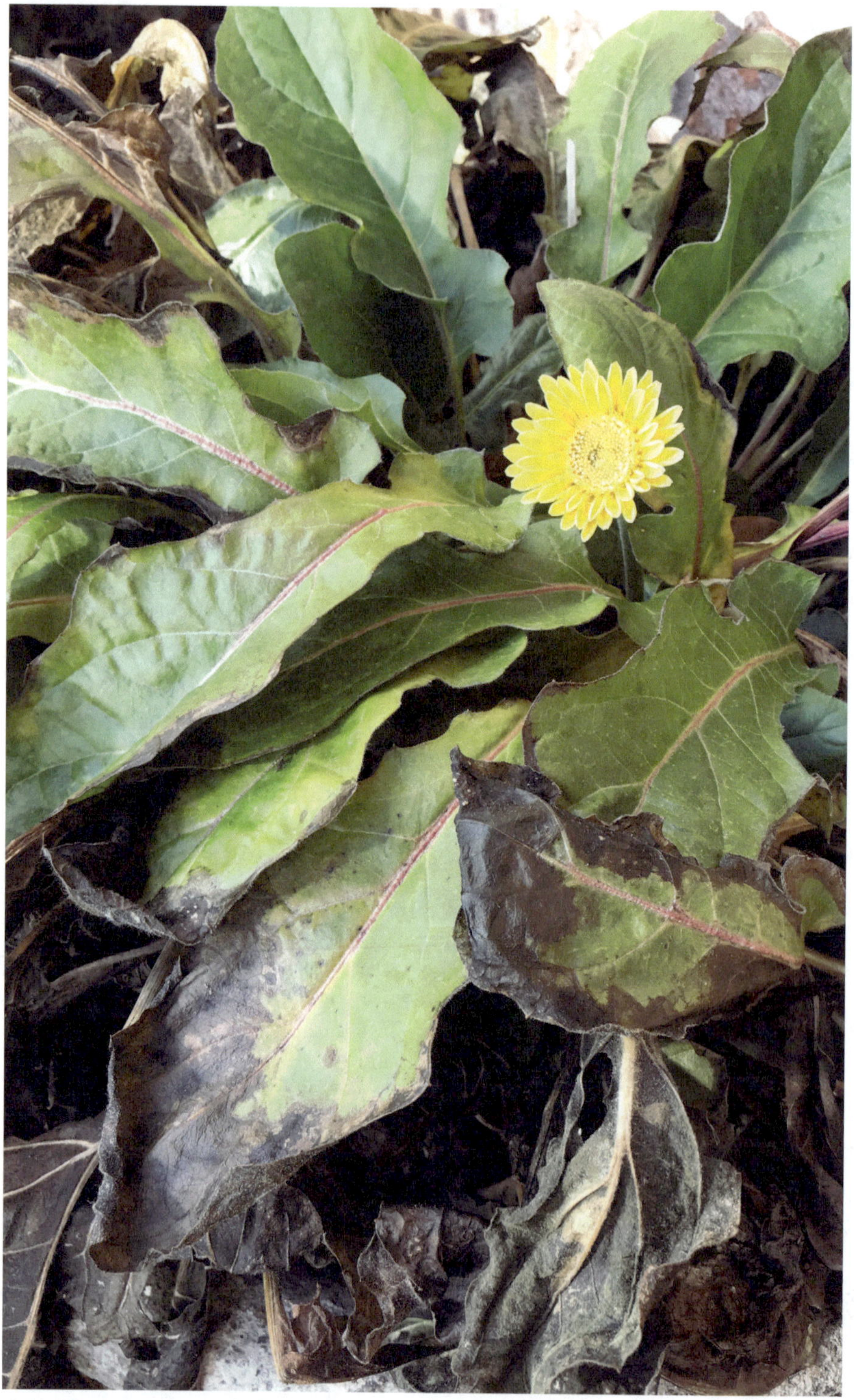

Overcomer!

1 John 5:4. "...because whatever has been born of God conquers the world. This is the victory that has conquered the world: our faith."

In two large concrete planters on my front sidewalk, I have Gerbera daisies planted. They've survived there through the winters and summers for over five years now. During a recent January cold spell, I wasn't sure they were going to make it. We had several days of very cold weather with single digit temps overnight. I covered them in hopes that I wouldn't lose them. The picture shows the damage done by the frigid cold, though, and I was already thinking about visiting the garden center in spring to get new plants. It was rainy for a few days and I didn't look at them, until one day to my surprise, I saw a new stem with a bud and then this bloom opened in a couple more days.

God used this new growth from the old, dead leaves, to remind me that we're not finished here until He's finished with us. Even when we've been left with great damage from the harshness of this cold, hard world, He still can bring renewal and cause us to reflect His glory. All He has to do is touch us with His light to bring out our usefulness again. He shines His love on us and if we're His children, we respond to the warmth of His grace and mercy and bear fruit as we are meant to do. Never give up on yourself even when you've been damaged by the cares of daily life in this broken world. Our God specializes in healing, restoration and coaxing the beauty hidden deep within us to bloom once again. He's the Creator, Sustainer and Master Gardner.

'And why do you worry about clothes? Learn how the wildflowers of the field grow; they don't labor or spin thread. Yet I tell you that not even Solomon in all his splendor was adorned like one of these!' Matthew 6:28-29. He's not finished with you yet my friend. Bloom on!

Notes: _____

_____

_____

_____

_____

_____

_____

_____

I'm Wanting To Go Fishing

Matthew 4:18-20. "As He was walking along the Sea of Galilee, He saw two brothers, Simon, who was called Peter, and his brother Andrew. They were casting a net into the sea, since they were fisherman. 'Follow Me,' He told them, and I will make you fish for people.' Immediately they left their nets and followed him."

I love to cast a rod and reel in hopes of catching a fish. Honestly I enjoy doing that even on a sunny day when nothing bites. Sometimes, just fishing without catching anything, is enough to make me happy.

Today is one of those teaser days in February where the temperature is predicted to be 70 degrees. I hear the birds singing this morning. I imagine they are about as happy to have a nice day as I am. While the birds will probably be out looking for worms, I will be stuck inside today at work. Although I'm very thankful to have my job, while the birds were singing, I thought "I'm ready to go fishing," Thoughts of fishing causes a smile to slowly spread across my face. You can ease inside any bait and tackle store on the Gulf Coast to watch fishermen of all abilities drool over new lures, reels, rods, tackle boxes and nets. We love to look at all the latest and greatest equipment to catch the elusive fish.

The thought of fishing led to another thought. I should be fishing every day, but for people not fish. Jesus calls us all to different things but one thing he calls us all to do is fish! Now, before you take that as an excuse to miss work on a sunny day to take a pole and bucket of worms to the lake, let me explain. As Christians, fishing for opportunities to tell people about Jesus should always be on the top of our minds. Our relationship with Jesus is the most important one we will ever have. Yet, there are still so many people, even in the US, who have not heard the gospel. You are probably wondering how that is possible, with so many churches available to be viewed on TV and social media. The thing is, the best way to reach people is still one by one. People still tend to listen to the story of what Jesus can do for them when it's discussed by someone who's telling them individually what HE has already done for them. Let's all be sure we never miss an opportunity to go fishing!

Notes: _____

_____

_____

_____

_____

_____

Waiting For God

Psalm 37:7-9. "Be silent before the Lord and wait expectantly for Him; do not be agitated by one who prospers in his way, by the man who carries out evil plans. Refrain from anger and give up your rage; do not be agitated - it can only bring harm. For evildoers will be destroyed, but those who put their hope in the Lord will inherit the land."

How can you be content with the struggles of this world? How can you be content when you've buried someone you love dearly? How can you be content when you are unhappy at work, where you live or in your current financial status? How can you be content when you are angry about something in your life right now?

In Philippians 4:11, Paul tells us that he has learned how to be content in whatever circumstance he is in. Paul was in jail for preaching the gospel when he wrote Philippians. How was he content in jail? How was he not angry and agitated? Paul waited on God. Psalm 37:7 says to wait EXPECTANTLY on God. (Emphasis on expectantly is mine.).

Waiting is hard. Nobody likes to wait. We live in a fast paced world where nobody has to wait anymore. We have fast food that we can pick up without getting out of our car. If we have to wait more than five minutes in the drive through line, we fuss about it. We have microwave ovens to heat our food or drink in a matter of seconds. We surf the Internet and get responses in a matter of seconds. We have "instant" messaging that allows us to communicate with someone in another state in less than a second. We are a people that have lost our ability to wait patiently for almost anything. I include myself in that group. Even our photography is instant now. Gone are the days of making a picture and having to wait a week for the film to be developed to see how it turned out. As a people, we have mostly lost the ability to wait, but Psalm 37:7 says to wait expectantly on God. Those of us who are older, will have to relearn how to wait, but for some of you, learning to wait is a first time experience. How do we learn to do that?

When you compare waiting with waiting on God, it feels incredibly different! Waiting on the results of a medical test is stressful, because you don't know if the outcome will be good or bad. When you are waiting on God to work, you know HE will do what is best. When we are praying and waiting on God to do something, we wait with expectation. We can be thankful for what He's going to do BEFORE He does it. Colossians 4:2 gives us instructions on praying for something. "Devote yourselves to prayer; stay alert in it with thanksgiving.". A good example of being thankful for God's answer before it took place can be seen in 2 Chronicles 20:17-19. We see Jehoshaphat and the Levites bow in worship as a response to what they have been told God is going to do. Their worship was based on the fact that when God said HE was going to act, it was as good as done! That is waiting expectantly on God. We know HE knows the outcome of a situation before we start. When we don't know the outcome of our circumstances, isn't it comforting to know the One who does know the outcome? HE loves us with an everlasting love. We can turn to Him in prayer while we wait on Him.

He knows our hurts, frustrations, fears and pain. We can be honest with the One who hung the stars because HE can see inside our hearts too. We can worship Him during this time of waiting. Worship is one of the best things to bring us comfort. We can worship during the pain. Worship is not something you do just when everything in your world is happy and feels right. Worship during pain and suffering is a choice to obey, and it is some of the best worship we can do. Worship done during the waiting produces trust in God. It exhibits the choice to have faith. So, pray honestly and openly to God while you wait. Study scripture. Psalms has some great verses prayed to God during trials and it's okay to borrow those prayers in the scripture. Sing to God. He loves to hear our praise and it will lift your heart. Thank Him for everything you can. There's always something we can be thankful for. Doing these things takes our focus off of our problems and puts it where it needs to be—on Him!

Notes: _____

Ministry Is Personal

2 Corinthians 1:4-5. "He comforts us in all our affliction, so that we may be able to comfort those who are in any kind of affliction, through the comfort we ourselves receive from God. For as the sufferings of Christ overflow to us, so through Christ our comfort also overflows."

Most pastors live in the community near the church they serve. God puts some pastors in churches close to where they already live and others He calls to relocate to a new community, state, or even country to serve the people in a particular church. We see that with missionaries also. It's very difficult to serve a group of people without being involved in their lives on a weekly or some type of regular basis. Luke 2:8 "In the same region, shepherds were staying out in the fields and keeping watch at night over their flock". The shepherds live with the sheep. The sheep see the Shepherds daily. They know their voice and what they like to do. Moses had to leave Midian and go back to Egypt to lead God's people out of Egypt. Moses traveled with the people and lived amongst the people all the way to the Promised Land. The people would have known Moses well. They would have seen the flaws that Moses had. He shared his life with the people. It was personal.

Let us never forget, that Jesus gave up being in Heaven to walk this earth and go to the cross for our sins. HE gave His life to save you and me. There is nothing more personal than that.

Before we decide this is written for pastors and quit reading, let's remember that we all have a calling or a ministry of some sort. 1 Corinthians 12: 4-7 says "Now there are different gifts, but the same Spirit. There are different ministries, but the same Lord. And there are different activities, but the same God activates each gift in each person. A demonstration of the Spirit is given to each person to produce what is beneficial:". Uh oh... that sounds like we all have a ministry of some kind to do. We all have to serve. We each have a God given gift or talent that is needed in the church. You may serve by teaching, singing, keeping the nursery, greeting people as they come in the door, or you may serve in a more quiet way. You may be the one who reaches out to encourage people one on one, away from the church building. You may send cards, or you might call or text. Today, there are many ways to reach out to people with a little encouragement. You may be the one people count on to pray. There are many types of ministry but they all have one thing in common. It's personal. You have to interact with people in some way to minister to them.

When God comforts us while we are going through a trial of some kind, it's so we can share that comfort with someone else. It helps us to hear from somebody who knows how we feel, and the only people who can know how we feel during a trial, are the ones who have experienced the same type of trial. That makes the comfort we receive personal. That type of comfort touches our hearts in a way that someone who hasn't experienced the same thing can't possibly do.

We have all faced trials in our lives. If we turned to God for comfort, HE gives it to us. Then, whether we think we are or not, we are qualified to share that comfort with someone else who is struggling. When we reach out to comfort another person who is hurting, we share part of our heart, and that is personal.

How many of us have a favorite teacher that we remember from growing up? Maybe you have fond memories of someone who took you fishing as a teenager, or taught you to crochet. Maybe you remember a particular Sunday School teacher that taught you about Jesus. These people shared something personal. All throughout our lives, there are people who pour into us somehow, even after we are grown.

    We need to use the abilities God has given us to pour into others also. It can be done in many ways. Sometimes just smiling at a stranger in the check out line changes the tone of their day. If you are saved, Jesus lives inside of you. I encourage you (and me) to listen to the nudge of the Holy Spirit to share the comfort you have received. Sometimes it may be painful to share in another's hurt. Remember, God comforts us, so we can comfort others. If you have been through a painful trial, let it bring you comfort to know that the pain can be used for a purpose. Then, minister to someone else. What Jesus did for us was personal, and our ministry should be also.

Notes: _____

_____

_____

_____

_____

_____

_____

God Gave Everybody A Story

Joshua 4:1, 4-7. "After the entire nation had finished crossing the Jordan, the Lord spoke to Joshua. So Joshua summoned the twelve men he had selected from the Israelites, one man for each tribe, and said to them, 'Go across to the ark of the Lord your God in the middle of the Jordan. Each of you lift a stone onto his shoulder, one for each of the Israelite tribes, so that this will be a sign among you. In the future, when your children ask you, 'What do these stones mean to you?' you should tell them, 'The waters of the Jordan were cut off in front of the ark of the Lord's covenant. When it crossed the Jordan, the Jordan's waters were cut off.' Therefore these stones will always be a memorial for the Israelites."

For further study read Joshua 3 and 4

Have you ever noticed that everybody alive has a story? Before you laugh, I mean really, we all have a story of something that has happened to us. For those of us who are saved, we can't deny having a story. Joshua 4:1 says the entire nation crossed the Jordan. The Jordan river was at flood stage when this took place. God gave Joshua specific instructions on how to cross this river. Those instructions might have seemed a little strange at first... have the priests carry the ark of the Covenant and go stand in the water and the water will be cut off. Rivers don't have a faucet that you can just turn the water on and off, at least none that I've ever heard about. Yet, God told Joshua the waters would stop flowing. Can't you just hear the chatter amongst the Israelites before the priests stepped into the water? "Do you really think that water's going to stop flowing when the priests step foot in it?" Now, when God tells you something, you can count on it being so. Joshua obeyed God, and the Jordan river did stop flowing. It happened just as God said it would. It must have been absolutely amazing to see. I imagine the chatter amongst the Israelites was very different after they crossed than before. I bet they couldn't stop talking about what they had just experienced. And that's what God intended. HE didn't want them to ever forget what happened. HE didn't want them to stop talking about what HE had done for them. HE knew they would if they didn't have something to remind them. So HE instructed Joshua to have 12 men carry 12 stones from the middle of the Jordan river. I'm sure the priests questioned Joshua's sanity when he sent 12 men back into the Jordan to get those stones. But God had a great purpose for those stones.

Because children are naturally curious, God knew they would ask how those 12 river rocks came to be stacked on the bank instead of in the river. And that would provoke the parents to tell the children what God had done for them. That was a fool proof plan for the children to hear about the Lord.

What about us? If you are saved, God has worked a miracle in you. Actually, I feel sure, if you admit it, HE has worked more than one for you. We like to make pictures of our children as they grow up, so that we can reminisce about their childhood. As they grow up, and things happen, do we teach them that the time they almost got bit by a snake, but didn't, was because God protected them. Do we acknowledge His act of mercy when we walked away from the car accident unscathed? What about the time there was more month left than money and we still had bills? Do we write these events down somewhere so that we can be reminded of all the many blessings and miracles

HE has so graciously provided? The stack of river rocks was more than just something pretty to look at. It was proof of what God had done and a way to be sure the next generation would hear about the miracle God had done.

I pray we all keep records of the blessings that God gives us as we go through life, and that we use these records to teach the next generation (and anybody else who will listen to us) about how great our God is. God has so graciously given all of us a story (or two or three or four....). We must not waste these experiences. We have the example from Joshua to share our story, and all of these stories are really HIStory.

Notes: _____

_____

_____

_____

_____

_____

Safely Anchored In The Living Hope

1 Peter 1:3. "Praise the God and Father of our Lord Jesus Christ. According to His great mercy, He has given us a new birth into a living hope, through the resurrection of Jesus Christ from the dead."

When a dangerous hurricane is predicted along the Alabama coast, where I spend some of my time, you will find that most shrimp and fishing boats are moved up river and securely anchored in a safe harbor. The natural bends and curves of the river make for protected places where their boats will ride out the storm and hopefully avoid damage. These professional fishermen know where to go for protection from the wind and waves when storms roll in.

Sometimes in life, like the wise fishermen, about all you can do is flee to a quiet, secluded cove and put down your anchor to wait out the storm. Our scripture comes from Peter, a serious fisherman…one who made his living on his boat. Peter, along with his brother Andrew, were the first disciples Jesus called to 'Follow Me'. They were seasoned fishermen who knew what hard work was. Yet, they also knew what a safe harbor to anchor in could mean when the sea was stormy and the waves were overtaking them.

I often think that Jesus must have felt a special love for fishermen. Four of His disciples were called out of that rough life. They must have all felt a deep security in Jesus when He said 'Follow Me', because that's exactly what they did. I think they recognized that trusting Jesus meant anchoring their lives in the safest harbor of all. Peter's verse says we can have a 'Living Hope through the resurrection of Jesus from death'. Jesus is our Safe Harbor to Anchor our Hope in for eternity. Just think! One day, if we do that, we'll get to be there with God, our Father, and Jesus, our Savior, but also with 'ole walk-on-water-Peter', and the other fishermen called by Jesus to fish for a bigger catch...the souls of men. I wonder if we'll hear some of their 'biggest catch' stories? The stories that count will be stories of souls who were reached for God by His fishers of men! How exciting it will be to hear Peter and the other disciples telling of their catches!

Notes: _____

_____

_____

_____

_____

_____

A True Family Legacy

Deuteronomy 6:4-9. "Listen, Israel: The Lord our God, the Lord is One. Love the Lord your God, with all your heart, with all your soul, and with all your strength. These words that I am giving you today are to be in your heart. Repeat them to your children. Talk about them when you sit in your house and when you walk along the road, when you lie down and when you get up. Bind them as a sign on your hand and let them be a symbol on our forehead. Write them on the doorposts of your house and on your gates."

How did the Israelite children know to follow God down through the generations?

We have this tradition in our family about Christmas Eve. It starts at midnight on Christmas Eve. If you see, call or text someone else in the family, you start off by saying "Christmas Eve Gift.". Whoever can say it first, causes the other person to "owe" them a gift. Now, we don't take the gifting part real serious but the competition to say it first is fierce. It's not just in my immediate family either. It goes to extended cousins, aunts and uncles because I know it went back at least as far as my great-great-grandmother. I really think it went way farther back than that. It's a fun way we celebrate Christmas and being family. It's one of the ways we honor our ancestors and remember them. We have continued to pass this down to all living generations, including anyone married into our family.

That's fun, but what else are we teaching our descendants? Another thing that our ancestors passed down to their descendants was their faith in God. Now, I'm not saying you can inherit salvation from your ancestors, nor am I saying that every one of their descendants were saved. That is simply not true. We must all chose to accept Jesus individually, but they DID make it a priority to teach their children, who taught their children, who taught theirs and on down. We do have a large number of family members who are saved, and a fairly high number who serve as pastors, missionaries, Sunday School teachers, music ministers, and in other capacities at church. I know my Christian ancestors did not live to see the birth of all of their descendants who are living for Jesus now. Will the descendants we have living in 70 years (if Jesus doesn't come back sooner), be saved? Honestly, that is not a question that any of us can answer, but we can look at what God told the Israelites about how to teach their children about Him. I think the instructions still apply to us today.

God instructed them to love the Lord your God with all your heart, with all your soul and with all your strength. We are to love Him with everything we are. We are to read and study the Bible so much that it is soaked into our beings through and through. It is to be in our hearts and on our minds constantly. We tend to talk about what is on our minds and in our hearts, so if the scriptures are there, we will talk about them a lot. Deuteronomy 6:7 says to repeat the words that Moses gave them to their children. Our children watch us constantly and imitate us more than we can imagine... sometimes in ways that we would prefer them not to. That's why it is so important to have the scriptures soaked into our hearts, because what's in the heart comes out of the mouth usually.

We see a number of examples in the Bible of people whose faith stood the test of time and trial. Let's take a look at Enoch. Genesis 5:24 says that Enoch walked with God and then he was not there because God took him. That sounds like a pretty close relationship to me. If you keep reading in chapter 5 on down through several generations into verse 31, we find Noah being born. I'm sure you remember the story of how Noah stood against the evil on the earth with only his wife and sons standing with him. His father and ancestors were no longer living at this time. Apparently, Enoch stressed the importance of walking with God to his children, who taught their children, down through the generations to Noah.

Even though it only takes a few minutes to read chapter 5, a lot of years and several generations passed by in those few sentences.

Let's look at Moses. He was adopted as a baby by Pharoah's daughter, who paid his birth mother to nurse him until he was weaned. His parents obviously made the most of those few years they had with him in their home, because when he was grown he chose to stand with his people rather than enjoy the riches of Egypt. We know that Moses made a few mistakes, but overall he got it right.

Although there are many examples in the pages of scripture, the next one I want to mention is Daniel. Daniel was 15 years old when he was taken captive to Babylon, given a pagan name, and forced to serve in the king's court after 3 years of culture and language training. Yet, even through all of that, he held onto and lived his faith. Daniel was in his 80s when he was thrown into the lion's den for his determination to pray to God. Even then, his faith was strong enough to influence the king that he served.

There are many, many other examples in the scriptures of people whose faith was a priority they lived by in everything they did. It wasn't just on the sabbath. It was so ingrained into everything they did. As they ate, as they walked along the road and in their homes. What about us today? Does our faith drip out of our pores like sweat as we spend time with our children? Do we think about what our children will remember and teach theirs? Chances are at least some of us will have an opportunity to influence our grandchildren and maybe even our great grandchildren, but what about the generations to come? Oh, parents, grandparents and great-grandparents, don't under estimate the opportunity you have to influence not only the next generation but the generations to come after that. What you do and say matters! Make those opportunities to bring Jesus into your conversations with those little and big ones.

You have way more influence on the generations to come than you can imagine! Think about the joy of worshiping Jesus in Heaven together with all of our ancestors and descendants! What a glorious day that will be!

Notes: _____

Foggy Night

Psalm 16:5, 11. "Lord, You are my portion and my cup of blessing; You hold my future. You reveal the path of life to me; in Your presence is abundant joy; in Your right hand are eternal pleasures."

Last night my husband and I left home about 6:15pm, headed to Gulf Shores, Alabama. Typically, it is still dusk dark this time of year, but due to heavy fog, it was completely dark. Visibility was extremely low. Quite frankly, you could barely see where you were going. As it got later into the night, it became harder and harder to see. We travel this way fairly regularly and are familiar with the road, but most of the way down, it was hard to actually SEE the road. I knew the road was there or I thought the road was there, but you couldn't actually see very much of the road at a time. I had good headlights. I had a good vehicle. I had the equipment I needed, but there was still no guarantee of seeing much of the road at a time. The fog was just too thick. The only way to see the next patch of the road, was to keep moving forward.

    Sometimes life is like that too. Actually, it's probably more the norm not to be able to see very far in life, we just don't always realize it. We think we know what is coming next, but we really don't. We can't see past the minute we are in. We get up and get dressed to face the day. We make our plans. We purchase the gift for the birthday party next weekend, only to get up with the stomach virus the day of the party. We make a reservation for the ski trip, and then twist our ankle. We get a cast instead of skis. We get up planning to clean the house this afternoon, but go to the hospital for the birth of our grand-baby instead. We prepare for the next day, the next week, the next month, and often the next year, only to have circumstances beyond our control cause those plans to go down the drain with last night's dishwater.

It's easy to become disappointed when things don't go like we've planned. Often our plans do become reality, but don't let that fool you into thinking you know what the future holds. We don't. We can't see the future any more than I could see the road ahead through the thick fog. So, where's the comfort in all of this? We are not left to just navigate alone through the thick fog of life. God holds our future in the palm of His hand. Even though we can't see the future, HE can. HE knows what the path ahead is like. HE knows the road we are traveling. We know if we keep walking forward with Him, HE will light up the path of life for us as we need to see it. We did eventually see the entire road we traveled, just not all at one time. We saw each inch of the roadway but only as we moved forward in faith that our headlights would continue to light the path ahead. We didn't see as much of the road at a time as we expected last night, but our headlights did reveal what was right in front of us through the entire trip. Sometimes it was scary and I did get weary before we arrived. Sometimes my progress was slower than others, but I kept pressing forward and we did safely arrive at our destination, despite the fog. For those of us who are saved, God will lead us through the thick fog of life to the safe destination of Heaven. We just have to exercise the faith that HE will continue to reveal each step of the path as we move forward with Him.

Notes: _____

_____

_____

A Good, Good Father

Psalm 103:13. "As a father has compassion on his children, so the Lord has compassion on those who fear him."

Proverbs 22:6. "Teach a youth about the way he should go; even when he is old he will not depart from it."

Ephesians 6:4. "Fathers, don't stir up anger in your children, but bring them up in the training and instruction of the Lord."

Hebrews 12:7. "Endure suffering as a discipline: God is dealing with you as sons. For what son is there that a father does not discipline?"

Psalm 86:15. "But you, Lord, are a compassionate and gracious God, slow to anger, and rich in faithful love and truth."

Isaiah 54:10. "'Though the mountains move and the hills shake, My love will not be removed from you and My covenant of peace will not be shaken,' says your compassionate Lord."

2 Corinthians 6:18. "And I will be a Father to you, and you will be sons and daughters to Me,' says the LORD Almighty."

God has the ultimate Father's heart. His heart is full of love for His children. To know Him is to know His perfect love. He loved us first, even before we knew and loved Him. He loved us so much that He gave His only Son as the ultimate sacrifice so that we, undeserving sinners, can be adopted into His family as one of His children. If we accept His offer of salvation, we become heirs to His estate in Heaven. There, we can feel His unconditional love forever. He instructs and disciplines us adopted children out of His everlasting love for us - not out of anger but for our own benefit. He doesn't want to see us stray off into a sinful lifestyle and suffer the consequences that come with sin. All we have to do is believe in Him, accept His Son as our Savior, and trust His guidance and Will for our earthly lives and we have a guaranteed eternity with Him and Jesus in Heaven. He places a Peace within us that cannot be explained while we wait to be with Him in Heaven. It's such a simple plan and yet so many don't accept His invitation. Life here is so short and eternity is forever...don't miss out on being with your good, good Father!

Notes: _____

_____

_____

_____

_____

No Equal To God

Isaiah 40:25-26. "'Who will you compare Me to, or who is My equal?' asks the Holy One. 'Look up and see: who created these? He brings out the starry host by number; He calls all of them by name. Because of His great power and strength, not one of them is missing.'"

Even though I spend most of my days inside working at a desk job, there are some things outside that I really enjoy.

One thing I love is to look up at the stars on a clear night. The stars are so beautiful and the night sky seems to have an endless depth to it. I look up at those stars and wonder what God sees from the other side. This has become especially meaningful to me since my Daddy joined Jesus in Heaven. The stars seem so far away, yet so close at the same time. I look at the night sky, and I know beyond any doubt, that it was created. It didn't "just happen." As vast as the night sky is, what kind of ability did it take to create that? My God created that night sky, and His unlimited ability makes me worship Him even more.

Another thing that I love to do is sit in a chair at the beach on a warm sunny day and watch the waves roll in. Some days the waves roll in gently almost like a whisper. Other days, the waves bound ashore, almost in a playful fashion. Then there are the days the waves violently crash ashore. There are days the waves do not stop on the shoreline but come much further in doing damage to everything in their way. There's a unique beauty in each type of wave, even the violent ones. Although I'm very sorry for anyone's loss caused by the waves, the shear strength of a wave is incredible. There is one thing that all waves seem to have in common; they roll in one after another after another, each one just a little different than the last one. Who could be powerful enough to control such force? Who could be endless enough to create waves that continue to roll ashore since the beginning of time? God is the only one who can set things in motion that last throughout time.

The last thing in today's list is the amazing size difference between things in our world. We have Mount Everest which rises up 29,029 feet, but we also have tiny purple flowers that are the first hope of Spring. The flowers are so tiny we barely notice them in our yards but if you stop to look, you see the petal of each flower is perfectly created. Many of us favor either large things or small things but who has the ability to create things the size of Mount Everest, yet still possess the precision to put the parts of an ant together? My God, that's who!

Our God has limitless abilities and strength. HE was, HE is and He always will be! And HE is worth every ounce of our worship. As amazing as the things HE has created are those things are but a drop in the ocean.

Notes: _____

_____

_____

_____

_____

Peace, When We Learn To Trust

Isaiah 12:2. "Indeed, God is my salvation; I will trust Him and not be afraid, for Yah, the Lord, is my strength and my song. He has become my salvation."

Last night it stormed. It rained hard. There was wind. There was thunder and lightning. There were sounds of small limbs and small debris hitting the roof. It sounded rough, but we were safe and dry. My husband and I knew that.

Now our dog, Gilligan could not understand that he was safe. No matter how many times I tried to tell him that he was safe, he could not relax. He would not lay down and sleep. He's very afraid of storms and even just a little rain. He was actually downright petrified. Needless to say, there was not much sleep in our house last night. Gilligan went from one side of the bed to the other, back and forth between myself and my husband, panting heavily. He trembled all over. I got up and tried to get him settled on his bed, only for him to get back up trembling and panting. I even tried resting my hand on his head as he stood by the bed. I thought surely my touch would make him trust what I was telling him. He just couldn't bring himself to believe it when I was telling him that he was okay. I felt really sorry for him as I witnessed his fear. It was also frustrating for him not to trust what I told him.

As the night wore on, God began to remind me that I am a whole lot like Gilligan when it comes to trust issues. Jesus tells me that HE will always be with me. HE tells me that He will never forsake me or leave me. He tells me that I can trust Him to take care of me. Yet, I still have fears. I feel His touch but I still worry.

As the rain continued to fall and Gilligan continued to stand by the bed panting heavily in my face, I felt the increasing pressure of guilt crushing my toes. Gilligan could have had a peaceful night of sleep if he had only trusted my husband and I. How many nights of peaceful sleep have I lost because I didn't trust Jesus to carry me safely through the storm? It's amazing how easy it was to see God's perspective on my lack of trust in Him as I watched Gilligan last night. I could see the effects of not trusting Jesus to carry me through the storms of life as I forced my tired self out of bed this morning with the 5 am alarm snoozed the third time. I showered, packed a lunch, poured a much needed mug of coffee and spent my time with the Lord. Gilligan sleepily snuggled under his blanket on his bed while I told him he would be fine and dashed out in the rain to go to work. Wouldn't life be easier if we all just trusted Jesus to take care of us and got a good nights sleep?

Notes: _____

_____

_____

_____

_____

Completing Our Work

Read Genesis 1:1-31-2:3 and John 3:16.

Genesis 1:31. "God saw all that He had made, and it was very good. Evening came and then morning: the sixth day."

John 3:16. "For God loved the world in this way: He gave His One and Only Son, so that everyone who believes in Him will not perish but have eternal life."

When an artist finishes his painting, or a potter finishes his work on the clay he's molding, when a needlework artist finishes her project or an author puts the last period on the last sentence of her book, these creators sign their name to their work. It is identified then as their idea; a creation they planned and finished in the way they had envisioned and they're usually happy with their accomplishment and proud to put their name on it. Signing your work is a finishing statement saying this is your creation and you take not only credit for it, but responsibility for it also. It's a reflection of you. It's part of your heart.

In that same way, the Master Artist of the universe, God the Father, Himself, has signed His creation and He is proud of the accomplishment. He looked upon it and pronounced it 'Good!' when the creation of the world was done. That creation process included us, the people He created in His own image. He breathed into our lungs, looked upon us and called us 'Good'! This statement of ownership of His creation means that He is claiming the idea, the creation and finishing work of creating us. He is therefore willing to take credit for it but also to take responsibility for it.

When the first created man and woman fell to Satan's temptation, and committed sin against their Creator, it broke God's heart. However, rather than destroy His good creation, He chose to give up even more, His only Son as a sacrifice for mankind's sins, so that we might have the choice to live. He had designed, created, finished and claimed His creation and He took responsibility for providing a way of salvation so that we could still be His beautiful and useful works of art, rather than being destroyed by our sins. It was only due to one thing: His great love for His prized creation. I'm filled with gratitude that He has such great love, grace and mercy for us.

Notes: _____

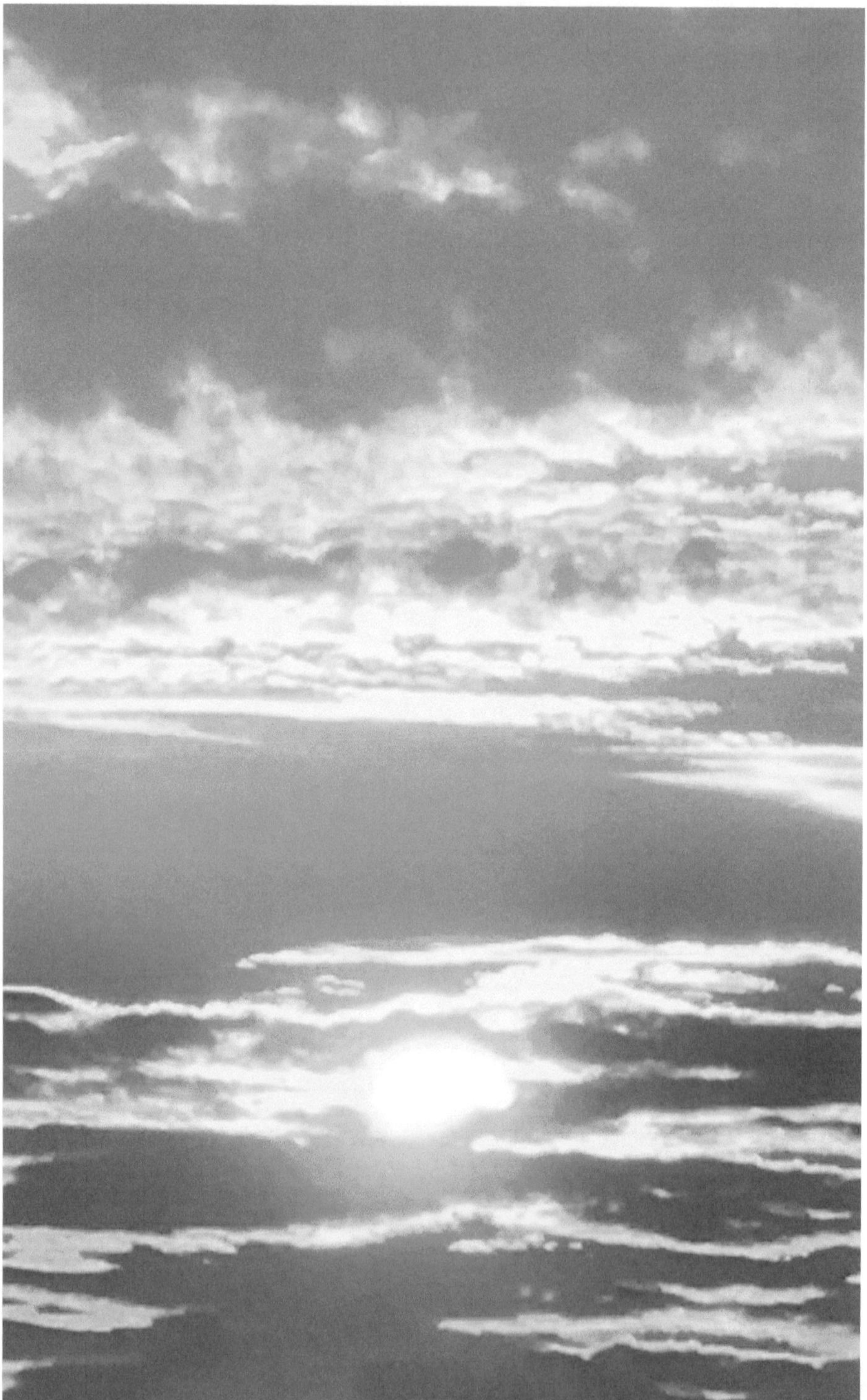

Homecoming!

John 17:24. "Father, I desire those You have given Me to be with Me where I am. Then they will see My glory, which You have given Me because You loved Me before the world's foundation."

I got up this Saturday morning with several thoughts jumbled up in my mind.

Tomorrow is Homecoming at our church. The person who will be bringing the message tomorrow is someone who grew up in our church. He no longer lives in this area. He is coming home to preach tomorrow. He has family in our church that I know will be glad to see him and hear him preach. My own son preached a homecoming service at our church a few years ago, so I know the joy they are feeling as they anticipate tomorrow.

My friend, Kim is from New Mexico. She now lives around the curve from me in Mississippi. Anyone who has looked at a map, knows that Mississippi and New Mexico are a long distance apart, but Kim still knows how to get there. She recently flew to New Mexico for a visit with her family. Some of her family prepared a room in their home for her to stay in while she was there. She is back now, but I saw a few pictures from her trip. We love Kim here in Mississippi, but the rest of her family in New Mexico love her also. Every picture I saw of her with her family had people, including Kim, with big smiles. It struck me how much she and her family miss being together. The joy Kim and her New Mexico family had while she was there, did not keep her husband and friends here in Mississippi from missing her while she was gone.

    Monday will be seven years since my Daddy passed from this world into the arms of Jesus. Although he is never far from my thoughts, he has been on my mind especially all this month. I miss my Daddy terribly, even after seven years, but I know he is rejoicing as he praises Jesus in Heaven. Anyone who has ever lost someone dear to them (who was saved) understands all the different emotions that go with those thoughts. I miss him every day. There are things I need to ask him, things I would like to show him, family events I wish he could be at and things I would like to discuss with him. Quite often, I just long for one of his hugs that made me feel so loved. I would also like to tell him one more time just how much I love and appreciate him. He was a good daddy. As I think back over all the memories I have of him, I am thankful that God gave him to me as my daddy. No matter how much I miss him though, I always know that he is much happier in Heaven than he could ever be here on this earth, even with all of his family that he loved so dearly. Why? Because he is HOME! He is with his Father, who is also my Father. He is with Jesus who saved him and saved me. He's home! That is why I have such mixed emotions of sadness because I miss him and great joy because I know where he is. Jesus prepared a home for those of us who are saved. Although I have a house here that I call home, it can't compare to what it will be like when I actually get to my real HOME in Heaven. The more time I spend with Jesus, and the more I study His Bible, the better I understand. I look more and more forward to Heaven. The longer I live, the closer I am to going HOME, not just for a visit but for eternity with Jesus! Thank You Father for Your indescribable Gift of Salvation through Jesus!

Notes:

About the Authors

Jennifer Sessums Stockman is a wife, mom, and soon to be grandma, who loves Jesus and studying her Bible. She believes the Bible is the most exciting book ever written and loves discussing it with others. She's excited to see what God does next in her life!

Carol Alawine Sessums is a Christian, (saved by God's Grace), Mom of a daughter and a son, Granny to four, Great-Granny of two, (with another coming soon!), and a widow learning a new way of living. She believes you are never too old to just obey and follow what God gives you to do because He doesn't send us out alone.

We may not know you, but we know that you are like us and most other people. Sometimes you have hurts, pains, sorrows, doubts, fears and questions...often lots of questions! So do we.

We didn't start this journey with writing a book as a goal. We were simply doing our regular Bible studies and making our notes. Then we both felt God telling us to share the truths HE was teaching us with others who might be encouraged by them. One thing we've learned is that when God says DO something, we'd best obey!

We hope something in our book will renew your hope and encourage you in your walk with God. If even one person finds something that blesses them in Anchored By This Hope, we will consider it a success!

We appreciate you and we pray that God will bless your life abundantly!

Made in the USA
Columbia, SC
31 March 2025